Michael O'Leary

ABOUT THE AUTHOR

Matt Cooper has had a thirty-year career at the heart of Irish current affairs journalism. He presents the daily drive-time show *The Last Word* on Today FM and co-presents *The Tonight Show* on Virgin Media 1. Before becoming a broadcaster Cooper was an award-winning print journalist (two-time national print journalist of the year) and newspaper editor (at the helm of the *Sunday Tribune* for six years). He is now a leader page columnist with the *Irish Daily Mail* and contributor to the *Sunday Business Post*. He has made a number of economic and political documentaries for television and is also an experienced TV sports host (anchoring TV3's Rugby World Cup coverage in 2015). Having accompanied the former US basketball star Dennis Rodman on his extraordinary goodwill visit to North Korea in January 2014, Cooper narrated the cinema-released feature documentary about the trip, *Dennis Rodman's Big Bang in Pyongyang*. He is the author of three bestselling books, *Who Really Runs Ireland?* (2009), *How Ireland Really Went Bust* (2011) and *The Maximalist: The Rise and Fall of Tony O'Reilly* (2015). Originally from Cork, he lives in Dublin with his wife and their five children.

Michael O'Leary

*Turbulent Times for the Man
Who Made Ryanair*

M A T T   C O O P E R

BUSINESS

PENGUIN BUSINESS

UK | USA | Canada | Ireland | Australia
India | New Zealand | South Africa

Penguin Business is part of the Penguin Random House group of companies
whose addresses can be found at global.penguinrandomhouse.com.

First published by Portfolio Penguin 2018
Published in Penguin Business 2019
001

Copyright © Matt Cooper, 2018

The moral right of the author has been asserted

Set in 11.88/14.1 pt Garamond MT Std
Typeset by Jouve (UK), Milton Keynes
Printed and bound in Great Britain by Clays Ltd, Elcograf S.p.A.

A CIP catalogue record for this book is available from the British Library

ISBN: 978-0-241-31563-7

www.greenpenguin.co.uk

MIX
Paper from
responsible sources
FSC® C018179
www.fsc.org

Penguin Random House is committed to a
sustainable future for our business, our readers
and our planet. This book is made from Forest
Stewardship Council® certified paper.

As always, to my family, Aileen and our children,
Andie, Aimee, Millie, Zach and Harry

Contents

Prologue: Turbulence

Michael O'Leary treated the letter from pilots demanding his resignation as chief executive officer at Ryanair with scorn.

'We suggest you leave now, and we call on the board and investors to engage a new CEO to return this airline to its rightful place,' the letter demanded. It was signed on behalf of the European Employee Representative Council (EERC), an unofficial body established by disgruntled Ryanair pilots in 2017 – apparently thousands of them – as part of their campaign for better working conditions. The group had enjoyed considerable success in putting the airline, and its boss, on the back foot, and was looking to press its advantage.

O'Leary read their demands and was angry. Once the anger subsided, he decided that he would punish this impertinence. As far as he was concerned, he was back in control and he would not be undermined again, especially by pilots. To him, this letter was a sign of weakness on their part, a desperate plea from people who thought they had him where they wanted him. So he decided that he would let these troublemakers know, again, how little he thought of them, and that he would do so publicly.

It was late February 2018, and the fallout from the most difficult year of O'Leary's professional career was ongoing. He dictated a statement for publication in his defence, insisting that the EERC 'had no legal standing or validity' and therefore would be ignored. The contents of the letter he'd received, which claimed a mass exodus of unhappy Ryanair pilots, were said to be 'ridiculous' and 'bizarre'. Given O'Leary's public behaviour over the previous decades, it wasn't hard to imagine that, had it been a vocal rejoinder, he would probably have added the words 'and they can fuck off'.

He hated them and they hated him. Their demand for him to resign might have been genuine, but it was also naive. Notwithstanding thirty years of conflict with O'Leary, they failed completely to understand their adversary, or that he continued to hold the balance of power. It was typical of O'Leary to be so confrontational, even if he had been giving regular interviews since 2013 promising to be nice, implying that he was a more mature and measured individual now. It wasn't that he was annoyed that the pilots had implored him to 'do the decent thing now and leave before you do any further damage' and made their demand public. He just didn't respect or fear their analysis.

The pilots – or at least those represented by the EERC – claimed that the airline would face a future of flight cancellations because so many pilots were resigning, despite the significantly improved pay on offer from Ryanair. After the very public debacle of 2017, when Ryanair experienced the humiliation of cancelling thousands of flights, the pilots seemed to think that O'Leary would do anything not to endure that experience ever again.

O'Leary was confident that he was on top of the situation and had enough pilots on his side to ensure further flight cancellations at Europe's largest airline wouldn't happen. He would not be threatened. He was prepared to confront strike action if necessary, believing that he could face down the pilots and not suffer public opprobrium if even more flights didn't take to the skies. As many pilots had already taken the enhanced pay deals on offer, involving as much as €20,000 extra per year, and as they were divided between those who had taken the money on offer and those who were gambling they could get more, he felt he could convince the public that the EERC pilots were just being greedy. The public would be angry with them, not with him or his airline.

Admittedly, O'Leary had previously misjudged the strength of his collective opposition. That uncharacteristic miscalculation had led to the cancellations and the extraordinary concession of trade-union recognition in late 2017, something he had sworn would never happen, in any circumstances. To the onlooker, it seemed all of these blows must have dented O'Leary's reputation and Ryanair's recent efforts to improve its brand image. To O'Leary, it was just another wave to ride out. He disdains conventional thinking, believing that it is too often emotional instead of rational. His way of looking at things is different from most people's. He never bows to the wisdom of crowds, or the demands of the mob or the media. The record shows that he is almost always right. This has given him enormous self-confidence, which his enemies see as arrogance. Yet he has enough self-awareness to realize that what he has always done is not what always should be done, and that there are times when he has to shift course. He doesn't care if he is criticized for changing his mind or his actions, regarding that as irrelevant. He shifts with the shape of the airline industry's paradigm.

As a result, O'Leary remained confident that his vision for Ryanair would be realized. His was an airline that had flown about 130 million passengers across the Continent in the twelve months to the end of March 2018, in spite of the very well-publicized problems during that period. He knew he would report profits of just over €1.3 billion for the year. He was running over 2,000 daily flights from 86 bases across

33 countries, connecting over 200 individual destinations, and those numbers were growing. Ryanair had a fleet of 430 Boeing 737 aircraft in use, and a further 240 on order to buy. O'Leary's ambition was to lift the number of annual customers to 200 million by 2024, and to raise his profits in line with that. This was a company worth over €18 billion. He spoke of its becoming the world's largest airline, and he meant it. He certainly wasn't going to turn his back on all of that just because a bunch of pilots didn't like him.

He remained relentless, even if he was turning fifty-seven in March 2018. His consistent success in an industry, where major losses and airline closures are common, was put down to his obstinate obsessiveness in keeping costs at the lowest level possible, lower than those of all his competitors. Investors and industry operators knew him as the young man who had saved the airline from extinction in the late 1980s, and then grown it year on year into Europe's biggest and most profitable short-haul carrier. It was all in the numbers, as the accountant in O'Leary knew. O'Leary didn't see insoluble problems, just wrinkles to be ironed out.

Yet others, both inside and outside Ryanair, felt that a cloud hovered over him. Nobody in business lasts forever. There were whispers that he might be losing his touch, even if they were uttered quietly and without much conviction. It wasn't that he was going soft – even if he was trying to pretend that he was nicer than his reputation – but the events of the previous six months meant he had to prove that his attention and ambition weren't wavering. Questions were being asked: was Ryanair struggling with its size, having grown so fast? How would it cope with the further route growth required by the large number of aircraft on order? Would O'Leary's emotional intelligence allow him to deal with the modern necessity for more understanding relationships with his staff? Did he have the right management in place to support him? Had the rebellious O'Leary become part of the establishment himself, so that his attacks on it appeared hypocritical? Had he become so predictable as to be boring, or was he best ignored?

Suddenly, people were talking about Ryanair without O'Leary. It may have been wishful thinking on the part of those who wanted to see him go away, and preferably humiliated to boot, but it was a real and legitimate conversation nonetheless. And yet it was almost unthinkable. O'Leary and Ryanair seemed interchangeable, as if the person and the corporate entity shared the same DNA. What would Ryanair be without O'Leary? And who would he be without Ryanair? For the first time in thirty years, the idea took hold that O'Leary's grip on Ryanair might be loosening, that arguably Ireland's greatest ever businessman and the airline he had built could, and would, be separated.

PART I
Changing course

1. The Ryanair way

'What part of no refunds do you not understand? We don't fall over ourselves if they say, "My granny fell ill." You are not getting a refund, so fuck off.'

That was it in a nutshell – the Ryanair way, the Michael O'Leary way. It has long been one of the most fascinating aspects of the airline's success that it has made so much money, and acquired so many customers, when it treats those passengers with an attitude that borders on contempt – and sometimes spills over into actual, expletive-laden abuse.

So many people have a Ryanair story. There were stories about lengthily delayed or suddenly cancelled flights, with no compensation offered for rank inconvenience or genuine distress. There were tales of rude and dismissive staff – in the air, at the airport check-in desks and departure gates, and, if you could get them to answer when trying to make a complaint, on the phone. Passengers on flights within the same country were baffled to discover they were not allowed to board without their passport, which was the only form of identification accepted. The stories described widespread, regular and wilfully antagonistic behaviour that was the very antithesis of the business cliché that the customer is always right.

Ryanair wasn't just unapologetic; it was confrontational in its response to criticism. The example was set from the very top, with O'Leary taking to the airwaves, if necessary, to stick it to their critics. 'People say the customer is always right, but

9

you know what – they're not. Sometimes they are wrong and they need to be told so,' he said. If flights were delayed or cancelled, Ryanair was most often unsympathetic. 'If a plane is cancelled, will we put you up in a hotel overnight? Absolutely not,' O'Leary declared. 'If a plane is delayed, will we give you a voucher for a restaurant? Absolutely not.' In another interview he said: 'No, we don't provide accommodation for people if their flight is cancelled. It's not part of our service. It's unreasonable of passengers to turn up at the airport and expect to be provided with a free cup of tea. People got an apology and the airport restaurant was open.'

That attitude became a major problem for passengers at airports served only by Ryanair, as often happened in its earlier years. This was especially the case if there was no other Ryanair flight due for days and no guarantee of being able to get a seat on it. At these far-flung outposts, there was no alternative airline to take a booking, and hotel accommodation might not be available because of the airport's rural location. In fact, even food services at the airport might be limited, but, as far as Ryanair was concerned, that was not its problem.

When EU consumer legislation was introduced in 2004, it got this response: 'Are we going to apologize when something goes wrong? No, we're fucking not. It doesn't matter how many times you write to us complaining that we wouldn't put you up in a hotel because there was fog at Stansted. You didn't pay us for it.' One of his spokesmen put it more tactfully when he said, 'A hotel bill alone will dwarf Ryanair's fare, and this runaway compensation culture in the Commission will clearly lead to higher fares and less choice for consumers.'

Unlike others in the industry, O'Leary was not romantic

about air travel. For him, it was a taxi service. There was no exclusivity or luxury about flying. People would get what they paid for and no more, not even a smile. He saw it in purely functional terms, getting passengers from point A to point B as efficiently as possible. 'I don't give a shite if no one likes me. I am not a cloud bunny, I am not an aerosexual. I don't like aeroplanes. I never wanted to be a pilot like those other platoons of goons who populate the airline industry.'

There were none like him in the industry, at least not on this side of the Atlantic. O'Leary loved making outrageous statements. He suggested pilots should engineer a bit of turbulence to boost on-board drink sales. He advocated the introduction of charges for using the toilets: 'One thing we have looked at is maybe putting a coin slot on the toilet door, so that people might actually have to spend a pound to spend a penny in the future. If someone wanted to pay £5 to go to the toilet, I would carry them myself. I would wipe their bums for a fiver.' He speculated about providing pornography on rented screens on late-night flights, suggesting that he would be the airline's best customer. He put forward the notion of flying casinos. He suggested standing tickets: 'I'd love to operate aircraft where we take out the back ten rows and put in hand-rails. We'd say, if you want to stand, it's five euros. People say, "Oh but the people standing may get killed if there's a crash." Well, with respect, the people sitting down might get killed as well.'

When Ryanair repainted its aircraft in December 2003, it issued a statement saying that O'Leary had ordered that the yellow angel on the logo was to get a breast enhancement, to offer customers a more uplifting experience – guaranteeing plenty of free coverage in Britain's biggest-selling tabloid paper, the *Sun*, as well as other publications. He meant little or none of it; what he wanted was publicity and he got it, in spades. He was a pioneer in fake news. But all this also highlighted one of the many paradoxes about O'Leary: he was full of bullshit, yet his public image simultaneously traded on his apparent ability to cut through it, too, to the benefit of his customers. He was the antithesis of political correctness and there has long been a market for populist championing.

While his antics were often laced with good, if sometimes questionable, humour, they were also occasionally accompanied by a dismissive, ugly sneer. He berated passengers for taking up too much space: 'Nobody wants to sit beside a really fat fucker on board. We have been frankly astonished at the number of customers who don't only want to tax fat people but torture them.' If people had issues with the website, he refused to believe that the problem was at the Ryanair end, suggesting in some cases that impatient people had logged in and out of the site prematurely and been charged twice as a result. According to O'Leary, any customer who couldn't find a cheap deal with Ryanair was 'a moron'. And when the opportunity arose – such as for major sports fixtures – Ryanair was never slow to up its prices dramatically. It was simply a case of charging what the market would bear.

To everyone's surprise, bar O'Leary's, the approach actually worked. Year after year, despite seemingly never-ending complaints, more and more customers flew Ryanair, creating a consistently bigger, more profitable airline. O'Leary was not far from crowing in many of his media encounters. He knew better than the so-called experts, both in marketing circles and the media, what consumers really wanted: low fares. Nothing else mattered, apparently. While the complaints rumbled on, the proof of his model was there in the steadily climbing graphs for passenger numbers and profits.

'Our customer service is about the most well-defined in the world,' he explained once. 'We guarantee to give you the lowest fare. You get a safe flight. You get a normally on-time flight. That's the package. We don't and won't give you anything more on top. We care for our customers in the most fundamental way possible: we don't screw them every time we fly them. I have no time for certain large airlines that say they care and then screw you for six or seven hundred quid every time you fly.'

He believed that if passengers were paying only a small amount for a ticket, they should not expect anything in compensation should something go wrong. He was asking them to take a gamble, with low odds of anything going wrong. He wasn't offering in-built insurance, not when the ticket prices were so low. His belief was that the only way airlines such as Ryanair could consistently offer low fares was by not having any means of dealing with complaints.

'Our strategy is low fares, high capacity at busy times, flexible tickets,' he said, in his early days as CEO. 'There are only three layers of management. No secrets. No dogma. No unions. I drive buses at the airport, check in passengers, load bags and get a good kicking when I play for the baggage-handlers' football team. The only thing I will not do is fly aircraft.' Cleverly, O'Leary was showing that, while he was up for anything and not too proud to do anything relatively menial or trivial, he knew his limits. He was also subtly reminding people that Ryanair was not so cheap that he would take risks with their safety when it came to flying the aircraft.

Other than on that important point, Ryanair benefited from lowered expectations. Complaints received short shrift, not just from the airline but from fellow passengers, too.

People got what they paid for, that was all, and what they had paid for was a cheap seat. When people expect nothing else, they are not disappointed. When they expect things to be bad, they are pleasantly surprised when things go well. As aviation marketing expert Marco Serusi from SimpliFlying argued: 'The airline consistently under-promises and over-delivers, thus creating a positive brand experience.' Serusi also believed that critics of airlines like Ryanair tend to be people who 'don't like what they've heard about it, but who haven't actually flown with it. On the other hand, its strongest advocates are actually those who have, and continue to fly, the airline.'

Meanwhile, so-called legacy airlines, like Ryanair's traditional Irish rival, Aer Lingus, were pilloried if they did not match the standards expected of them, partly prompted by their advertised promise that they offered a superior service. Efforts by what are usually state-owned or formerly state-controlled airlines to reduce costs – so they could reduce fares to Ryanair levels – involved reducing the quality of those services, a move against which customers rebelled. They were caught in a Catch-22 bind.

The British comedian David Mitchell provided one of the most insightful commentaries on Ryanair in a column published in the *Observer* in November 2013.

Ryanair's public relations, until now, has been a work of rare clarity. The underlying principle was that, when it comes to air travel, it isn't necessary to make your customers like you. As O'Leary said in response to a survey naming Ryanair the worst brand for customer service: '99 per cent of people don't think, what's my favourite brand, they look for the cheapest fares.'

Exactly. Most customers of airlines want to get to distant places cheaply, quickly and safely and that's all they care about. Armed with that insight, the company was able to harness the awesome power of negative publicity . . . [it] is always free and, as long as it didn't seriously undermine any of the three pillars of cheapness, speed and safety, it did no appreciable harm . . . the thousands of column inches reporting how nasty, amoral or penny-pinching the company was not only kept up its profile, but also repeatedly subliminally associated it with value. 'They will do anything to keep costs down' was the perpetual subtext . . . So, members of the public disgusted by Ryanair's treatment of the disabled one day, became customers checking its website for bargain flights the next.

The approach was relentlessly consistent. In September 2012 Ryanair went to war with a passenger called Suzy McLeod. She wrote on Facebook about her experience of having to pay €300 at Alicante Airport for boarding passes to allow her access to a return flight to Bristol from a family holiday in Spain. 'I had previously checked in online but because I hadn't printed out the boarding passes, Ryanair charged me €60 per person! Meaning I had to pay €300 for them to print out a piece of paper! Please "Like" if you think that's unfair.' More than half a million people did so, a number that would terrify most business bosses and bring about immediate grovelling apologies.

Instead, O'Leary was scathing in his response. 'We think Mrs McLeod should pay 60 euros for being so stupid,' he said. 'She wasn't able to print her boarding card because, as you know, there are no internet cafés in Alicante, no hotels where they could print them out for you, and you couldn't get to a fax machine so some friend at home can print them and fax them to you. She wrote to me last week asking for compensation as a gesture of goodwill. To which we have replied, politely but firmly, thank you Mrs McLeod but it was your fuck-up.'

McLeod, who was travelling with her two children and her parents, said she had been unable to print out the boarding passes for her return flight because her holiday had been for fifteen days and Ryanair only permitted passes to be printed out fourteen days in advance of departure.

The story brought plenty of media publicity, with additional mentions of the £6/€6 per person 'admin fee' that was added to every ticket price, as well as the £6/€6 'web check-in fee'. It was noted that Ryanair had introduced an 'EU261 levy' of £2/€2 per ticket to offset the potential cost of paying compensation for delays and cancellations, and also an additional 'ETS levy' of 25p/25c per ticket to cover the cost of the EU's Emissions Trading Scheme, under which airlines are fined for exceeding carbon-emissions limits. The information that Ryanair passengers wishing to check in a single bag were charged between £15/€15 and £40/€40 per person, depending on the time of year, their destination and the weight of their luggage – with sports or musical equipment costing another £50/€50 – was repeated again and again.

However, there were signs that O'Leary was becoming slightly more concerned about Ryanair's image. In September 2013 Ryanair did a deal for a provocative advertising campaign with Ashley Madison, a dating website for married people who wanted to cheat on their spouses. The plan was to paint a Ryanair plane pink, with a large slogan on the aircraft body reading LIFE'S SHORT, HAVE AN AFFAIR. This pink plane would fly for six months between Barcelona and London Stansted, and Ryanair would receive €120,000 for the branding. At the last minute, O'Leary changed his mind and voided the contract, turning down the easy money.

In June 2013 Ryanair's head of communications, Robin Kiely, wrote to various newspapers and travel websites, insisting that 'The claim that Ryanair is a "no-frills" airline is entirely misleading and outdated, given that we offer all-leather seats, reserved seating, industry-leading punctuality, online check-in and on-board catering for those who wish to avail of it. Ryanair is a low-cost airline and I would appreciate if you would refrain from describing Ryanair as "no-frills" in the future and amend your article to reflect this fact.'

Something was changing, it seemed. After all, when O'Leary had once spoken of what business class would include on any putative long-haul service, he said Ryanair would offer 'beds and blowjobs'. In 2012 Ryanair was ordered by the UK's Advertising Standards Authority (ASA) not to repeat two 'sexually suggestive' newspaper advertisements. The first ad, published in the *Guardian*, showed a woman in her underwear. She had one hand on her hip and was pulling her pants down slightly with the thumb of the other hand. The headline stated: RED HOT FARES AND CREW. ONE WAY FROM £9.99. The text in the copy advertised the airline's 2012 cabin-crew calendar, a charity affair in which female members of staff posed in skimpy outfits. The second ad, published by the *Daily Telegraph* and the *Independent*, showed a different woman in her underwear, with a similar text. The ASA, having received complaints that the adverts were sexist and offensive, concluded that, while the images were 'not overtly sexual in content', they were sexually suggestive and 'likely to cause widespread offence'. It also declared that most readers would interpret the images and text as linking female cabin crew with sexually suggestive behaviour.

Complaints were about more than sexual content in the company's advertising, and it wasn't just in Ireland and Britain where Ryanair annoyed the authorities. The Italian competition regulator Codacons attacked Ryanair's pricing information on its website and fined it €350,000. Ticket prices should be 'clearly and fully indicated from the very first contact with the consumer in such a way as to make the final price immediately clear', it ruled in April 2013. It was particularly annoyed by the presence of a 2 per cent credit card commission that Ryanair introduced in 2012, ostensibly to comply with a UK Office of Fair Trading ruling, and that it applied to all flights across Europe.

A narrative was taking shape, one that was highlighted by a survey published in *Which?* magazine just weeks before Ryanair's 2013 AGM. It asked consumers to rate 100 leading companies in the UK according to staff knowledge, attitude and ability to deal with issues. Ryanair scored two stars (out of a possible five) for each category. This produced an overall rating of 54 per cent, by far the lowest of all the companies surveyed. Only TalkTalk, a mobile phone provider, and npower, an energy supplier, came nearly as low, at 59 per cent.

'Passengers appear to agree with Ryanair CEO Michael O'Leary's open admission that price is a priority over customer service,' said *Which?* 'One said of his recent travel with Ryanair that he found it: "aggressive and hostile towards customers. Staff are rude and unpleasant." Another flyer related their poor in-flight treatment, lamenting "rude air stewards who make you feel like a nuisance rather than a customer". Others are unwilling to be treated badly, whatever the savings. "I now prefer to pay £50 extra for my flights and to be treated like a human being," concluded one of their experience.'

Ryanair had a typically tart response ready for the inevit-able questions from the media once *Which?* had put the information into the public domain. 'We surveyed over 3 million passengers on the Ryanair website last night,' a spokesman said. 'Only two of them had ever heard of *Which?* and none of them had ever bought it or read it. Ryanair's survey conclusively proves that *Which?* magazine hasn't got a clue about what air-travel consumers actually do, because they're too busy booking Ryanair's low-fares, on-time flights to waste time filling in *Which?* magazine's tiny surveys.'

Behind the scenes, however, the survey only confirmed for O'Leary what he had been coming to believe, particu-larly as analysis of figures from easyJet, one of his main rivals, showed a pattern of changing customer behaviour. Previously, O'Leary had scoffed at such reviews, but he was savvy enough to realize that a generational shift might mean that things like this actually did matter. The profile of the bookings data he had seen over the last year worried him. New customers were being attracted, but not necessarily in the large numbers that he wanted and, given his ambitions for growth, needed. Maybe low fares – allied to punctuality – were not all that mattered, especially to the younger generation of new frequent flyers, the millennials who said that they valued 'experiences'. It may even have been more basic. Risk had become a major issue for many flyers, not the risk of the flight crashing but that a holiday would be ruined by delays, missed connections, lost bags and other perceived horrors – which O'Leary, of course, saw only as inconveni-ences. The expectation was that flying with Ryanair could be a miserable experience, and that the savings provided by cheaper fares were not worth the risk of what the costs would be if something went wrong.

O'Leary is like a magpie when it comes to picking the shini-est aspects of what his competitors have to offer. He regularly mocks and belittles the performance of other airlines – a way of spreading the idea that Ryanair does it all better – but is never slow to take from rivals what he can use to his own advantage. The performance of easyJet always held a particu-lar fascination for him. It was founded by Stelios Haji-Ioannou, a scion of a Cypriot shipping business, who also courted con-troversy to garner attention for his business. In 2010 easyJet changed course. It appointed a new chief executive, Carolyn McCall, the former chief executive of Guardian Media Group, publisher of newspapers such as the *Guardian* and the *Observer* that O'Leary derided for their liberal political positions – and constant criticism of Ryanair. O'Leary dismissed McCall as a 'media luvvie'. He didn't think she would be able to deal with the chaos she would find at easyJet, as the airline struggled to provide enough flights to meet the demand from its existing customers.

It turned out that McCall had identified a strategy for growth before O'Leary and Ryanair did. She targeted the business market, provided more flexible tickets and promoted easyJet's brand. She managed to reposition the public percep-tion of easyJet as value for money, instead of merely cheap, increasing passenger numbers and revenue per passenger in doing so. She provided reasonable customer service at a low-fares airline and, using this model, was able to expand the business. Quietly, O'Leary began to understand and admire what she was doing and to consider that there might be benefit in Ryanair executing a similar change of course.

O'Leary may have been consistent in his attitude while it was paying dividends, but, when it comes to business, he is first and foremost a pragmatist, so if that attitude was no longer working, he would ditch it – he's unsentimental in the extreme. He is often criticized for being stubborn, but he is flexible in his thinking when assessing methods and profits. What he was coming to realize was that his brazen approach might not work for the next thirty years.

There was one particular incident that really called into question the Ryanair way. The top-down attitude of never giving an inch had worked brilliantly in financial terms, but in 2013 it was brought to its logical conclusion by a staff member and resulted in a passenger being treated in an appalling manner.

On 13 September 2013 Dr Muhammad Taufiq al-Sattar, a Dublin-based neurosurgeon, received a call from East Midlands Police in England. His wife and three children lived in Leicester, and he commuted to and from the family home. He had his ticket home booked for that evening, for his weekly visit. The police called to give him the horrifying news that there had been a fire at his home and asked him to travel back quickly. Dr Al-Sattar rushed straight to Dublin Airport, to try to get a flight leaving at an earlier time than the one he was booked on.

While in the queue to change his ticket, he received a second call from the police. Fearful that he would learn the news via social media before he reached Leicester to be told in person, they had decided to tell him what had happened: his entire family had died in the fire. They were the most unfortunate victims of a case of mistaken identity; their home had been targeted by an arsonist who had meant to set fire to a nearby house.

Dr Al-Sattar stumbled, crying, to the Ryanair desk. Clearly distraught, but trying to compose himself, he explained as best he could that he had just been told that all his family had been killed, and that the local police wanted him in Leicester as quickly as possible. He had to be on the earliest possible flight. 'Please, help me,' he pleaded.

'Certainly sir,' he was told by a Ryanair employee at the service desk. 'We can't transfer your existing ticket, but we can get you on board a flight that is going very soon. That'll be €188 for the new ticket.' Deep in shock, Dr Al-Sattar didn't argue. He just handed over his credit card, entered his PIN to confirm the payment, grabbed his ticket and raced to his flight.

It wasn't until the days after the funeral that the cruelty of his treatment by Ryanair sank in. 'I don't want to make a big deal about it, but it did shock me,' the doctor said in an interview he gave to the *Irish Daily Mail*. 'I really did not expect them to charge me. I thought, given the circumstances, they might just let me transfer flights, as I had already paid for a return fare.'

The newspaper contacted Ryanair to ask for its response to this claim. The paper's editor, Sebastian Hamilton, anticipated a denial and possibly threats of legal action from Ryanair if such a potentially damaging allegation was put into print without substantiating proof. Despite being more than willing to dish it out to competitors, Ryanair had a long-standing reputation for responding to negative comment with criticism of its critics, usually finding some excuse to kick back or change the nature of the argument. It rarely, if ever, admitted fault. If it did, it was often in a begrudging or tongue-in-cheek fashion. Up until this point, that tactic had usually worked. On this occasion, however, Ryanair couldn't do that without making things worse. To Hamilton's surprise, Ryanair responded promptly, not only confirming what had happened but apologizing for it. In a statement, the airline said: 'Ryanair offers its sincere condolences to Dr Sattar and confirmed that in the circumstances it will provide a full refund of any monies paid last Friday.'

The rest of the media fell upon the story once the *Irish Daily Mail* published it, with all of the damning newspaper headlines and radio talk-show condemnation one would expect. There were plenty of expressions of outrage, too, on an increasingly influential social media. Ryanair had gone too far this time.

Ryanair didn't just grovel once for this appalling error. As it happened, the report – and a subsequent radio interview with the bereaved surgeon on Sean O'Rourke's extremely popular RTÉ Radio 1 show – coincided with the airline's AGM for shareholders, which took place, as was required by stock-exchange regulations, in a public forum in Dublin. O'Leary – the high-profile face of the company, the man who always counter-attacked – had planned to use the occasion to roll out his campaign for a 'nicer' Ryanair. Now he had to pass an immediate test of that declared new approach.

'The staff were implementing our policy, but I think you have to make exceptions in cases like that,' O'Leary admitted at the AGM. 'And we clearly made an exception . . . once we became aware of it last night, we immediately refunded to Dr Sattar the money that we regret having taken from him in such tragic circumstances . . . We've already written to him to apologize and to sympathize with him in the circumstances he found himself in last Friday.'

Questioned further by the media after the AGM, O'Leary spoke of Ryanair projecting a 'softer image', but admitted there was no intention of applying this policy to similar cases. 'We simply deal with them on a case-by-case basis,' he said. 'When you're carrying 81 million passengers across 120 airports, you can't run something on the basis that you'll make an exception when there's an exception.' His staff had been told to implement airline policy 'without exception or variation', so when he said, 'We want to respond sensitively to these cases', many of them wondered just how they were supposed to do both.

To his many critics, this story underlined the culture he had cultivated at his airline. It was one that was so unyielding and so unforgiving, and that instilled such fear of deviating in any way from company policy, that staff had no freedom to be compassionate, believing or flexible in dealing with passengers. Michael O'Leary might not have agreed entirely with that analysis, but he is an astute operator, and he realized that something had to change.

2. Plotting a coup

Michael O'Leary might have been thinking in terms of change, but he first had to deal with some pressing and highly irritating distractions. He and Ryanair spent the summer of 2013 engaged in a public spat with pilots and the media. A number of them joined forces with a documentary producer in a move that, to O'Leary, was tantamount to high treason.

Secrets from the Cockpit was an exposé planned by the independent company Blakeway Productions, for broadcast as part of Channel 4's *Dispatches* series. Blakeway wrote to Ryanair, detailing twelve specific concerns raised by pilots over working conditions and the amount of fuel they had to carry, and how this impacted on safety.

That word – 'safety' – was like a red rag to a bull. It was a major concern of O'Leary's. Ryanair could not be perceived as a cheapskate when it came to safety procedures. The long-held fear was that any crash involving fatalities would not just be catastrophic in itself but ruinous for the airline overall. 'It doesn't matter how good you think you are in the airline business,' O'Leary said. 'We live every hour of every day with how do we avoid ever having an accident. I never want to have an accident on my conscience or any of our consciences.' O'Leary was credited within the company as being rigorous in that regard.

There was one potential weak point, however. Ryanair instructed its pilots to manage the amount of fuel they carried for each flight – and 'manage' was regarded by many as 'minimize'. More fuel obviously costs additional money: a heavier fuel load requires the burning of extra fuel in order to carry it. The official Ryanair policy was that captains could take on up to 300kgs more than the amount set by the official flight plan, and extra only with a proven good reason.

This fuel policy had caught the attention of the media, because there had been several controversial incidents that called it into question, mainly involving busy flights to Spanish airports. In 2010 a young pilot who had not taken on extra fuel got into difficulties when he was diverted from Alicante to Valencia. On his approach he had to declare a 'Mayday' emergency – which involves fire and rescue services being put on full alert – because his fuel was below the final reserve he had declared. In the summer of 2012 similar incidents had occurred with three Ryanair aircraft approaching Valencia – having been diverted from Madrid because of thunderstorms – that also had to call in a Mayday, two of them within three minutes of each other. This attracted intense media coverage, much to Ryanair's frustration.

The issue of flight safety brought to the surface the toxicity of the relationship between Ryanair and some of its pilots, particularly those represented by organizations such as Irish Airline Pilots Association (IALPA) and the trade union IMPACT (Irish Municipal, Public and Civil Trade Union). O'Leary was among those who suspected that other agendas were at play in their complaints. The pilots had gripes about the status of their contracts, the lack of guarantees on flying time, the fact payments were made only for hours flown, the amount of unpaid leave, and having to pay for their own initial training and uniforms. Some pilots claimed they flew when unwell, simply to make sure they got paid. O'Leary was dismissive, believing they were being led by employees of other companies who were seeking to destroy Ryanair's competitive advantage by upping its costs.

Once Blakeway sent its letter of intent, Ryanair reacted immediately and aggressively. It had been through this before with Channel 4 and *Dispatches* in 2006. That time, Ryanair had launched a media campaign to discredit the programme, and it had paid off. The 'revelations' – which were nothing that hadn't been aired publicly before – had failed to stall Ryanair's growth. 'We know how to deal with this,' O'Leary told his colleagues. Robin Kiely, head of information, was a recent hire, so many of the responses he sent to Blakeway in the coming days were overseen by O'Leary personally.

The first objective was to undermine the programme-maker's confidence in what it intended to broadcast. Kiely attacked Channel 4 for 'having previously made false and unsubstantiated allegations against Ryanair (using actors to "simulate" cabin crew)'. He claimed: 'It's surprising that *Dispatches* are again inventing false and unsubstantiated claims – presumably again using "actors" – to make what are manifestly false claims . . . airline safety is a matter of fact and evidence . . . These so-called "pilots" you have interviewed have misled you. Ryanair's fuel policy clearly establishes that the final discretion on fuel lies with each captain.' He offered an interview with O'Leary, on condition it was broadcast in full and unedited. Blakeway rejected all of the claims and also rejected the interview as impractical.

The letters flew back and forth, and Blakeway wrote that their research came from a survey of pilot attitudes, conducted among 1,000 captains and first officers, and commissioned by the Ryanair Pilot Group (RPG), which was not recognized by management but claimed to represent more than half of all pilots. Kiely was scathing in response: 'The Non-Ryanair Pilot Group (NRPG) is quite clearly a PR front for pilot trade unions of Ryanair's competitor airlines. A so called "survey" fabricated by these ECA pilot unions, which does not have access to or contact with the entire 3,000 plus pilots employed by Ryanair, lacks any independence, objectivity or reliability. It is another failed attempt by ECA pilot unions to use non-existent safety "concerns" to advance their 25-year-failed campaign to win union recognition in Ryanair.'

Despite the bombardment from Ryanair, Channel 4 aired the programme. It featured three pilots who spoke anonymously. One stated that three quarters of the airline's pilots were on 'zero hours' contracts, meaning they could work only for Ryanair but had no guaranteed hours of employment. The survey found that more than eight out of ten pilots said Ryanair did not have an open and transparent safety culture, and that two thirds felt uncomfortable raising safety-related issues at Ryanair. Nearly 94 per cent believed the Irish Aviation Authority (IAA) and its European counterpart should investigate the impact of Ryanair's employment practices on safety. Nearly all of them said they did not have access through Ryanair safety channels to details of every incident involving Ryanair aircraft over the previous 29 years.

O'Leary fired off a response: 'Ryanair rejected the false and defamatory claims made by the Channel 4 *Dispatches* programme which wrongly impugn and smear Ryanair's outstanding 29-year safety record based on nothing more than anonymous hearsay claims made by individuals whose identity was concealed, and/or by representatives of pilot unions of Ryanair's competitor airlines masquerading as a Non-Ryanair Pilot Group.' He also contacted the IAA and asked it to issue a public statement. It did. It called the documentary a 'misguided attack' because Ryanair's safety record was 'on a par with the safest in Europe'.

Ryanair began defamation proceedings against Channel 4's *Dispatches* programme and against the *Daily Mail*'s UK edition for its reporting on the programme. It also sacked, with 'immediate effect', long-serving pilot John Goss, a member of the interim council of the RPG, and started a separate legal action against him because he had been identified as a speaker in the documentary. The relationship with Goss had been bad for a long time, going back to 2005, when Goss tried to have O'Leary and two of his management colleagues, David O'Brien and Ray Conway, jailed for an alleged contempt of court, for failing to comply with a previous order to allow his return to flight duties from a suspension. On top of that, not long before the *Dispatches* programme, Goss had given a newspaper interview about aircraft safety, for which he was disciplined by Ryanair.

The airline settled its case with the *Daily Mail* quickly, with the paper agreeing to making a statement in court in which it made a grovelling apology. Ryanair seized upon it immediately. Speaking afterwards, Ryanair chief pilot Captain Ray Conway said: 'I wish to emphasize that Ryanair cannot and will not tolerate what were totally unjustified and inappropriate allegations in relation to our industry-leading safety. Safety has been and always will be the absolute priority of Ryanair.'

O'Leary went further: 'Generally speaking we are content to allow the media or anybody else to make whatever claims they want but not inaccurate claims about our safety. We must and will continue to vigorously defend our outstanding safety record.' But it was equally important to him that he put his pilots and their unions in their place. Ryanair might have notched up that battle as a win (though, as this book goes to print, the Channel 4 case is ongoing), but it had by no means addressed the resentment seething under the surface. The war with pilots was far from over.

It was an unwelcome distraction from O'Leary's desire to focus on Ryanair's need to expand, and how he would do it. There was a scheme in the offing that would be a serious game-changer: buying the iconic Aer Lingus. O'Leary had a grand plan for the airline – if only he could gain control of it.

This was proving difficult to achieve. He first tried in 2006, when the Irish government floated Aer Lingus on the stock exchange. The decision was taken reluctantly by the Bertie Ahern-led Fianna Fáil/Progressive Democrats government, which would have preferred to keep the airline fully in state ownership; but, as Aer Lingus was constrained in raising capital as a state-owned entity by EU rules, floating part of it became a necessity. The state would keep a 28 per cent shareholding, while employees were gifted 15 per cent through a share-ownership trust. Shares in Aer Lingus were made available at €2.20 each, valuing the company at €1.2 billion.

The shares rose immediately after trade began, making everyone happy. But what nobody had spotted was that the price was being driven up by Ryanair's active purchasing of the available shares. Just one week after the flotation, Ryanair announced that it had bought 16 per cent of the shares – at an average price of €2.42 – and was willing now to buy the rest for €2.80 each in cash, valuing the airline at €1.48 billion. 'This offer represents a unique opportunity to form one strong airline group for Ireland and for European consumers,' a statement from O'Leary read. It was not hard to imagine him laughing as he wrote it, a cat setting the pigeons into panicked flight.

There was widespread consternation at this unforeseen turn of events. The idea of Ryanair getting its grubby paws on the pristine Aer Lingus upset many people. The opposition berated the government for having allowed it to happen. The trade unions weighed in heavily on the criticism, too. The Aer Lingus pilots decided to use part of their pension fund's assets to buy their own 2.24 per cent stake, in an attempt to block any takeover. The Irish Pensions Board quietly asked questions as to the appropriateness of the investment.

As the drama unfolded, many industry watchers were baffled as to what O'Leary really wanted. Taking control of Aer Lingus would mean an unholy fight that would distract his attention from other matters. Would the financial return really be worth all the bother? Yes, it would deliver him a bigger company, but it would also open him up to a highly unionized environment, one that he had prevented from developing at Ryanair. He would either have to break down that culture and structure at Aer Lingus, or allow it to become the norm at Ryanair. If Ryanair could establish a greater monopoly presence on the Ireland–Britain route by controlling its main rival, that would bring benefits, but few could see the regulators approving this.

Many suspected that O'Leary was merely causing mischief, and that he intended using his position as a substantial minority shareholder to handicap Aer Lingus to Ryanair's advantage. This seemed confirmed when he brought Ryanair's shareholding up to just under the 29.9 per cent maximum shareholding allowed by stock-exchange rules before triggering a mandatory takeover bid (which differs from an offer). At worst, it seemed that Ryanair would profit from a rising Aer Lingus share price.

O'Leary subsequently admitted that the shares were

purchased almost on impulse, an idea he dreamt up as he read through the Aer Lingus flotation document. It was another indication of the hold he had over the Ryanair board that he quickly persuaded his fellow directors to allow the enterprise when it had relatively little chance of success – at least if a full takeover was the intention. Declan Ryan, son of the founder Tony Ryan and who had soldiered alongside O'Leary in its early loss-making years, rang O'Leary and jokingly told him, 'Now I know you're bored.'

The offer wasn't merely rejected by shareholders. The European Commission (EC) would have none of it either, on competition grounds, failing to be impressed by O'Leary's arguments that an enlarged group, with more than 50 million passengers each year, would be better able to compete with behemoths like British Airways, Lufthansa and Air France. O'Leary promised that Aer Lingus would continue to be run as a separate company, but claimed that, as part of a larger group, it would have access to lower cost aircraft and cheaper financing. He also promised to upgrade its transatlantic fleet and improve long-haul services. The EC's 500-page response could be summed up in one word: No.

Aer Lingus denied Ryanair board representation, despite the size of its shareholding, which encouraged O'Leary to air his criticisms publicly: 'As the current wave of European airline mergers and takeovers gathers pace, it is clear that Aer Lingus is being marginalized on the sidelines of European aviation, losing money, with no apparent strategy to return to profitability. Its independence strategy, which over the past year has delivered higher fares, a six-fold increase in its fuel surcharges, route closures in Ireland, and a lurch to substantial losses, has failed its customers, its staff and has, we believe, failed to secure Aer Lingus's long-term viability.'

In spite of his low opinion of the Aer Lingus management, O'Leary made another bid to buy it in 2008. He offered €748 million in cash, or €1.40 a share, which just happened to be half the value of Ryanair's previous offer. The Irish government was dealing with its own difficulties – such as the late September 2008 decision to offer a guarantee over the debts of all six Irish banks, to be known colloquially as the 'Bank Bailout', with disastrous consequences for the state's finances – so O'Leary reckoned the time might be right to forge a deal on Aer Lingus. But he had underestimated the deep-seated hostility that remained towards him personally and his airline by extension – no matter how much circumstances had changed. The government had enough troubles without being seen to capitulate to O'Leary. Knowing this, Aer Lingus swiftly rejected the offer as 'not capable of completion'.

O'Leary was left to take flak from critics that he had wasted his shareholders' money on an egotistical folly that had no chance of success. Ryanair was down hundreds of millions of euro on its ill-fated investment. For that reason, the surprise third effort to buy the airline, in mid 2012, was seen by many as a ploy to flush out a buyer for Ryanair's near-30 per cent shareholding: and, once Ryanair's offer was rejected, another party did come in to buy Aer Lingus. However, there was far more significant intent behind it than that. O'Leary really wanted to buy his great rival because he had a use for it.

O'Leary's idea was that Ryanair would continue on its same path, with its low-price, low-service offering, but that Aer Lingus would be used throughout Europe – and far beyond its existing network of routes – to offer customers the choice of using primary airports and receiving a friendlier service. He saw that about 70 million passengers were travelling point-to-point on short-haul European markets, mainly to primary airports, and paying higher fares, but not with Ryanair. O'Leary was also confident that he would be able to drive down costs at Aer Lingus if he had control, thereby achieving a superior profit margin because of Aer Lingus's already higher ticket fares.

First, he had to get his hands on Aer Lingus. He would need to offer a good enough price, and address all the issues that had stymied his previous attempts, particularly in relation to competition. Colleagues also suggested he play the public-relations game a bit more subtly, not insulting the people he needed to sell to him. The belief was that money would conquer any misgivings. It was a tall order.

Politically, it was all change again. Fine Gael was now the lead party in a coalition government, although it was controlled by the rules set down by the Troika: the European Commission, the European Central Bank and the International Monetary Fund. It had provided the finance to stop the Irish state from going bankrupt in late 2010, but one of the conditions was that the government sell non-essential state assets to raise cash to repay them. The remaining 28 per cent shareholding in Aer Lingus was an obvious option. The government said it would sell 'at an appropriate time', and then Minister for Transport Leo Varadkar said he would not sell for less than €1 per share.

Ryanair went for it and put in its third offer, pitched at €1.30 per share, which was 46.7 per cent higher than the average closing price of an Aer Lingus share over the past six months. O'Leary devised all sorts of ways to mollify those opposed to the idea of him owning Aer Lingus. It was a lengthy list, headed by the government and Aer Lingus itself. They were supported by the EU, the British and the Irish regulators, all of which felt it unwise to allow Ryanair a monopoly out of Ireland and in other countries, too. Yet O'Leary continued to lobby and offered a wide range of concessions to persuade the regulators. In an unusual move he brought into his management an Irish aviation expert – stockbroker Joe Gill – to work not just on persuading investors to sell but also on devising the remedies that would be acceptable to the EC.

To the relief of the Aer Lingus board and management, the EC was not impressed by the concessions offered, claiming they would lead to higher fares. Ryanair was furious and accused the EC of acting unfairly and failing to apply its own competition rules and precedents to Ryanair's 'unprecedented' proposals: 'We regret that this prohibition is manifestly motivated by narrow political interests rather than competition concerns and we believe that we have strong grounds for appealing and overturning this politically inspired prohibition.' It alleged the decision was a political one, to protect the interests of the Irish government. It accused the EC of holding it to a 'different and considerably higher standard' than any other EU-flag-carrier airline. 'Accordingly, Ryanair has instructed its legal advisers to prepare a comprehensive appeal against this manifestly unjust prohibition.'

Ryanair's response drew a tart response from Varadkar: 'Ryanair spends a lot of time and money in the courts and generally doesn't get much success from their actions . . . The government's view very strongly was that we want to see lots of airlines flying in and out of Ireland, lots of competition, and lots of routes.' But there was a good reason for him not wanting a Ryanair appeal: tying things up in the courts could scare off other potential buyers of Aer Lingus and frustrate the government's efforts to sell its shares to raise money.

O'Leary was no doubt thoroughly frustrated that his efforts

were thwarted at every turn, but his failed Aer Lingus caper also left him with a problem. He had a deal with Boeing to buy new aircraft, but he needed more passengers to fill them. He had captured the bottom part of the market – those interested in price above and beyond service – but he wanted to capture the next tier. There were plenty of people who would pay an extra €10 per ticket or more to fly with one of Ryanair's competitors on exactly the same route because the service made it worth the extra cost. Other airlines were able to charge a premium. Aer Lingus would have given him a brand that could target those passengers and gain access to the primary airports that Ryanair didn't currently serve. He had needed it more than he had let on. It meant Ryanair would have to find another way to grow its market and attract more customers. O'Leary needed an alternative strategy.

3. Nosedive

Most airlines lost their shareholders loads of money, just as Ryanair did at the start. Warren Buffett, arguably the world's most successful and most famous capitalist, turned his sights on the industry in 2013 and said that 'investors poured their money into airlines . . . for 100 years with terrible results . . . It's been a death trap for investors.'

Under O'Leary's stewardship, Ryanair had more than bucked that trend. It was producing annual profits of over €500 million by the end of March 2013. This was from an inauspicious beginning in 1986, when it started operations on a single route between Waterford, on Ireland's south-west coast, and England. It had joined the stock market only in 1997. So to have reached this scale of business so quickly – and after many years when the financial generosity of its founder, Tony Ryan, was all that kept it in the air – made it an aviation sensation. It was the most successful international company ever developed out of the island of Ireland, an unlikely location on the furthermost western periphery of Europe. What's more, its profitability and level of carriage had been achieved despite an avalanche of bad publicity – of the type companies were told to avoid at all costs for fear of damaging their brand. O'Leary seemed to have founded a new business model: the anti-brand.

So if everything had worked beautifully up until now, why would O'Leary change? More importantly, would change jinx its success? It might have spooked investors, but O'Leary

37

knew by now that Ryanair had to do things differently, and he wouldn't be deterred from that.

The first time O'Leary publicly signalled his change of heart was at an aviation conference run by Goodbody Stockbrokers in Dublin, in September 2013. It was attended by some of the industry's most senior executives, with airline bosses, airport chiefs and corporate investors among them. O'Leary's presentations at such events were always a highlight, even for those who didn't like him or his airline. He was always worth listening to for the fun and outrageousness of what he might say, whether or not he could be believed.

Instead of giving a speech, O'Leary was interviewed by his host in a so-called fireside chat. He declared that, in future, his staff would smile and ask passengers how they were enjoying their experience of flying with Ryanair. It would be hardwired into the overall business. Customer service would be paramount. Ryanair was going to treat customers with, at the very least, respect. It would listen to complaints and act upon them. It would make customer service one of the core principles of its business, while not, of course, forgetting its concentration on costs and prices. The flight path he had charted, defended and extolled was not the optimal one. From now on, he and Ryanair were going to be 'nice'.

Audible guffaws greeted O'Leary's claims. Experience had taught everyone present not to take his pronouncements at face value. He often said things for effect, for publicity, and then did exactly the opposite. He was into the delivery of fake news long before Donald Trump made the phrase well known. Equally, though, he often did exactly as he said, even when nobody had anticipated he would. He enjoyed wrongfooting rivals and causing chaos. So maybe this time he was telling the truth, and about something quite fundamental?

After O'Leary's presentation, some of the attendees sought out other Ryanair officials in an attempt to get clarity on the proposed changes. Surely he had told them? He hadn't. Well, not quite. He had been talking about it a bit, they said, but not in a way that was entirely convincing. Howard Millar, O'Leary's deputy chief executive at the time, out of his boss's earshot, rolled his eyes when asked if this change would really come to pass. 'I'll believe it when I see it,' he told one interested party.

The prior experiences of the Ryanair executives suggested that a Damascene conversion on the part of their boss was unlikely. Here's just one example: each Wednesday there was a rigorous review, at headquarters in Dublin, of the extra revenues Ryanair had pulled in over the previous week. At one stage the focus was on income from customers who had attempted to board with cabin bags that were bigger than the allowed 10kg maximum weight. Their oversized bags were taken from them at check-in, and they were charged an extra price for them. O'Leary occasionally would turn up and was known to shout and roar at his executives if those aggregate numbers for income derived from excess baggage did not meet his expectations. Giving up this specific money-making activity was one of the things he was now talking, in public, of abandoning.

Within days, however, O'Leary had started enforcing the new mantra. A team was put in place to respond to complaint emails, and the website was revamped to make it more user-friendly. A new digital strategy would be implemented, making access easier, in a bid to copy the improvements made by competitors such as easyJet. Ryanair would no longer charge for its mobile app, reduce online booking times and embrace social media via Twitter. O'Leary promised an end to the practice of fining customers whose carry-on baggage was just millimetres larger than the guidelines specified.

It wasn't quite a case of 'the beatings will stop once morale improves', but staff were told to be nice . . . or else. The Wednesday management meeting became something entirely different: a review of how helpful the staff were being to customers. While many executives were relieved and happy with the new outlook, some were disconcerted by the demands that were now being made of them. They had been so deeply conditioned by O'Leary's previous behaviour that they found it hard to adapt to this U-turn. This was cultural change writ large.

O'Leary doubled down on his promises, reiterating them publicly at an international aviation conference in London, and then again at the company's AGM in September, the one at which he apologized to Dr Al-Sattar. In the presence of shareholders and the media, he revealed a whole range of measures that, if implemented, should make travelling with Ryanair a far more pleasurable experience for the customer. He also did something else that was almost unprecedented for him. He admitted he had been wrong, and that he had often misbehaved in the past.

'I am very happy to take the blame or responsibility if we have a macho or abrupt culture. Some of that may well be my own personal character deformities,' he said. There were gasps from the audience as he admitted that he had no idea 'just how stressful' it had been for many people to fly with Ryanair. From now on, he would conduct its business in a 'softer, more sensitive and caring manner'. The airline would 'try to eliminate things that unnecessarily piss people off': 'We have to improve significantly those aspects of our customer service that irritate people. They irritate us as well. Some of our policies are implemented with a degree of robustness that isn't warranted. A lot of those customer-services elements don't cost a lot of money. It's something we are committed to addressing over the coming year.'

He wasn't entirely contrite. He defended the old rules about baggage and boarding passes as warranted, but then conceded that 'we overdid it. We had people inventing new rules at boarding gates . . . and we were putting our staff at points of conflict with customers.' O'Leary paid tribute to his ground and cabin staff, and said it would be wrong to suggest there was something seriously wrong with the airline's conduct. But he acknowledged that there remained 'something to improve, and we're very conscious of it'.

This softer, more sensitive and caring Michael O'Leary caught the attention not just of employees but of investors, rivals, media and the travelling public. To those who wondered if the new approach would cost money – and therefore damage profitability – O'Leary said the airline could afford to take advantage of its market-leading position. Ryanair had just become the first European carrier to pass the 9-million-passengers-in-one-month mark – and it had done it from a low-cost base.

Some of the more cynical media commentators thought that the announcement might have more to do with counteracting the negative publicity associated with the treatment of Dr Al-Sattar earlier that month. That incident no doubt made O'Leary pause and think, but to put the change of direction down to that alone might be crediting him with too much compassion. The decision to change had been made before that tragedy; the two merely coincided. There was another pressing reason to review the company's procedures, and it was one that was far closer to O'Leary's heart: profit.

Yet this fundamental shift was somewhat overshadowed

by other events, and when it was acknowledged, it was mis-understood or underplayed. O'Leary's many critics were sceptical of the promised changes and, myopically, many were interested in emphasizing the negatives instead of wondering what bigger picture O'Leary could see. That said, it is easy in retrospect to see why their attention was snagged on the immediate scene. September 2013 was a month of almost continuous bad news for, and from, O'Leary and Ryanair, far beyond customer satisfaction issues. For the first time in a decade, there was speculation about O'Leary's future at the airline.

It started publicly on 4 September with a 'profit warning' – a formal announcement to the stock market that the airline wasn't going to achieve the expected level of profits – the basis on which investors buy their shares. Projections of a profit of €640 million in the twelve months to the end of March 2014 were too high. At this stage, the company 'guided' to stock-market investors that it would produce pre-tax profits of somewhere between €570 million and €600 million, and probably at an even lower level than that.

To the casual observer that might seem like no big deal, but some investors panicked and headed for the exit chutes, selling all or part of their investments in the airline. The share price fell by 14 per cent on the day of the warning, taking more than €1.3 billion off Ryanair's market value, meaning it was now worth 'just' €8.3 billion. There had been days in the past when the share price had taken an even bigger tumble – such as in 2004, when it fell by 30 per cent in a day, again because of a profit warning – but Ryanair was much smaller back then, so the absolute amount knocked off the company's value was less dramatic. Clearly, the airline had flourished in the aftermath of that panic, but this was one of the biggest one-day falls ever in the market value of an Irish company and could not be shrugged off as 'one of those things'.

The immediate future did not look bright: Ryanair admitted that bookings for September, October and November 2013 were lower than expected and, on top of that, the average price being paid per ticket was below expectations. The pessimists saw it as the start of a trend. Any profit warning casts a spotlight on the CEO and his/her responsibility for what had happened to cause it. Inevitably, the questions began to roll: had O'Leary promised investors too much? Had he misread the market? Was he running the company in the wrong way? Was he able to deal with the changed marketplace and customer demands? Had he entered into commitments that could hamper the company's ability to nimbly adapt?

In Ryanair's case, investors worried that the airline had committed enormous sums to the purchase of new aircraft that might not now be filled, or that would be filled but not at sufficiently good revenues to reward the capital investment. In April 2013 O'Leary had agreed and signed a deal – subject to approval by shareholders, such was its size – to buy 175 new Boeing 737-800 aircraft. The value of the combined order came with a list price of $15 billion, but O'Leary was believed to have secured an extraordinary discount of more than half that amount, making it simultaneously a bargain and potentially an enormous risk.

The problem was that to get the full value from its order – no one outside of Ryanair (and its banks) and Boeing knew the exact figure, but speculation was that the bill was at least €7 billion – it would have to find new routes and then fill those aircraft with additional passengers. How exactly could this be achieved when it was losing custom on its existing ones?

An unmistakable gloating tone greeted the bad news in

sections of the media, and among the public. To some, O'Leary and Ryanair were getting their comeuppance. His critics argued that his bad manners and outrageous comments, as well as the airline's poor record of customer service, had more than outlived their usefulness, if indeed they ever could have been excused. It gave some people, perhaps ignorant of the firmness of O'Leary's grip on the company, the opportunity to raise questions about the sense of keeping him at the helm. Others asked more rational and fundamental questions: could it be that the model that had been so successful in the rapid growth of Ryanair was no longer capable of attracting the required number of customers to deliver its long-term ambitions?

O'Leary offered explanations, not following the old maxim of Irish business that 'When you're explaining, you're losing', preferring instead to persist in his belief that 'There is no such thing as bad publicity.' He said the declines were 'marginal and around the edges . . . We're not talking about some collapse or catastrophe, but it is weaker than we had expected it to be.' Ryanair had always done well in securing double-digit fare hikes for passengers who booked last-minute flights, particularly during its peak summer season, but a 2013 summer heatwave in the UK saw a fall in demand for Continental breaks. A decline in the value of sterling didn't help either, given that a quarter of Ryanair's revenue was generated in the British currency. O'Leary also blamed continuing austerity and weak economic conditions in Europe, which meant consumers had less money to spend on travel. This, in turn, meant Ryanair and other airlines were having to reduce fares at a time of increased seat availability in the British, Scandinavian, Spanish and Irish markets.

However, the contrarian in O'Leary believed that what

went down would go up again . . . for him, at least. O'Leary is wise to the desires of stock-market investors, who want consistent and smooth increases in profits from quarter to quarter, but he is also assertive enough to challenge their assumptions and demands. His form over the years has proven that O'Leary thinks longer term, which means he is prepared to take short-term hits to profits in order to fulfil larger ambitions – and to suffer the consequences of Ryanair losing some of its overall stock-market value, albeit temporarily. It's a strategy that requires nerves of steel for any CEO, but O'Leary is not a man to doubt himself.

That might explain why he let it happen again. In November 2013 O'Leary announced the company's second profit warning of the year. Instead of expecting a profit of somewhere around €570 million in the twelve months ending 31 March 2014, Ryanair admitted that the figure was more likely to be somewhere between €500 million and €520 million.

If the first profit warning was blamed on weak demand and the euro–sterling exchange rate, it was lower air fares – and a 'perceptible dip' in bookings – that got the blame now. O'Leary argued that fares were down 9 per cent in the last three months of 2013 and would be down about 10 per cent in the first quarter of 2014, pushing down customer yields because costs per passenger could be cut by only 7 per cent. Even a slight rise in actual numbers could not overcome the net effect that those sales would generate less profit. Regardless of how good his argument, in response the shares fell by 13 per cent in value on the stock market, to €5.33 per share, valuing the company at €7.6 billion.

Immediately, there was debate as to whether there was more to Ryanair's problems – whether, in fact, the low-fares strategy was becoming redundant. If the notion that the market had shifted gained ground, alongside the doubt surrounding O'Leary's ability to bring about the promised sharp improvement in customer service, even more investors might just be persuaded to bail, with the result that the share price would drop even further. It felt like dangerous times.

Much of the media commentary focused on comparisons between Ryanair and easyJet. The British airline – Ryanair's biggest competitor in the short-haul, low-fare market – was preferred by many of those loudly offering opinions because it was perceived to treat its customers better and to fly to more conveniently located airports for much the same price. Carolyn McCall was fêted for her manners as much as for her ability, in a pointed rebuke to O'Leary's carry-on. O'Leary was later to admit, on her departure in 2017, that 'I clearly underestimated her and I was proved wrong. She forced us to up our game on customer service. EasyJet and the industry are better as a result of her tenure.'

But he wasn't saying that publicly in late 2013. It was a more loose-lipped Howard Millar – who gave a series of interviews in 2014 as he departed Ryanair (although remaining as a part-time director) – who was more forthcoming about how McCall got under Ryanair's skin. 'I saw her being interviewed on *Newsnight* one time and she got a nice little run in, a few easy little questions,' said Millar in one of those interviews. 'If we'd been on it, we'd have got a stake through the heart.'

It got worse. Within weeks, easyJet announced a 51 per cent jump in profits to €673 million (£478 million). This didn't come as a surprise to Ryanair, which had been conducting detailed reviews of the publicly available figures. It noted that its rival was doing well in increasing both passenger volume and profitability. A strong October had seen easyJet passenger numbers increase by 5.4 per cent, with a load factor of 89.4 per cent. It was expected to carry 61 million passengers in 2014, which was about three quarters of Ryanair's estimated total.

Long before the 2013 profit warnings, however, there had been plenty of internal discussion at Ryanair as to whether its own strategy of offering low fares at the expense of customer service was still realistic. The slowly dawning realization was that they might have to offer both. Millar admitted that the Ryanair product 'had got run down over a number of years' and conceded that: 'We were too aggressive. We were trundling along. Our load factor was flat, our fares were slightly up or down, so we knew there was something going on. We started to look more closely at how easyJet was managing its fares and how it was pushing the whole customer relationship.' By contrast, the Ryanair management concluded that their airline had become 'rules-based'.

'We set the rules and we pushed people to implement them and if you didn't implement them, we penalized you,' Millar said. 'The buck has to stop somewhere. Management made those decisions, but we absolutely went too far. We could see that the excess-baggage take was rising, people were being caught for €50 at the gate, the grief we were getting on the boarding-card reissue thing – all of these things were cumulative.'

Not for the first time, O'Leary had allowed the impression to form that his airline was in trouble, that it could not sustain its profitability. This was not deception, because he put accurate information into the public domain and he could not be responsible if the herd interpreted it in a particular way. On this occasion, he created a situation where investors thought, Well, if that's happening to Ryanair, which knows what it is doing, what's going on at its rivals?

Why did he do this? O'Leary likes creating chaos and crisis within the airline industry. It is a defining aspect of his personality and business strategy that he is not afraid of what turbulence will do to him or to Ryanair, as long as he feels he is the one in control of the situation. He believes his stirring of the pot can do great damage to his competitors, or enemies, which will deliver long-term benefit to Ryanair and its shareholders. He is always playing the long game, and that's a point many commentators seem to miss as they exclaim over his latest whimsy or outrage.

Historically, Ryanair always reacted quickly to adverse conditions, and the November 2013 profit warning was no different. It prompted O'Leary, in addition to the customer-service improvements he had promised in September, to engage his tried and trusted approach: he announced a marketing blitz with seat sales to fill aircraft. He decided to ground up to 80 of the 300 aircraft for the winter, as against his previous plan of about 50, because it was better to incur the cost of mothballing them than have them in the air losing money, especially with the oversupply bringing overall prices down even further. O'Leary's decisive actions would cut available seats by about 750,000, allowing him to better maintain overall prices and yields on other flights.

In a trademark show of bullishness, O'Leary did not hide and nor did he show any lack of confidence in his ability to deal with what was going on: 'What we tend to do in these periods when pricing is weak – as we did after 9/11, as we did after the London bombings, as we did after any other events – is lorry out loads of cheap fares. If a couple of competitors get blown up as part of that process – well and good.'

On a conference call with stockbroking analysts, he held up his winning formula: 'You go back to the fundamentals, the Ryanair model. We take whatever price we get as long as we fill our planes to 82 per cent, 83 per cent on a year-round basis. And if this is one of those five or six years where prices fall, let's capitalize on it and be out there with aggressive pricing, driving up traffic and putting pressure on the competition.' Some saw it as bravado, but others suspected he was more in control of the situation than the majority of his rivals. O'Leary argued that Ryanair was partly the 'author' of the reduced-profit guidance: what he meant was that he was taking control of the market in response to the increased competition and weak economic conditions by cutting fares, and that some of his rivals would fail as a result.

Stockbrokers decided it wasn't a bluff, and they bought the O'Leary sales pitch. The Dublin-based Goodbody cautioned clients about 'short-term weakness' in the shares, but also assured them that the long-term fundamentals of the company remained positive, especially going into 2015. Investec noted that traffic would 'pause' for the next twelve months, but that O'Leary's commitment to beating everyone else on price was 'bad news for competing airlines across Europe'. Davy cut its twelve-month price target for Ryanair from €8 to €7 – compared to the €5.68 price immediately after the latest profit warning – but also stated that the airline was laying building-blocks for future growth and that it would make up for lower ticket fares with cost decreases in time.

It wasn't a surprise that O'Leary had convinced them to come around to his way of thinking. Not all investors get the same treatment. The professional investors at most public companies – with large holdings – get reasonably regular briefings from Ryanair senior management, and stockbroking analysts, on behalf of investors big and small, get to hear and see them, too. They get to see more of the real O'Leary, a man who is measured and controlled and not saying things just to grab publicity – the clown's mask removed. What they had come to understand was that O'Leary could micro-manage his business but at the same time see the big picture, that while he was rigidly consistent in some things – such as managing costs – he was flexible enough to change the things that he realized were going wrong, to introduce new things even when they involved something he hated, such as incurring costs.

Professional analysts and investors know that many corporate bosses are stubborn, resistant to change and criticism, confident that they can carry all before them by doing as they have done before. As such, they watch for the signs of inflexibility because it's a red flag. When the chief executive is a dictator – and all the evidence suggests that O'Leary was and is – those dangers may be magnified. But, at the same time, any chief executive who has previously steered a course through the toxic cloud of a profit warning may be skilful enough to do so again. They have garnered the relevant experience. And, in addition, O'Leary really did seem willing to embrace the proposed changes for the good of the company. So they watched to see if he would practise what he preached. If he didn't, that would be their red flag – a warning that it might be time to head for the exits.

However, those investors who were surprised by the profit warnings had good reason to be, and, if they didn't believe the positive spin being put on things, they had good reason to be angry, too. That very year, only three months before the first profit warning, O'Leary had been required to host an EGM of shareholders to confirm the biggest contract in the history of the airline. The latest deal to buy new aircraft was being negotiated at a time when Boeing was launching its all-new 737-MAX aircraft. Ryanair was able to use both its own market power and the argument that it was not buying the most up-to-date model to get a deal on incredibly favourable terms.

Not for the first time, O'Leary had driven Boeing to near-distraction. Talks about the new contract had gone on for years, but throughout this time O'Leary had publicly courted the European manufacturer Airbus and the Chinese entrant to the market, Comac. O'Leary took a day trip to China to display to Boeing his interest in a possible relationship with this competitor, and he spoke of his requirements in aircraft design at a press conference at the Paris Air Show. At one stage he publicly derided the designs of a Boeing plane as a 'dog's dinner of a design' that 'had been drawn on the back of a fag packet'. That, almost inevitably, was the plane he ended up ordering.

The deal was the biggest capital investment of any kind ever announced by an Irish company. While his critics worried that Ryanair would not be able to fill the planes with enough passengers, O'Leary was sure he knew better. There was great profit available to him once he filled those cheaply acquired aircraft, with their bigger capacity, especially as his operating costs would not rise. He reassured nervous investors at the June EGM, promising them 'renewed growth', boasting that 'current trading' at the airline was 'excellent' and claiming that the airline had been 'inundated' with requests from airports in Europe to add new services.

That was an important angle, because having aircraft was one thing, but having airports in and out of which they could fly was just as essential. Stansted had become the airline's most important airport – even more so than Dublin – but, while Ryanair had used it as a hub to service other secondary airports, it knew Stansted also had the potential to link up with primary airports all over Continental Europe.

Ryanair's approach towards management at the British Airports Authority-owned Stansted was aggressive over the years, and it often lobbied the Civil Aviation Authority over the prices charged at the airport. To Ryanair's delight, Manchester Airports Group bought Stansted in February 2013 in a £1.5 billion deal. Ryanair had encouraged it to do so, promising more business for the airport, as long as it got reduced fees per passenger. It was a hefty price tag, and MAG was under pressure to turn around the long-term decline in traffic at Stansted. Total passenger numbers had been falling since 2007 and were now at about 17 million annually, making it the third-largest airport by passenger numbers in the London region.

MAG wanted to build a second runway – to support a range of business and leisure, low-cost and premium, long- and short-haul flights – to initiate a shift away from being purely a base for cheap flights to Europe. It started an £80 million terminal redesign in order to improve its security checks and airside shops in a bid to attract airlines to fly long-haul routes. None of this investment impressed Ryanair, particularly if it was expected to pay for it. The plan was for the airport to increase passenger numbers to 30 million within ten years, but the catch was that it would be impossible to achieve without Ryanair.

Despite Stansted's importance to Ryanair's future, O'Leary engaged in more brinksmanship to sweat better terms out of the deal. He realized that, much as he needed Stansted, its new owners needed Ryanair more, because MAG was immediately reliant on the income it would get from Ryanair to make the finances of its acquisition work. One of Ryanair's first moves with Stansted under new management was to cut its flights from the airport by 6 per cent in protest at the price structure MAG had inherited. The point having been made,

Ryanair's deputy chief executive, Michael Cawley, negotiated a deal with MAG and presented it to O'Leary for approval. To Cawley's horror and shock, O'Leary said the terms were still too generous to Stansted and that he would sign only if Cawley secured a further 15 per cent reduction in the proposed fees. Cawley objected, saying O'Leary had been aware of how the negotiations had been progressed, but O'Leary insisted Cawley return and do the deal again. Cawley did, MAG buckled, and O'Leary got the terms he wanted.

The details of the new deal with Stansted went unreported, but management within Ryanair were cock-a-hoop with what Cawley eventually extracted. Insiders said this was almost as important to the airline's growth plans as the order for new aircraft. Analysts at Citibank estimated that Ryanair paid Stansted €8.40 per passenger, and a 10 per cent discount would deliver Ryanair savings of approximately €11 million a year. In return, Ryanair would increase the number of aircraft based at Stansted from 37 to 43 and add four new routes – Bordeaux, Dortmund, Lisbon and Rabat – to make a total of 120. The deal also required Ryanair to work with MAG to develop its flight network and to encourage other airlines to add long-haul flights from the airport. 'We would offer a network of flights unrivalled by any other airline at any other London airport,' said O'Leary. 'We would serve more destinations from Stansted than BA would serve from Heathrow and Gatwick combined.'

It was an interesting contrast: the media was talking doom and gloom, forecasting the end of the Ryanair model; O'Leary was upbeat, energetic and forward-looking. Someone had to be right, and someone had to be wrong.

4. A new departure

There were plenty of signs in November 2013 that, despite two profit warnings, O'Leary was confident about where Ryanair was heading; but the media is often more interested in apparent bad news than it is in seemingly mundane announcements about intentions that are actually crucial to the future. Ryanair announced nine new routes from Dublin and increased the frequency of eight existing services, creating 300 jobs and promising an additional 700,000 passengers through the airport every year. The new routes included locations that many would never have dreamt there would be a sizeable market for: Almeria, Bari, Basel, Bucharest, Chania, Comiso, Lisbon, Marrakesh and Prague. It brought to 85 the number of services that Ryanair operated from Dublin Airport. It also increased the frequency of the Dublin to Birmingham, Bristol, Edinburgh, Glasgow, London Stansted, Madrid, Manchester and Nice routes, bringing the number of flights from 300 to 400.

In addition, having lobbied the new Fine Gael/Labour coalition government to remove a travel tax that the previous government had introduced during the recession, Ryanair introduced eight new routes out of Shannon Airport in the west of Ireland, with a promise to nearly double the annual number of passengers. O'Leary also demonstrated his confidence in the company's finances by continuing to return money to shareholders by way of a €1 billion share-buyback programme, his preferred alternative to paying dividends, because by buying back shares and cancelling them, the value of the remaining shares increased. Ryanair hadn't issued a profit warning in a decade. For ten years O'Leary had under-promised and over-delivered. Now he was telling investors that 'It's one of those years', when the company had to take a financial hit to maintain its competitive advantage for the sake of future profitability. As Millar said: 'We are still going to make over half a billion this year. That's a good perform-ance from any company.'

Not everyone agreed, though. Chief Executive Christoph Mueller of Aer Lingus was particularly vocal in criticizing Ryanair: 'For the first time someone has explored the dark side of the elasticity curve. They have cut prices by 20 per cent, but only gained 5 or 6 per cent in volume. That's a new phenomenon.' This raised the notion that Ryanair had satur-ated the European short-haul market and driven both costs and prices down to their productive limits. What Mueller may not have realized, however, was that O'Leary, in his meticulous way of sizing up the market, had gone beyond that consideration.

Instead, O'Leary decided to do something difficult, some-thing that risked changing the existing Ryanair brand – even if he claimed not to believe in branding – and that might not convince the travelling public. He decided to re-engineer Ryanair itself, keeping all that he regarded as best about it, but adding a new dimension: improved customer service. It was the 'be nice' campaign, and it was even going to have a catchy title: *Always Getting Better.*

In an uncharacteristic move, Ryanair held a formal, bells-and-whistles launch for the new campaign at the end of March 2014. It was to be implemented by a new member of staff, Kenny Jacobs, who joined Ryanair in 2014 and who was encouraged to quickly take up a position of public prominence, easing some of the burden on O'Leary. A graduate of University College Cork, Jacobs had worked outside Ireland for many years, with companies like Tesco and the German retailer Metro Group. At the age of forty he wanted to return to Ireland, so he left his job as chief marketing officer of moneysupermarket.com to join Ryanair. O'Leary tasked him with re-establishing the brand by adding better service to its unique selling point of low ticket prices. Jacobs was given responsibility for marketing, communications and sales, but, crucially, he was also given the job of marrying the new ethos to improvements in digital technology, which would be overseen by other managers who would be hired. It was effectively a brand-new role, with a greater emphasis on marketing at a senior level than ever before. Jacobs's appointment – and the importance attached to it – was one of the biggest signs that O'Leary was determined to prove that he and Ryanair were evolving.

The location chosen by Jacobs for the big announcement – and to which O'Leary reluctantly agreed – was the Design Museum on the banks of the River Thames in London. Ryanair had always held press conferences, but usually in cheap hotel conference rooms, airport meeting rooms or its own offices, all to keep the costs down. If reporters got a cup of tea or coffee, it was because the hotel had provided it. Not so for *Always Getting Better*. Ryanair flew in many of the seventy-plus invited journalists and plied them with free baked sea bass, smoked salmon and pumpkin risotto, washed down with copious free Prosecco and other complimentary drinks. It was like a return to the era of Ryanair's first chief executive, Eugene O'Neill, which O'Leary had brought to an end in the late 1980s as the airline's losses mounted in an orgy of flash expenditure. When O'Leary joked that the 'expensive yuppy London venue' was turning his stomach, he may well have been serious ... and that was even before he was presented with the bill.

It was a day for turning on the charm, for attempting to change the perception of O'Leary that had formed and hardened among the media over the years. Was he up to the job of behaving himself in a mannerly and mature fashion? He couldn't quite manage it. He toned down the bad language, but he couldn't eliminate it entirely, so a few expletives crept in. One female journalist drew attention to the decision to populate the venue with attractive, blonde Ryanair hosts wearing skimpy blouses and tight black pencil skirts. 'Skye has assured me she's not that cold,' shot back O'Leary, who was standing next to one of the women. 'I will, of course, do everything in my power to warm her up.' Only some in the audience found it amusing.

A picture of a smiling O'Leary, holding and petting a Labrador puppy, was projected on to a giant screen on one wall. Some of those present wondered if the photo was of a real animal that O'Leary had held for the photograph, or was a stuffed prop, or a Photoshopped image. Trained by experience to apply a large dose of salt in all dealings with O'Leary, they wondered if this cuddly image was yet another example of him taking the piss.

It was put directly to O'Leary that people might find it hard to believe he could be friendlier and less confrontational and controversial, that a smiling, puppy-stroking O'Leary might not be believed. 'It's not an image,' he responded. 'It's real. I've always been a nice guy, just misunderstood.'

There were plenty of announcements to be made that afternoon. As part of *Always Getting Better*, O'Leary announced that the new website would be launched on 10 April, with the phone app following in May. Seats would now be assigned at booking, bringing a second bag on board would be free, and families would be allowed to prebook seats together. It was the night of the *volte-face*. Having denigrated frequent-flyer clubs and bonuses for decades, he now unveiled the My Ryanair Club, which offered discounts and free flights to members. In his speech he said that 'We had locked ourselves into a position of "We're cheaper, nastier and we don't care." But there were millions of passengers saying, "I don't care how cheap you are." We should try to eliminate things that unnecessarily piss people off.'

He admitted that the company had imposed 'overzealous restrictions on bags' in the past, to 'incentivise people to travel with less'. Now he announced that additional charges for luggage over the summer months – seen as a tax on family holidays – would be scrapped. Extra charges for heavier bags were to be abolished, along with escalating fees for second, third and fourth items. 'By getting rid of baggage check-in, we got people checking in on the website,' he said. 'We got rid of check-in-desk rental charges, check-in staff, baggage-handling staff and lost-bag departments – and we reduced ticket prices as a result.'

The airline decided to offer a range of discounts for parents travelling with children, a Family Extra service that included a free 5kg infant bag allowance, reduced infant fees, a 50 per cent reduction on allocated seating charges for children and discounted priority boarding. The new service also offered in-flight bottle warming and baby-changing facilities, as well as the ability to bring two free pieces of infant equipment, such as a buggy or a cot.

'Hell has frozen over,' O'Leary said, laughing. 'Ryanair is

doing TV advertising, distributing through travel agents and being nice to customers. For twenty-odd years our focus has been to stack the product high and sell it cheap. We're still going to do that, but we're going to let the customer relax in the process. Just imagine how many more people we're going to carry and how much more money we're going to make when we give customers more of what they want.'

And yet . . . the question remained as to whether people would believe him. If they didn't believe him, would this hurt Ryanair? The impression was created that Jacobs was going to be more to the fore as the new, customer-friendly face of Ryanair, with O'Leary making fewer, and more restrained, public appearances. (Later that year, Millar would say that he had persuaded O'Leary to be more 'presidential', aloof from the fray.) The idea was encouraged that Ryanair had come to believe that the airline's brand was too tightly wound up with O'Leary's personal version – and that, as he deeply divided opinion, he was alienating the airline from those who didn't like him, costing it potential revenues. 'When I go around saying *mea culpa, mea maxima culpa*, I'm sorry for what I've done wrong, well, this generates huge publicity. Is it just a PR stunt? I'm no longer going to be dressing up in silly costumes to generate free publicity,' O'Leary said, playing the chastened man.

So was this it, then? Was Michael O'Leary ready to settle down, grow up and assume a suitably CEO style of behaviour and management? The vision being dangled before investors and the public was tantalizing: that of a reliable airline that matched low prices with high standards. What could be better? If O'Leary was indeed determined to see this through, and could pull it off, there could be a golden age ahead for Ryanair.

PART 2

Man and businessman

5. Foundations

Michael O'Leary has become an actor. He plays a part – very effectively, if increasingly repetitively – in a corporate soap opera, performing as expected for his audience, delivering punchy lines that engage and even enthral them. He is the big personality in a world that the general public perceives as a succession of dour people in grey suits. O'Leary draws attention to himself deliberately, defying political correctness with his often incendiary comments, making mischief, but also telling truths that others evade. For those who aren't listening, he isn't afraid to provide visual stimulation, dressing up in costumes as he mugs for the cameras in all sorts of daft positions or even, on one occasion, stripping to his shorts to pose for photographs with Ryanair air-hostesses in their bikinis.

He is easily the best-known Irish businessman of his generation, and, while readily and interchangeably identified with Ryanair, his notoriety is not necessarily for what he has done with the airline's name but for what he has done with his own. There are many 'characters' in Irish life, but few enough of them in Irish business circles. His fame is such that he was the first person approached when the producers of the Irish version of *The Apprentice* sought a high-profile 'boss' to fill the Donald Trump role. As a real businessperson, rather than a figurehead, O'Leary had no truck with such nonsense, but it was easy to see why the producers wanted him. He divides opinion, but, more importantly, he also attracts it. He comes across as down-to-earth, someone most people would like to have a beer with, even if the truth is that he is not a great socializer. And yet it shouldn't be forgotten that he is, at core, somebody who had an accountant's training and whose main interest is in making money – that everything he does in public is with the aim of persuading his audience to spend money with his airline. But it doesn't necessarily mean the public sees the full picture: that of the family man who lives in the area where he grew up, eschewing high-profile social circles, and who is a regular local Mass-goer at the Catholic church where he was married.

All sorts of things made him the man he is: his family, his schooling and his mentors. O'Leary went to a local primary school in Mullingar, County Westmeath, but his formative education was at Clongowes Wood College in County Kildare, a private boarding school run by the Jesuit order (whose most famous member is Pope Francis). A Jesuit education is seen as a huge asset among the business and professional classes. It is preparation for taking a place among the elite, for making the connections that will endure throughout life. While many of the school's ambitions for its pupils seem boilerplate – 'intellectually competent, socially able and culturally aware, physically and emotionally developed and committed to strive for excellence' – there are some less-standard aspirations that pupils are encouraged to fulfil. There is a strong emphasis on social awareness. Students are encouraged to 'develop their sense of conscience and to become men who can discern what is right and have the courage to do the right thing' and also 'to be compassionate, to respond to those in greatest need and to have a strong sense of empathy'.

Clongowes is all about money, too, even if it pretends otherwise. It is a Catholic boys-only boarding school that receives and educates Ireland's richest sons. The annual fees of over €20,000 ensure that it remains an elite school – and it is the school for O'Leary's own sons, too. O'Leary has tried to downplay its exclusivity in interviews, claiming that its popularity with the rich is a phenomenon that developed only after he left. This isn't the case. Clongowes has long been associated with privilege, following an ethos that was, and is, deliberately developed to ensure that Ireland's future leaders come from the right stock and are adequately pre-pared. It could be described as an Irish Catholic version of Eton or Harrow, if not quite as stiff and formal. Its roll call of famous past pupils, before and since O'Leary's time, speaks for itself: James Joyce; former taoiseach (prime min-ister) John Bruton and his brother, Minister Richard Bruton; Tánaiste (deputy prime minister) Simon Coveney and his brother Patrick, the Greencore chief executive; John Red-mond, leader of the Irish Parliamentary Party from 1900 to 1918; Tom O'Higgins and Thomas Finlay, both former chief justices of the Supreme Court; U2's manager, Paul McGuin-ness; and international rugby players Gordon D'Arcy and Rob Kearney. The multimillionaire businessman Tony O'Reilly, although schooled by Belvedere College (another Jesuit insti-tution), sent his sons from America to Clongowes, such is its power to impress on a resumé.

O'Leary went to Clongowes in 1974 from his family's farm in Mullingar, County Westmeath. Unlike many of his peers, he wasn't of Clongowes stock, in that he wasn't the son of a past pupil. O'Leary has suggested that he may have been a little intimidated by his surroundings, but he seems to have handled it in a way that very much speaks of his future self: 'Don't ask me why, I was not precocious, but I was always a loudmouth. In my first year at Clongowes I used to get killed by the sixth years, mouthing off at them. Boarding school is very good in that it teaches you to shut up occasionally.'

He spent six years at the school, playing in various sports activities alongside his academic studies. He was a competent cross-country runner and played rugby as well, although he wasn't good enough for the school's first team. His real love was golf and he was fortunate that the school had its own private course. O'Leary used the facilities regularly and enthusiastically, and was regarded as well able. He was able also to turn his hobby to profitable use. During his summer holidays, he would earn money at Mullingar Golf Club by caddying for the adults. His favourite client was the nationally famous show-band singer Joe Dolan, a local. O'Leary wasn't a known fan of Dolan's music, but Dolan tipped generously for carrying his bag of clubs, and O'Leary made sure that he was the one who got to caddy for him. He showed an instinct for having his own money from an early age.

He made a good circle of friends, but by his own admission he didn't make a particularly big impression at Clongowes. Interestingly, his fellow students remember him as quiet, reserved and, surprisingly, conformist. He was regarded by some as an introvert. He was never marked out as the one who would succeed greatly, let alone to the extent he has, or who would conduct himself in the high-profile and often combative manner he has chosen. One friend recalls that Mick – as his friends called him – got up early many mornings, without complaint, to go help the priests prepare the celebration of Mass. Some of those schoolmates look at the adult O'Leary with a degree of bafflement. He has become one of Ireland's most celebrated and controversial businessmen, and they wonder how he became so brash, ebullient, loud and confrontational. 'Where were the clues?' said one, mystified.

O'Leary could thank his parents for giving him the start in life that only Clongowes could bestow. He was the second of six children, and his parents had certainly never had the benefit of a first-class education. His father, Timothy (known to all as Ted), and his mother, Gerarda (he remains close to his mother and is somewhat in awe of her), were originally from Kanturk in County Cork, where their own parents farmed, but they moved to Mullingar when Ted had an idea for a business he wanted to set up. O'Leary senior was interested in earning more than farming could bring him. He went through a string of businesses, having started in textiles and then moved into agricultural supplies. His working life had what has been described euphemistically as 'many highs and lows'.

O'Leary has always been careful not to reveal too much about private family matters – out of respect for the wishes of his mother and siblings – but in one rare comment about his late father he said: '[My father] was great at starting up businesses, but crap at running them.' Elaborating on this during another interview, he said that 'The trouble, like with a lot of entrepreneurs, was that once he had set up a business he started to lose interest in it, or lose money, which was even worse.'

O'Leary was still at Clongowes when the family textile business, Tailteann, was put into receivership in 1976. It had been struggling in the recession for years prior to that, and Ted had tried desperately to keep it afloat. How aware O'Leary was of the situation is not clear, although there were signs that the children could not miss. Apparently, O'Leary's father's track record in business meant that 'When we went bust, he would sell the house, and when he made money, he would buy another house.' The O'Leary family moved three times when Michael was growing up, living in Mullingar's Harbour Street until 1972, then moving to Clonard House, the former residence of the Bishop of Meath, for a year, before moving again, this time to the village of Lynn, outside Mullingar.

'We were comfortable,' O'Leary told one interviewer. 'The wealth came more from the fact that we had a very good family life. We never went on foreign holidays or anything like that, but I never in all my childhood memories remember ever wanting for anything and certainly not when time came to educate us and there were six children within eight years. By that standard we were very well off and we were very well taken care of.'

O'Leary learnt much from his parents and their values and choices. Knowledge of his father's experiences seems to have informed much of his subsequent career in business. While O'Leary has never been afraid to make a big bet in business, he has rarely done so from borrowed money. He is a man who ensures he has large cash reserves in place, both corporately and personally. He has something of the old-fashioned farmer about him: he likes to have cash and to haggle about the price of things, much as his father did. He is also obsessive about costs and managing costs, which may stem from his father's failed businesses. If, as he said, his father wasn't an adept manager and he paid for that by going bust time and again, undoubtedly that lesson stuck hard with his son. The Ryanair ethos of low costs might well have its origins in Ted's losses. But, although he may have made mistakes, O'Leary's father was hard-working and ambitious. That's another lesson O'Leary took with him into life: 'I learned from my parents the value of hard work, and I think that will always stay with me.' In Mullingar, there are people who say that ethic was particularly true of his mother, who is regarded as a formidable figure. Certainly, her son remains somewhat in awe of her.

There was an interesting pen-picture of O'Leary senior given by Philip Reynolds, businessman and son of former taoiseach Albert Reynolds. Ted supplied the Reynolds' company, C&D Pet Foods, with materials, so Philip dealt with him regularly. In an interview with biographer Alan Ruddock in 2007, Reynolds said of O'Leary senior: 'One: he was a difficult man to deal with, always considered himself to be the expert and never wrong. He would not accept criticism of either his service or his product. Two: he knew the value of a pound and never accepted damaged or spoilt credit notes, and he made it his business to find a reason to visit around the time for payment and so collected his dues in person. And three: he was always looking for an angle, trying to do better, to do things different and do more and more business.' The apple certainly doesn't fall far from the tree.

Ireland is such a small country that connections are often made readily, and Clongowes was designed to enhance that. At the school, O'Leary had already encountered a family that would have a life-changing impact on him. Cathal, Declan and Shane Ryan were sent by their father, Tony Ryan, to board at the school, two of them during O'Leary's time there. None was in O'Leary's class, but he knew them, and Declan was in his brother Eddie's class. Their father was on his way to becoming a celebrated figure in Irish business circles. He had come from an Ireland far removed from the hallowed hall of Clongowes, but would work his way up to a life of fantastic wealth. O'Leary couldn't have known then, of course, but the Ryans were his future.

After Clongowes, O'Leary studied for a business degree at Trinity College Dublin, another establishment institution. He has downplayed his time at TCD as being more about enjoying the social side than concentrating on his education, but, again, this was part of his subsequent myth-building. He worked hard and was lucky in that he enjoyed privileges not readily available to the majority of students in that era. He received a very generous weekly allowance from his parents and the use of a family apartment in Dublin that he shared with two of his sisters. He topped up the allowance further by working as a barman at his uncle's Dublin hotels. He discovered that he wasn't afraid of working long and unsocial hours, and that he liked having his own cash. 'I knew that I wanted to make money,' he said. That was an important realization because it guided all of his subsequent decisions.

He left university not just with a degree but with money in the bank, an unheard-of achievement in the Ireland of the 1980s. His degree was good enough to secure a graduate place at Stokes Kennedy Crowley (SKC), one of the country's leading accountancy practices, which numbered many of the country's biggest companies and richest individuals among its clients. (It has since been renamed KPMG.) There he came under the wing of Gerry McEvoy (who just happened to be Tony Ryan's tax adviser). O'Leary was gaining in confidence and in McEvoy he found the perfect mentor, someone who was willing and able to encourage a more maverick thinker than many who took up the profession. Although O'Leary knew that he needed accountancy training to fulfil his ambition of making even more money, he did not foresee a future in which he would work his way up to being a partner at SKC. To him, that sounded boring, and not a path to serious wealth. Although former SKC trainees of his intake remember him as almost obsessively hard-working, he had no interest in sitting the exams that were needed to gain full accountancy qualifications. It seemed he had inherited his father's entrepreneurial instincts: 'I wanted to work for myself because that was the only way to make money in those days. The money was in newsagents, pubs and property.'

So, just as he would many years later, he assessed the market, reviewed the options and made his choice: newsagents. He opened a shop in Dublin, opposite the Kestrel corner, on Walkinstown Roundabout in the south-west suburbs of the city. Remarkably, given his age and the depth of the recession at the time, he persuaded his bank manager at AIB to give him a £25,000 (nearly €32,000) overdraft, at an annual rate of interest of 28 per cent. That provided a powerful incentive to make enough money to make his repayments, and have some left over.

It was an era of high unemployment and little disposable income. While O'Leary was in competition with the supermarkets, there were far fewer convenience stores about the place and the supermarkets opened very limited hours. He learnt all the practical skills of managing stock and cash flow and the buying habits of customers. He was able to squeeze an additional margin out of providing a service from a limited amount of stock. 'You learn from day one that my costs are this, my sales are that, and what's in the middle is my profit. So you are driving down costs, increasing sales and increasing your margins.'

Just as he had while moonlighting as a barman at college, he worked long hours, with the shop open from 7 a.m. to 11 p.m., under his micro-management. As he grew the business, he learnt how to delegate by hiring good managers and he bought into another two outlets. For years afterwards he loved to relate the story of how one Christmas Day he decided to take advantage of the fact that every other premises was closed. He remained open, bought in a massive stock of chocolate, cigarettes, batteries and other household essentials, raised the prices threefold and sold out of everything. His normal daily turnover was £1,000, but on this miraculous Christmas Day he made £14,000. 'I have never had a sexual experience in my life like it. The feeling of having one wad of notes pushed down one side of my trousers and another wad of notes down the other, waddling out of the newsagent in Walkinstown with about fourteen grand, hoping I wasn't going to be mugged going to the car.' He had read the market's needs before it even knew it had needs, and reaped the rewards.

It was a superb grounding for his later career. He learnt the impact on the bottom line of driving turnover upwards while simultaneously driving down costs. His tendency to micro-manage was striking, especially when it came to his staff. When he had three shops on the go, he couldn't be everywhere at once. To ensure his staff didn't rip him off, he put a sterling £5 note in the cash till each day, then made sure it was still there when he did the cash tot at the end of the day. If it was missing – given to a customer instead of an IR£5, which the till operator then pocketed – he would sack whoever had been manning the till that day. Whether someone had given him reason to be so suspicious and distrusting isn't known, but it does point to a man who subscribed to the idea that offence really is the best defence.

O'Leary was now in retail full time and his future looked bright, but, in an echo of his father's career, and just as had happened at SKC, he started to find it 'boring'. He wouldn't stay in retail for long.

6. Working for nothing

Tony Ryan was one of Ireland's most high-profile business successes. He was a self-made man in the old tradition, born into poverty in a working-class family and attaining immense wealth thanks to his own intelligence, eye for an opportunity others couldn't see, hard graft and sheer bullheadedness. It's a familiar description and brings O'Leary to mind – although O'Leary's family gave him a leg-up and he started much further up the ladder.

While O'Leary was at Clongowes, Ryan was a senior manager at Aer Lingus, in charge of Aer Lingus operations at JFK Airport, a role he had filled previously in Cork and Chicago. He had sent his sons back to Ireland for their education, and in 1973 he decided the whole family should follow.

There was no obvious role for Ryan within Aer Lingus back in Ireland – which had not been particularly interested in accommodating his relocation – so he was put into a division that managed the financing of aircraft, one of the biggest expenditures for an airline. Aer Lingus was going through a difficult time. Tourism into Ireland had slumped in the early to mid 1970s because of the international attention paid to 'The Troubles', the violent conflict in Northern Ireland. This was exacerbated by the soaring price of fuel during what was known as 'the Oil Crisis'. Ryan was given instructions to rid the airline of the two Jumbo aircraft used to service the Dublin–Shannon–New York route. Ryan's solution was to lease the aircraft to other airlines that had a greater need. He managed to achieve this, much to the delight of his impressed bosses. His wife, Mairead, wasn't as impressed because it also meant he had to bring the family out of the country again, this time to Thailand, to manage one of the planes on behalf of Air Siam.

The experience had planted a big idea in his mind. He could see an opportunity for a sizeable business. Many airlines might not be able to afford ownership of aircraft, but they needed them to operate. Wouldn't they jump at the chance to lease them from a specialist owner? Subsequently, Aer Lingus insiders would argue that Ryan had claimed credit for an idea that had been given to him by his employer. Whatever the exact origins of the venture, Ryan was the driving force: he took a big personal risk to establish it, borrowing £5,000, secured on a new mortgage on his home, to buy a 10 per cent share. Craftily, he got the other investors to agree that his shareholding would never be diluted by subsequent investments of new capital, something that backs up the assertion it was his idea. With the assistance of Aer Lingus and the private bank Guinness Mahon as his major shareholders, each holding 45 per cent, Ryan established a company called Guinness Peat Aviation, later GPA. It would purchase aircraft and rent or lease them to airlines that could not afford the massive upfront capital cost of buying them outright. The new company was based in Shannon, on Ireland's west coast, to take advantage of the tax benefits specific to the region. The business became very profitable very quickly, making him personally very wealthy.

Ryan's swift rise was noted by a sometimes admiring and curious Irish media. They detailed his back story: his decision to ditch a secure, pensionable state job at the age of thirty-nine – something few would have done at that time – to engineer a new start-up; his hectic working lifestyle that involved flying all over the world to make big money deals. They recounted how he hired the brightest and best young lawyers, actuaries and accountants, and made salesmen of them. They chronicled the arduous working hours, as the executives flew around the world between Monday and Friday, and of Monday-morning management meetings in Shannon, where they were berated and sometimes humiliated as an often angry Ryan demanded even better performances. Ryan became known to his staff as 'the Seagull': he flew in, shat on their heads and flew off again. The rewards for those who stayed the pace were considerable as the profits rolled in and GPA became an ever more valuable company. Ryan himself drew multi-million-pound annual dividends, which were largely tax-free.

Ryan decided to enjoy his wealth through investment and consumption. He developed a more cultivated accent (which reverted to its original roots when he was angry), wore the most expensive Savile Row pinstripe suits or white linen suits with a trilby, became a patron of the arts, and spent his money on expensive food, wine and property. Over the next decade he assembled a portfolio of magnificent homes, including his main base, Kilboy House, a 300-acre estate in County Tipperary, where he kept Irish wolfhounds and a herd of Blonde d'Aquitaine cattle. He kept houses in Monte Carlo, Ibiza and Mexico, and on Eaton Square in London; he also owned a Kentucky stud farm. Amid all that new-found wealth and success, his marriage to Mairead broke down, although they never divorced. He began a string of relationships with women, including, most famously, Miranda Guinness, Countess of Iveagh, who had married into the famous brewing family. Over time, having been absent much of the time while they were growing up, he became much closer to his sons.

Michael O'Leary – or Mick, as he was to the Ryan family – became like a son to Tony Ryan, too. They had long been aware of each other, especially during O'Leary's time at SKC, when Ryan had tried to poach him, but then O'Leary had veered off into the retail business. When he decided to leave that, he looked around at his options. He had money in the bank, so financial security wasn't a pressing concern. What he needed now was to understand how to make the leap from earning a large amount of money to accumulating serious wealth. That's how O'Leary came to offer his services to Ryan for free, so that he could be near the kind of success he wanted for himself, and to watch and learn. Ryan had always hoped to reel in O'Leary, so he agreed readily to the simple terms: O'Leary would get 5 per cent of whatever he earned for Ryan personally in a twelve-month period.

Starting in 1988, O'Leary became Ryan's personal assistant, with a brief to manage Ryan's personal wealth while he concentrated on the continued expansion of GPA. O'Leary was not the first person to hold that role. Previously, Ryan had employed Denis O'Brien in the same position, showing he had a good eye for what made a successful businessman. O'Brien was subsequently to become one of Ireland's richest, and most controversial, billionaires: a telecoms tycoon in Ireland first; and then, when he had sold his Irish business to British Telecom, in the Caribbean, with Digicel, a company he founded and owned. However, he became embroiled in a series of politically related controversies in Ireland over nearly two decades, making him a rival to O'Leary for the title of Ireland's best-known businessman but also serving as a warning as to how Ireland would not subserviently praise the wealthy for what they had accumulated.

Ryan's personal portfolio was broad and varied. He did

not merely invest in property or art, as many in his circle did. He became a major shareholder in the *Sunday Tribune* newspaper, for example. This damaged his friendship with Tony O'Reilly, the main shareholder in Independent Newspapers, who didn't want to see another tycoon exercise political influence in Ireland via a newspaper title. It was an ill-fated purchase, however, with Ryan in regular conflict with his rambunctious editor Vincent Browne as the losses mounted. Alongside the newspaper investment, he also bought a pub, the Pike Inn, on the main Dublin–Limerick road, which he rebranded as Matt the Threshers, a gastropub well ahead of its time, and he ran the Kilboy Estate as a major functioning farm, which was another revenue stream.

Now that they were finally working together, the relationship between Ryan and O'Leary blossomed quickly. Ryan was surrounded by too many lackies, yes-men who were afraid to confront or question the all-knowing, quick-to-anger boss. O'Leary had little fear, partly because he was financially independent and partly because he may have seen many of Ryan's traits in his own father, whom he had been less confident about confronting. Ryan liked O'Leary's straight-talking, but also his ability to bolster his arguments with a forensic reading of the accounts. Denis O'Brien had a similar desire to create new businesses while working for him, but O'Leary showed more interest in managing them, and Ryan quickly realized that he needed that support.

O'Leary was put to the test immediately, when a very high-profile investment threatened Ryan's success, and required O'Leary's attention.

In 1988 Ryan bought 5 per cent of one of Ireland's biggest banks, Bank of Ireland, for just over IR£30 million. It was one of those rare business stories that became front-page news at the time. There was speculation – correct, as it turned out – that Ryan was interested in taking control of the bank. He and O'Leary had identified all sorts of flaws in the management of the bank and thought that it could be run on a far more profitable basis if Ryan could force through change. Ryan joined the board of the bank – or court, as it was known – but the timing of the investment was spectacularly ill-judged.

Within months it became clear that there was a far bigger problem at the bank than Ryan and O'Leary had anticipated. The recent purchase of First New Hampshire Bank in the USA turned out to be a dud, costing Bank of Ireland tens of millions in unexpected losses and routing the share price. Ryan found the culture at the bank resistant to change, even though he was instrumental in removing its chief executive, Mark Hely Hutchinson. Frustrated, Ryan sold his shares within eighteen months of the original purchase. Although he never fully explained his decision to sell – which was as sudden and unexpected as his decision to buy – he was under pressure from his lending banks to repay what he owed them. What was kept quiet was that Ryan had borrowed $64.5 million from Merrill Lynch to buy the shares and that he had increased that loan to $80 million a year later, offering his shares in GPA as security. When Ryan used the proceeds of the sale of his Bank of Ireland shares to reduce his debt, he still owed Merrill Lynch $35 million. That was going to come back to haunt him within the next couple of years.

It was a blow to his ego, too. Engineering profitable change at Bank of Ireland would have been a feather in his cap and would have earned him considerable respect in business and political circles, as well as providing a massive return on his investment. O'Leary was in it for the massive return, and was unimpressed by the nature of his boss's ambition. In an interview twenty years later, he said: 'Tony was brave, but he was also an egomaniac. He had lots of money coming in, and he couldn't help it. It wasn't enough to run a successful company and make it bigger and better, like McDonald's. It was all about having political clout in Ireland when he shouldn't have given a shite.'

O'Leary was completely clear-eyed about what he wanted: 5 per cent of the considerable upside he had projected. He saw it as Tony's distraction by non-financial matters that had caused them both to lose out, which was an important lesson for him. It's easy to see how he has refused all distractions in his subsequent quest to build huge personal wealth. The fallout of the failed bid at Bank of Ireland meant that O'Leary now had to concentrate on another of Ryan's investments, one that was also proving costly to Tony's personal finances: Ryanair.

7. Slashing and burning

Ryanair wasn't Tony Ryan's first foray into setting up an airline – that had occurred in the early 1980s, when he had set up, via GPA, 'a cheap, no frills' airline called Irelandia. It was Ryan who first used that phrase – cheap, no frills – and for him it meant a cheap but cheerful flying experience that customers would enjoy, and therefore feel they'd got a real bargain. The plan was to fly from Shannon to the hubs of New York, Boston and London, and then expand from that base.

It was ambitious, but it was very much in keeping with the personality of the man proposing the idea. His instincts were right on the money, but he came up against an Irish government set on protecting the state carrier, Aer Lingus. Ryan's arguments about low fares and consumer choice didn't convince the state, and Irelandia's request for licences was turned down. As it happens, that was probably to Ryan's benefit, because the airline was likely too far ahead of its time and would have incurred enormous losses. It didn't deter Ryan from looking at other options, however, and he later tried to buy a licence from an existing Irish operator, the struggling Irish cargo operator Aer Turas. That didn't happen either, because Aer Lingus simply bought Aer Turas to frustrate Ryan's ambitions.

Eventually, in 1985, with the encouragement and help of Christy Ryan (no relation), an old friend from his Aer Lingus days who had joined him at GPA, Tony set up a new air-taxi service, flying passengers between the tiny Waterford Airport in the south-east of Ireland and Gatwick. He wanted to call it Trans Tipperary, but Christy – who made the application for the airline's licence in his own name – wanted to call it after himself. They eventually agreed that Ryan was a good name for an airline and Ryanair was born.

In 1986 Ryanair got a licence that would allow it to muscle in on the main Dublin–London route, going up against Aer Lingus, albeit via Luton on the outskirts of Greater London. Although Christy remained with the business – for the time being at least, before departing amid some acrimony – Tony provided the money and took control of the bigger operation. He put IR£1 million into the company initially, although it was owned equally by his sons, Cathal, Declan and Shane, through a trust fund. It was declared most emphatically that Tony Ryan himself had no ownership or involvement in Ryanair.

There were a number of regulatory and legal reasons for this declaration, although nobody ever really considered him anything other than the beneficial owner, even if legal sleight of hand made that impossible to prove. A financier of aircraft was not supposed to own an airline; it would create a perceived conflict with GPA's clients. More importantly, Aer Lingus was still a major shareholder in GPA, and Ryan was expressly precluded under his GPA contract from starting any airline. Those niceties were not going to deter Ryan, though, who was clearly in command of what was going on at Ryanair. The staff called him 'the man from Del Monte' – the Über-boss who was never seen but had the final say on everything.

There was a Denis O'Brien link to the early Ryanair, in that O'Brien's brother-in-law, Eugene O'Neill, was its second

CEO (after Liam Lonergan). O'Neill became the company's very public face, a willing interviewee for the media. Ryan had previously installed O'Neill as managing director at the *Sunday Tribune*, and also put him in charge of a failed hydrofoil-ferry venture, but that didn't stop him from giving O'Neill another shot at this project. O'Neill had an ebullient, can-do attitude that suited a new, ambitious start-up, and a very suave personal style that garnered attention and admiration. It was not necessarily an insult when he was nicknamed 'Mr Armani'. His staff loved him, and many willingly worked additional hours to get the airline moving. When he decided that Ryanair would pay for employee uniforms – whereas the original work code dictated they had to buy their own – his popularity soared. But everything he did cost money.

O'Leary started working as Ryan's PA in 1986, when Ryanair was in its first year. By mid 1987 it had flown 250,000 passengers, which O'Neill saw as a resounding triumph. The company was regarded as excellent in generating positive publicity for itself, partly due to O'Neill's profile and partly due to the backroom work of the PR executive, Anne O'Callaghan, a sister of the broadcaster Miriam. For all of the gloss applied, there was nonetheless a problem at the core of the business. O'Neill's profligate ways were undermining the bottom line and he lacked a thorough understanding of the industry. He introduced business-class services and frequent-flyer programmes while charging bargain prices. He was also in the crosshairs of Aer Lingus, which was determined to put obstacles in the way of Ryanair and unseat its chief executive. It watched approvingly as the government refused Ryanair a licence to operate a Shannon–Gatwick route and forced the Cork–Luton flights to touch down at Dublin Airport en route. In addition, Aer

Rianta, the state-owned controller of Dublin, Cork and Shannon airports, displayed a serious bias towards Aer Lingus and wasn't helpful in providing Ryanair with even basic facilities, such as check-in desks. It would take an innovative, wily CEO to steer a route through these conflicting problems.

Tony continued signing cheques to cover the costs of the rapid expansion of Ryanair, but the realization was dawning that the airline was not nearly as successful as O'Neill was claiming. Ryan became extremely worried when O'Neill made the near-fatal mistake of trying to compete with Aer Lingus on its favoured routes, instead of seeking out parallel routes that weren't being served. When tackled about it, O'Neill argued that Ryanair should sue Aer Lingus for its predatory behaviour. While technically he may have been correct in his argument, Ryan and his board knew that it would be more than counter-productive to sue, by proxy, the same state that held the power to issue and rescind the licences Ryanair needed to operate.

There was an instability at the heart of Ryanair now, and O'Neill was seen as the cause. When Declan, who was O'Neill's deputy as well as a board member, objected to one particular proposed investment, Ryan summoned O'Neill to a meeting at the Westbury Hotel in Dublin. At that meeting, O'Neill was sacked from Ryanair, a decision that enraged him and led to a flurry of legal actions that continued for years, and contributed to a serious decline in his own health, from which he suffered until his death in April 2018, aged sixty-two. But the Ryans were not for turning. They had come to the conclusion that O'Neill was operating almost recklessly, that he believed the family would always foot the bills and that they urgently needed a CEO more seriously inclined to cash management.

While Declan became acting chief executive, Ryan's first move was to send O'Leary into Ryanair to find out exactly how and why it was haemorrhaging money. Ryan's instincts, as ever, were correct: he had picked a bloodhound who could follow the trail of high costs with ferocious tenacity.

In May 1988 Michael O'Leary walked into Ryanair's central Dublin offices. It was, he said, 'like you'd arrived at the pearly gates'. He recalled 'gorgeous blonde chicks at every desk', plush carpets, expensive furnishings and a table in the chief executive's office that was so big, it couldn't be carried up the stairs. It had been brought in through the windows by a crane, once the floor had been reinforced to bear its weight. There were champagne receptions and specially commissioned crystal glasses distributed for every route launch. 'The place was a shambles and yet it was still amazingly sexy,' he confessed.

O'Leary was not impressed by the glamour and decided that nearly everything that was wrong was O'Neill's fault:

No one had a handle on the finances and money was leaking all over the place. Eugene appeared to have lost the run of himself, reading all that 'businessman of the month' stuff and believing his own BS that he was the next Tony Ryan or Michael Smurfit. One minute he was Mr Ryanair, the next he was out on the street . . . Ryanair needed the flash and the representation to get it off the ground, and Eugene looked good, talked a good story and generated huge publicity. But you look back and it was a piece of shite. He sold it well, but the product was crap. They had great PR, but where was all the money? They were producing accounts showing them making money, and yet there was a huge hole, with cash running out the door. They were making assumptions about passenger numbers and fares paid, they didn't seem to know what half the costs were, and there was hardly any accounting system.

It was to be an early indication of O'Leary's willingness to be blunt in offering an assessment of a situation and to be equally ruthless in offering a solution. O'Leary could see the problems O'Neill had created, and he wasn't slow to tell Ryan what he thought. (It is possible that O'Neill's brother-in-law and former Ryan aide, Denis O'Brien, was unimpressed by O'Leary's views. O'Leary and O'Brien's subsequent relationship suggested that no love was lost between the two Irish business stars. Eighteen years later, a Ryanair advert seemed to mock O'Brien's tax residency in Malta. The *Financial Times* commented: 'Michael O'Leary, Ryanair's chief executive, is known to take a hands-on approach to designing the company's ad campaign . . . The swipe at O'Brien has his fingerprints all over it.' Within weeks of the ad running, O'Brien bought a shareholding in Aer Lingus. Nobody doubted that he wanted to deny Ryanair ownership of the airline. 'Industry sources said Mr O'Brien's opposition to Ryanair stems from a newspaper advertisement in which the low-cost carrier lampooned the billionaire businessman,' the *Irish Independent* reported at the time of O'Brien's dramatic entry into the takeover battle. Elsewhere, O'Brien was quoted as saying he was 'not a fan of the Ryanair style of operation'.) It wasn't until later that O'Leary could also appreciate the good things O'Neill had done in providing the foundations for the later Ryanair. 'In a perverse way, if Ryanair had been run properly from the start, it would never have got off the ground. Eugene had a lot of faults, but he did a good job with the marketing and he gave it great credibility from a standing start. If it had been started by a bunch of accountants, it would never have gotten the credibility. And so, in a fucked-up, bizarre way, the best way to do it was to start with the panache and the style. Problem was, what they had built into the model was a cheque for ten million to pay for all this pizzazz.'

As a result, the more passengers Ryanair carried, the more money it lost. O'Leary calculated that in its first year of operations Ryanair had lost £4 million, another £5.5 million in 1986 and another £7 million in 1987. Yet it continued to increase passenger numbers, seemingly without regard for the costs. That lack of regard meant that increased sales equalled decreased income, which was mind-boggling for a penny-pincher like O'Leary. He just wanted it to stop bleeding cash. 'I think there was an implicit understanding within the airline: "Look, don't worry about the money, the Ryans will kind of pick it up." There was no malfeasance, but there was an assumption that there were deep pockets there so they would get the quality right and never mind the costs. They were opening routes fucking left, right and centre, the route network was nuts. They had no fucking schedule at all. It was madness. It was all planes, planes and planes and no airline.'

The shopkeeper in O'Leary spotted that the airline did not have a proper system for collecting money and had loads of bad debts owed to it. 'The numbers were rubbish. There was nobody collecting cash. We didn't know how much money we had, except we had nothing in the bank. The bottom line was that if Ryan didn't give us a million by the next Friday, we couldn't pay the wages. There was no cash in the company and that was the problem.'

O'Leary conducted a review of the operations and accounts, and, with characteristic decisiveness, swiftly made his recommendation to Ryan: the situation could not be salvaged, especially with a fares war with Aer Lingus on the Dublin–Stansted route draining what little resources were left, and the company should be shut down. He drew up the memorandum to close Ryanair and prepared it for a vote of directors at the company's forthcoming AGM. Declan Ryan agreed with O'Leary's analysis, and the two men decided to go to Kilboy together to confront Tony. In reality, he would decide, not the board.

On his way to Kilboy, Declan noticed a car pulled in at a lay-by near the house. It was O'Leary's car. Knowing O'Leary's strategic way of thinking, he reckoned his colleague was delaying deliberately so that Declan could deliver the bad news without him. When Declan arrived, he stalled for time and his father showed him a new fountain he'd had installed. 'I'm thinking of filling it with holy water for you,' Tony warned.

Once O'Leary had joined them, he and Declan set out all of the reasons why they believed Ryanair should be shut down immediately. Tony was furious and refused to countenance it, telling them to stop complaining and get back to work. It was a decision that defied commercial logic, but Declan knew what prompted it. 'Pride,' he explained, many years later. 'It wasn't that he knew how things would work out, but he didn't want to fail. His pride would not allow it.' That defeat would have been at the hands of Aer Lingus, given all the fights he had had with it, was too much for him. It didn't mean that he had a solution to offer to his son or O'Leary, though.

Ryanair's problems were not just the result of internal mismanagement. It was the victim of Aer Lingus's predation, ably assisted by the Department of Transport, sardonically referred to as Aer Lingus's 'downtown office'. Even though it ate into its own profitability and cash reserves, Aer Lingus increased capacity and reduced prices whenever Ryanair threatened one of its existing routes. It did so without cutting its own costs to provide the money to do this, knowing that history showed any incumbent government would bail out the 'national airline'. Aer Lingus benefited from the existence of a carve-up on its main Dublin–London route with British Airways, and a pricing structure that had to be approved by the Department of Transport as regulator. The arrangement with British Airways was presented as competition, but was, in fact, anything but that.

It was Ryan who took the lead in dismantling this blockade of Ryanair's operations. He targeted the minister for transport, Séamus Brennan, in a lengthy campaign to have his case heard fairly. Finally, his determination resulted in a meeting being set up between them. In the summer of 1988 Ryan and O'Leary went to Government Buildings. Ryan was fortunate that Brennan was one of the few politicians who realized the inherent contradiction involved in the government being both the owner of Aer Lingus and the regulator of its competition or, as Brennan put it, 'You can't be a referee and play on one of the teams at the same time.' He was prepared to listen, especially with regard to the issues of reduced choice for consumers and large-scale job losses.

Ryan and Brennan went back and forth on the issues, politely arguing points and counterpoints. It was an orderly meeting, until O'Leary, who had been on its margins, suddenly spoke up loudly and began banging the table. 'I do remember him being cheeky,' Brennan said afterwards. 'In fairness, I think he was the only one who called a spade a spade even then.'

Whether it was the polite argument or the table banging, Brennan emerged from the meeting with an understanding that the status quo had to change. His view was that Aer Lingus could have Heathrow and Gatwick, but it would have to give up Liverpool and Munich. Ryanair could stay at Luton and Stansted, and it would be allowed to offer direct services to the UK and Europe. However, Brennan was canny enough to realize that he had to get government approval for the plan before news broke and vested interests organized themselves in opposition. He surprised fellow ministers with a memo to Cabinet that Ryanair was on the verge of closure, that it would cost the exchequer IR£18 million to provide alternative employment, and that, in his view, no other operator would try to replace Ryanair for at least twenty years, which would guarantee Aer Lingus an anti-competitive monopoly. He received the necessary support.

'When I announced it there was absolute war,' Brennan recalled. Aer Lingus was furious and got considerable trade-union and political support. Brennan was accused of national sabotage. There was a picket at his constituency office, with banners suggesting Brennan had been bought, much to his fury. 'I don't claim any particular forward vision at the time except a gut feeling that competition was the way forward. Before Ryanair started flying it had cost up to £300 to fly from Dublin to London – in today's money that's about €600. There were no cheaper fares. I knew it would be stupid to let an airline close. I just wanted Aer Lingus to move over a bit.'

One of the biggest reactions came from the Federated Workers' Union of Ireland (FWUI), which accused the government of propping up a private company that had failed to compete with a state company – ignoring the fact that Ryanair's failing had much to do with the monopoly power exercised by this state company. The FWUI described the decision to favour Ryanair as a 'drastic blow to the workers who had facilitated Aer Lingus by agreeing to lower pay scales, increased productivity and changes in work practices'. Undoubtedly, O'Leary watched and learnt from this backlash. It informed his views on the role of trade unions, a view that was to become a defining aspect of Ryanair into the future.

The government's action meant that Ryanair was still a runner, so O'Leary went back in – again as a consultant rather than as an executive – to try to make it work. The problems he had identified were not immediately solved by the relaxing of Aer Lingus's stranglehold. In August 1988, just as the government made its decision, O'Leary told Ryan the airline needed minimum funding of £3 million to see it through to the following April/May. 'This company must now be profitable,' O'Leary wrote in a memo for Ryan. 'It has established a firm platform of profitable routes. All future efforts must centre around cutting costs and developing (strategically important) profitable routes.'

He listed immediate and widespread cuts, arguing that they should use 'the present financial crisis as a basis for action'. He proposed redundancies and salary cuts for management and support staff. He wanted to abandon the plush city-centre accommodation and work instead from 'Portakabin offices' in the executive jet terminal at Dublin Airport, because this would greatly reduce costs and improve morale at the airport. He recommended a major overhaul in the advertising and promotional budgets. He sought the elimination of what he described as 'abuses', such as cash payments, company cars, hotel use, free bars, family travel, free travel and taxis. He decided that anything that cost money had to be reviewed. Greater efforts were to be made to use competition and tendering to reduce fees for services provided to Ryanair.

One of O'Neill's mistakes had been a loose grip on the reins, which was directly opposed to how O'Leary did, and wanted to do, business. He called for a change of oversight to implement ongoing costs control. He wanted a new 'system of strict financial control and discipline' to be 'overemphasized' for the next six months, driven by 'a stronger system of management from the top down'. Management is paid to lead the company, he said. 'Do so,' was his peremptory instruction.

Ryan let him at it. Although O'Leary was not given any formal title at the company, he was allowed to do more or less whatever he wanted, go wherever he wanted. He wasn't impeded by Declan, who remained as interim chief executive – the two worked very much as a team – nor by P. J. McGoldrick when he arrived as the new chief executive in 1989. Instead of studying the industry by reading books or poring over financial statements, O'Leary behaved just as he had in the newsagents business. He put himself on the shopfloor and became hands-on, appearing at the baggage-handling department or the check-in desks, keeping watch. The brusque young man's presence was not appreciated by many, and staff regarded him as something of a bogeyman. Remembering that fiver in the shop till, it's not really surprising.

Given a largely free hand, O'Leary slashed and burned his way through Ryanair. In what was to become his trademark approach, he looked for problems, identified them and annihilated them. He could see costs everywhere that he wanted to reduce. Travel agents charged too much commission. Air-traffic control dallied and prevented quick turnabout of flights. Airports charged too much per passenger. Fuel suppliers overcharged. The list went on and on. He replaced the marketing department with an external PR agency, WHPR, although it worked very much to his command. His modus operandi was to get people to do more for less. Some of his suppliers refused to cooperate on his terms. Irish International Advertising, for example, resigned its contract two months after agreeing it because Ryanair was expecting far more services than provided for. O'Leary later noted that his non-titled position at the company was the perfect platform for this dirty work: 'I was all about getting rid of the lunatics who were running the asylum and putting some order on it. I was doing a lot of the ripping and burning and slashing at the lower end, which you couldn't have done if you were the CEO.' He had a level of freedom that allowed him to be ruthless. Not that he would have seen it as ruthlessness; it was simply common sense and good practice. It was just business.

His fearless certainty in his own analysis saw him start a fight with GPA about its terms for leasing aircraft to Ryanair. He was correct to do so. GPA had been taking advantage of the small airline, which had assumed wrongly that GPA was giving it discounts on account of its ownership. O'Leary was fighting with people everywhere, from staff to suppliers, and he didn't care if it affected morale. As far as he was concerned, he was safeguarding the airline's future, their jobs and his rewards.

One of his key changes was to instil discipline across the company, so that only money that had to be spent would be spent. He needed the staff and managers to think like him, at the micro level, aware of every penny. In a move that started a quarter-century of hostility, he cut pilot salaries by more than a third. The effect of the cuts started to be felt, and Ryanair began to take on a new shape. When, in a foretaste of future battles, Tony Ryan began to complain to O'Leary that the airline was starting to look just 'cheap' rather than 'cheap and cheerful', O'Leary asserted himself and, rather bravely perhaps, told Ryan, 'This is the way it has to be. You cut, you cut some more, then you cut more again.'

O'Leary and Declan Ryan worked closely together during this period, doing everything they could to stop the money haemorrhage while finding cash to pay the bills without always having to go cap in hand to Tony. They drove, separately, to Kilboy each Saturday to report on their week, and regularly received what were referred to as 'bollockings' for their troubles. They worked long hours, but neither wanted to be the boss. That was P. J. McGoldrick's job.

Appointed CEO in 1989, McGoldrick was an airline-industry veteran whose specialty was operations. O'Leary continued to hide behind the scenes, unknown to the media, while McGoldrick was the public face of Ryanair. He was regarded as having done a reasonable job in identifying and promoting the best routes for Ryanair to operate, but his relative success was only possible because of the work O'Leary and Declan were doing in the background. When Tony Ryan decided, just two years later, that the time had come to replace McGoldrick, Declan didn't want to step up, reckoning that the family name would be a handicap: 'Everyone would assume I had access to the Ryan family cash whenever money was needed.' To Ryan's anger, O'Leary refused to take the job. It seemed churlish, but O'Leary later said he wouldn't have been able to keep Ryan 'out of his hair'. Instead, O'Leary took the position of chief financial officer (CFO), while also retaining his role as PA to Ryan.

In December 1991 a former SKC accountant, Conor Hayes, arrived from Saudi Arabia to be chief executive for a crucial three-year term. Hayes imposed even more financial discipline, still not satisfied that the reporting systems were all that they could or should be. O'Leary was great at highlighting waste, but Hayes was strong at putting in place the measures to prevent it from being repeated. Information was now available in days and, at worst, weeks, instead of the months it had taken previously.

If Ryan had been a financial mentor, Hayes paved the way for O'Leary's ideas on how to manage people and suppliers. He impressed O'Leary with his willingness to make unpopular decisions. It was Hayes who insisted that no flight should take off without clearance from Brendan Berger, who was in charge of flight operations. The flight could only go if its revenues from seats sold more than covered the costs of running the flight. If they didn't, the flight was cancelled and combined with the next one. Anyone who failed to comply was fired. Flight consolidation, as it was called, only worked because of the frequency of flights, but it still seriously inconvenienced some passengers, especially those who were travelling for business.

O'Leary looked on in admiration, applauding the efficiency involved and the relentless way in which it was executed. He and Hayes were both unburdened by the need to be liked, and they had near-identical approaches to costs. Planes were now cleaned by cabin crews, not contract cleaners, and toilets were not emptied after each flight. They were continuing to improve productivity, while also reducing their cost base. It was exactly what O'Leary had been working towards.

As with McGoldrick before him, Hayes was very much the public face of the organization, but among staff there was an increasing sense of O'Leary's confidence and of Hayes reporting to him as a proxy for Ryan. The hard work and experience were bolstering O'Leary's position at the company and his sense of what could be achieved there. He was becoming more assertive in managing people, although in many environments his approach – screaming and roaring at staff, never sparing the expletives – would not have been allowed or tolerated. At Ryanair, it was just the way things were done, and got done.

Privately, O'Leary had a strong personal incentive to micromanage. He had done a secret deal with Ryan – unknown to Hayes or indeed to anyone beyond the Ryan family – where he would be paid 25 per cent of all Ryanair profits above IR£2 million. 'I thought if I could get it right, I would make some decent money, not a fortune. I thought in a good year, we'd make a couple of million and I'd get 250 grand, and there you go, I'd be rich. But at that stage, it was as likely to go bust as it was to make a million quid,' he said. O'Leary had learnt well: he had copied the deal Ryan had done for himself at GPA.

At that time O'Leary had no future vision for Ryanair, no notion of what it could and would become. He didn't have a huge gut instinct or dream that was guiding his actions. He wasn't thinking that this was his golden ticket and he should invest himself fully in it. On the contrary, he wanted out. Yes, he had put the foundations in place, as asked, but he didn't want to stay with the airline. It wasn't what he had signed up to do. He felt that he would be better off making 5 per cent of the other profits that could come from using Ryan's money. 'I had had four years of this place on the brink of bankruptcy; we had gotten back to making a small profit and I had had enough. It was a pain in the arse. My role in Ryanair from 1988 to 1991 was to stop it from losing money – it wasn't looking to make Tony money. I kept trying to get out. I thought it was a stupid business, and it was also very high profile. I didn't want a high profile. I wanted to make lots of money but not be known.'

It's a very interesting divergence not only from the career he would eventually pursue but also from his own image of himself, of the type of person he was. When he looked at himself then, he saw a private person, a backstage person, no limelight, no fuss. If he felt that this was his true character, as he must have, it's very far from the man he seemed to become. This person sounds more like the schoolboy at Clongowes that his classmates remember. He sounds like he would be greatly irritated by the antics of his future self. It suggests that when it came to making money, O'Leary was happy to go against his own grain in order to achieve what he wanted.

8. The disciple

O'Leary's moment of revelation has been very well documented. It came from Herb Kelleher and Southwest Airlines. The vision O'Leary hadn't had for Ryanair was handed to him on a plate by Kelleher, the former lawyer who founded the highly successful American airline in Texas. It was an early example of something that would recur throughout O'Leary's career at Ryanair: he was not an innovator, he was an adaptor. Some even called him a plagiarist, a shameless thief of other people's ideas, which he then claimed as his own. His vision for Ryanair may have been second-hand, but his unique skill was to manage it brilliantly. He had no romanticism about air travel, whereas Tony Ryan came from an era that did. To O'Leary, it was just another mode of transport, nothing more. In Southwest Airlines, he found the proof of this belief.

Ryan sent O'Leary to meet with Herb Kelleher in early 1992, to find out how he had created his airline, which was the first to brand itself as *the* low-fares airline. Whatever his model, it was working: Southwest had made profits of $27 million in 1991. O'Leary later told a story about how the relationship developed, although it's hard to know if it's deliberate myth-making or true. In an interview with the *Financial Times* in 1998, O'Leary described how 'I passed out about midnight and when I woke up again at about 3 a.m., Kelleher was still there, pouring himself another bourbon and smoking. I thought I'd pick his brains and come away with the Holy Grail. The next day I couldn't remember a thing.'

He'd already learnt all he needed. He had gone to Southwest with the intention of focusing on its operational issues. 'Some came here, but not in the same way as Michael,' Kelleher said in an interview for Siobhán Creaton's 2004 book about Ryanair. 'When we talked to Michael, he had a number of very significant questions. His questioning was always very incisive and very pointed. Michael was always very curious as to how we did things. Although he was pretty familiar with that, he wanted to know why we did them – why we did this this way, why we did that that way, why we didn't have assigned seats, why we didn't serve meals. I could go on and on, but he wanted to know what our thinking was – what our strategy was behind the things that we did do and behind the things we didn't do. He asked magnificent questions with respect to each one . . . I loved Michael. He's a lively lad. I realized within a very short time that he was a very doughty character and I kind of enjoyed his swashbuckling ways. He has a very forceful personality, very forthright, very outspoken.'

What Kelleher showed the eager O'Leary was that he ran his airline on a fixed set of strategic principles. The airline flew a single type of aircraft, the Boeing 737, to keep down engineering costs. It turned around the aircraft quickly – usually in under thirty minutes, as against ninety minutes at competitor airlines. This allowed them to make more flights daily, and they chose to use the less congested airports to facilitate this. It was usual to have five attendants, but if you had just two flight attendants on each 130-seater aircraft, and if they spent most of their time selling and telling people to clean up their own rubbish, which would save the airline on cleaning costs, then it was possible with that 25-minute turnaround to add maybe two extra flights a day. It did not board passengers according to seat numbers, again, to save on time. It was a free-for-all, like getting on a bus. Southwest specialized in flying short routes, typically about 400 miles or one hour apart, as many times in the day as possible. Onward connections were not facilitated. Economy class was the only option, and it served markets nobody else had even considered.

It might not have sounded like a successful approach, but Southwest grew by targeting cities underserved by existing carriers and where customers were paying high prices. It added routes and planes every year, but never let costs rise. There was constant cost reduction, and definitely no expensive air-miles loyalty schemes. It opened each route with very low fares to attract publicity, and that generated large numbers of customers quickly. Fares were promoted through provocative advertising, and Kelleher would personally act the clown or make outrageous comments to court publicity. It was possible to buy alcohol and peanuts, but the soft drinks were free. 'If you get your passengers to their destinations when they want to get there, on time, at the lowest possible fares, and make darn sure they have a good time doing it, people will fly your airline,' Kelleher said.

It's clear O'Leary adopted the Southwest strategy, but also that he adopted its style – or Herb's style, to be exact. He watched as Kelleher's very un-CEO-like behaviour scored interest and attention and free publicity – and passengers. He could see that the strategy succeeded because Southwest never veered from it, ever. There was a complete and total focus on cost reduction and delivering the cheapest seats in America. And it worked. Yet again, O'Leary watched and learnt.

'Southwest was a big guiding thing for me,' O'Leary said. 'Before I had heard about Southwest, I had seen two airlines in Ireland, Ryanair and Aer Lingus, both of which were blindingly incompetent. They had complicated check-in, business class this, travel agent that, all the rest of that crap, and were turning planes around in an hour. Then you went to Southwest, banging aircraft out after fifteen minutes. They were phenomenal, passengers loved it.'

O'Leary could see no reason why Ryanair couldn't repeat all of this in Europe. He was converted. He had been an unwilling participant in Ryanair until now, doing what was asked of him with one eye on the door, but now, suddenly, he could see a whole new future of possibilities rolling out in front of him. Contrary to what everyone said, it *was* possible to run a profitable airline. Ryanair could be the cash cow he'd been looking for all along.

O'Leary returned to Ireland and wrote a memo entitled, 'The challenge of replicating Southwest Airlines in Europe'. In it he wrote: 'The future of the international airline business, or more importantly its salvation, has arrived. In the US it is called Southwest Airlines.' He went on to describe a model with a 'constant focus upon challenging every received wisdom in the airline industry, and constantly innovating new procedures and systems with the sole purpose of increasing efficiency, heightening productivity, eliminating unnecessary frills, and above all reducing costs'. It was his Sermon on the Mount, and he was determined to make believers of the Ryanair staff and management.

He didn't need to convert Hayes, who was already intent on driving fares lower. But that could work only if O'Leary's cost agenda were implemented and sales volume increased dramatically, something most of the Ryanair management believed was not possible. O'Leary backed Hayes enthusiastically, and Hayes was buoyed by O'Leary's American optimism. Hayes borrowed the price on the lowest fare from a Southwest $29 promotion on the Dallas–Houston route and applied it to the Dublin–Luton route: £29 each way, with higher fares set at £10 gaps. He launched it as a 'Happy Days' promotion in February 1992. Such was its success, he was able to double services on the Dublin–Stansted route within a month using the same pricing policy, and then add a new Shannon–Stansted route in April.

Aer Lingus noted this audacious move and prepared to respond, but failed to realize that this pricing policy was to become a permanent feature of Ryanair's approach. It reduced its prices to match Ryanair's, but without reducing costs and without increasing capacity. In doing so, it ran up £10 million losses on the London route. Then it cut its Gatwick services and increased its prices into Heathrow, to Ryanair's delight, which now realized it had a niche as a low-fares airline.

It was almost a fluke, as O'Leary had yet to completely formulate his Southwest copy-cat strategy and Hayes was chasing volume rather than establishing an overarching plan. But that didn't matter. With only a limited number of aircraft available, Hayes was ruthless about shutting underperforming routes and he was not afraid to take the political flak for abandoning small regional airports.

It looked like they were set to start making some proper money. They had the vision, the belief, and Hayes and O'Leary were a formidable duo, confident of delivering on the potential they could now see. They had Aer Lingus on the ropes, and hoped their new strategy would keep it there. It seemed like the beginning of something exciting – until a crisis hit that threatened to blow the whole thing apart.

The crisis came directly from Tony Ryan. In 1992 Ryan's world came tumbling down – and there was little that O'Leary could do to help. The billionaire's financial crash was the biggest Irish business story of 1992 – and a major international one, too. Ryan had decided, after years of prevarication, to bring GPA to the stock markets, to allow for an open trade in the company's shares. The decision would give Ryan a major personal cash boost, worth tens of millions of dollars, as well as valuing his shareholding in GPA at over $250 million. Instead, he finished the year close to bankruptcy and O'Leary's personal plans, to make money from Ryan's investments, changed accordingly.

That Ryan decided to try to join the stock market at all in the summer of 1992 surprised many people. There had been speculation for years that the company might do so, but Ryan had always refused. In 1992 the push to float was internal, coming from key GPA executives who doubted the strategy being followed by Ryan of committing billions of dollars to the purchase of new aircraft. They wanted to raise new equity before spending such vast sums in investment. This time, Ryan relented, perhaps looking too much to his own personal needs. He could use the money to clear the Merrill Lynch loan he had repaid only partially the previous year when he had sold his Bank of Ireland shares.

In May 1992 GPA decided that it would hold an 'initial public offering' (IPO) in June, inviting investors to subscribe for newly created, additional shares. It intended to have the prices quoted on the Dublin, London and New York stock exchanges. It chose the Japanese bank Nomura to run the sales process. This was noteworthy – and, in retrospect, possibly mistaken – as it was the first time it, or any other Asian entity, had been chosen instead of a Wall Street or City of London bank to run such a major event. Nomura sought to sell shares worth about $850 million, an enormous amount. Yet there were many warning signs in the run-up to GPA's planned flotation that it was not going smoothly. There was adverse commentary in the international business media, especially in London, about the prospects for the entire aviation industry and GPA's apparent over-ambition. Ryan also insisted that he wanted to price the newly issued shares at $22 each, when they had been trading at a much lower level on the private market in previous months. His chosen price was also higher than the advisers to the float wanted, which was in the range of $16 to $18 per share. Ryan would not budge.

The flotation failed spectacularly. The company ended up with offers worth just $500 million, with no offers at all forthcoming for many of the shares. Ryan's reluctance to drop the asking price, because it would have impacted on his personal wealth, was regarded later as a major contributor to the IPO's failure, but it was not the only one. Subsequent events showed that potential investors were right to be wary: GPA's need for money had been far more urgent than many had realized. The $850 million it sought and failed to raise was only a fraction of the amount that it actually needed. It had a plan to raise another $3 billion in borrowings, which was now also ruined. Significantly, if it had tried to raise more equity but at a far lower price, it might have been able to reassemble the balance sheet sufficiently to protect the company.

It was a shambles, and, while he was sympathetic to Ryan's plight – and scathing about the performance of the bankers and brokers advising GPA – O'Leary was also among those who argued that Ryan was making a mess of things. However, this time he was largely peripheral to what was going on, because he was not employed by GPA. 'I'd have sold the shares at any old price just to get the thing away,' O'Leary said subsequently. 'Tony was going to collect a bonus on flotation of more than $30 million and I told him to forget about the price and just take the money, but he wouldn't.'

GPA went into a spiral. It attempted to raise finance at just $1 per share, but even that didn't work. Ryan looked to change management and wanted O'Leary to take control, with Declan by his side. O'Leary refused, saying he did not believe the existing other management was tough enough to do what was needed. It is more likely that he realized GPA was doomed. A year later it had to be sold, for a pittance, to the giant American multinational General Electric; all of Ryan's equity in the business was wiped out, and he was left with enormous debts.

It was a series of events that would have ruined him entirely financially had it not been for the efforts of O'Leary on his behalf, particularly in negotiating the settlement of the remaining $35 million loan from Merrill Lynch. The promise of repayment on this loan was secured by the perceived value of the shares in GPA. Now that these were worthless, Merrill Lynch would demand that Ryan sell other assets and give it the proceeds, or hand them over to the bank in lieu of a cash repayment.

Merrill Lynch demanded information on whatever was owned by Ryan's investment company Irelandia, as well as details of other assets held personally by his children and, in particular, those owned by the Ryan family trust, CDS, named after the initials of Cathal, Declan and Shane. This was important because CDS Trust provided the capital base for the operation of Ryanair. The American bank, with support from AIB, the Irish bank, which was also owed money, argued that it did not believe Ryan had no control over Ryanair and threatened to take legal action to challenge the previous transfer of money to the CDS Trust.

O'Leary took control of the situation, including the face-to-face negotiations. He fought loudly and angrily with the American bank, saying that his client, Tony Ryan, had written to his sons outlining the request from the bank that they should use their wealth to try to settle their father's loans, but, as they were separate legal entities, they were entitled to say 'get lost', as they had. Prompted by O'Leary, Ryan wrote: 'It is a matter of fact, and indeed legal record, that I have not, and nor have I ever, exercised any ownership or indeed control over Ryanair. Ryanair is owned, operated and controlled by my sons. Whilst I was the source of much of the finance for it during the early years, these funds were settled by me upon CDS Trust some considerable time ago, and indeed with the full knowledge of both Merrill Lynch and the banking group.'

Legally, it was correct, just about. The original set-up had been a ruse to maintain the pretence that he, as the chief executive of GPA, had not owned an airline in competition with Aer Lingus. Now it assisted in legally keeping his shares in Ryanair out of the clutches of the banks.

O'Leary proved himself invaluable once again as the crisis rumbled on. Crucially, he managed to hide from the lenders details of the real improvement in Ryanair's financial performance that was taking place under his watch. Ryanair declared profits of £850,000 for 1992, which just happened to be £1 profit for every passenger it had flown that year. The true figure may have been more like £3 million. Deliberately under-reporting or underplaying the true profitability of Ryanair was a big call for O'Leary to make, as his annual bonus was calculated as a share of the profits. In doing so, he showed the ability to prioritize long-term stability over short-term gains that has marked his leadership at Ryanair. He put aside his bonus and focused on the fact that he needed Ryan to retain control, because if Ryanair fell into Merrill Lynch's hands, it would derail O'Leary's personal incentive plan for future years. Had Merrill Lynch looked more closely at the underlying business – or entrusted AIB or Bank of Ireland with the task, as lesser partners on the syndicated loan – it would have seen the extraordinary cash generation that was taking place and the prospect for recouping a sizeable portion of the outstanding loan. The day that a Merrill Lynch executive said that the bank wasn't interested in Ryanair making up part-settlement of the loans is one that is still recalled with glee by the Ryan family and associates more than twenty-five years later.

Ryan held his nerve in the negotiations, helped greatly by O'Leary's mastery of detail and ability to act as an attack dog whenever required, and by the support of his son Declan. In the summer of 1993 Merrill Lynch indicated it would accept a repayment of $14 million in full and final settlement, but Ryan and O'Leary, sensing weakness, refused. They managed to get the payment down to a derisory $5 million with the promise that Ryan would be able to raise that amount of cash quickly. With the deal agreed, Ryan then provided only $4.5 million, to the bewilderment of the now worn-out bankers. It was late 1994 before all of this was sorted.

It was still money that Ryan didn't have, but O'Leary used Ryanair's resources to provide the necessary cash. O'Leary hatched a deal in which Ryan bought five Boeing jets for $20 million and then simultaneously sold them to Ryanair for $24 million, giving Ryan the cash from the profit to pay the American bank. It would not have been possible to have this sort of arrangement in a public company, but this was before the 1997 stock-market flotation and there were no other shareholders to whom the Ryans were answerable. O'Leary reckoned that, as Ryan had funded the airline for years, he was due this break. Of course, it also made Ryan somewhat beholden to O'Leary, but that went unspoken.

The episode, with Ryan near the brink of financial ruin, showed that there was more to O'Leary than merely being a manager. It had required O'Leary to keep a clear head, over many months, and to negotiate with ruthlessness when not necessarily in a position of strength. It taught him that others are not comfortable in dealing with aggression, even when playing with a stronger hand, and that taking unexpected positions can reverse any advantages the other side has. It all gave O'Leary a better understanding of how his goals could be achieved. In addition, the Ryans were almost like a new family for O'Leary, and he was loyal to them. There was an emotional context to what he was doing, not simply a financial or an occupational one.

There was another significant repercussion from all this. Given that he thought Ryan had made a mess of things, and with no Ryan investments available to manage and from which to profit, O'Leary decided it was time, finally, for him to step into the CEO role at Ryanair. It also convinced him that he had to assert himself even more than he had done to date. He wanted to take things to another level. Ryan's company was to become O'Leary's.

Conor Hayes's contract was due to run out at the end of 1993, and it became clear to everyone that he would not be re-employed as CEO. O'Leary was very visible around the Dublin HQ, and it was obvious he wanted to take the reins. Hayes was to find new employment quickly, as financial director at RTÉ, the state-owned broadcaster that O'Leary so reviled. Arguments raged in business circles as to whether or not Hayes received sufficient credit for his part in the salvation of Ryanair, and if the route flown by the airline subsequently was as much down to his plotting as O'Leary's. It is all supposition, of course, but it seems unlikely that Hayes would have had the force of personality to lead Ryanair as O'Leary went on to do.

Once Hayes was gone, the way was clear. O'Leary stepped formally into the position of chief executive of Ryanair on 1 January 1994. Through a mix of O'Leary's bullishness, cleverness and ruthlessness, the old order had been largely vanquished. It was time for a new era.

9. The messiah

From 2 January 1994, Michael O'Leary treated Ryanair as if it were his own company as well as Ryan's. He was invested, personally. He had steered Ryan through crises, stepped up to fight in the big league against international banks, stared down previous CEOs, who always blinked first – so he felt a powerful sense of 'rightness' about his appointment and his role. This was his shot at riches, and he wasn't going to miss. Of course, this attitude was inevitably going to annoy people, not least Tony Ryan.

O'Leary's first important announcement as CEO came at the end of January, when he revealed the purchase of six second-hand Boeing 737-200s, with a capacity of 130 passengers. The extra twenty seats, on average, in comparison with the aircraft presently being used, would allow the airline to chase extra ticket sales. A further five 737-200s would arrive later in the year. It was the start of a process by which Ryanair would replace all non-Boeing aircraft with this model. As he had learnt at Southwest, O'Leary knew that operating a single type of aircraft would allow for considerable cost savings in maintenance, crew and pilot training. It was regarded, in retrospect, as one of the most important decisions Ryanair, or O'Leary, ever made.

This was followed in February by a Valentine's Day announcement that customers would come to love – and rivals to hate. O'Leary abolished many of the arcane industry rules involving ticket purchasing. The cheapest tickets at Ryanair could now be bought up to a day in advance of the flight, instead of the industry standard of fourteen days. Better, Ryanair abolished the ridiculous rule that a passenger had to stay on the Saturday night in the chosen destination to avail of the cheapest possible return flight. If Hayes had been responsible for introducing the low-fare philosophy, then O'Leary was determined to expand it wherever possible. This copying approach became standard practice for Ryanair. O'Leary watched what others did in the industry and then shamelessly borrowed and tweaked it. The big difference was that he would implement it in a far more intensive way.

His focus remained Ireland and the UK for now, but he had Continental Europe in his sights. If he was to offer low fares, he needed low costs, and the prices charged by airports for access was one of his main bugbears. He had a good deal in place in Stansted, but he was engaged in a long-running battle with Aer Rianta over prices at the Irish airports it managed, constantly shouting that he would reduce fares if it cut its prices to him. He looked for more secondary airports in Britain to service and kept pressing them to offer him discounts against their listed prices, arguing that they would benefit financially from the additional passengers he brought them.

At first, there was resistance because airports saw nothing in it for them. If they were to reduce their prices for Ryanair, they would lose income, not believing that lower prices would bring about extra custom. But then it began to sink in that this strategy just might make sense. Prestwick in Scotland was an early adopter. It agreed to waive all landing, passenger and air-traffic control charges, costing it about £650,000 in its first year and £800,000 the next. The airport's logic was that it had not enjoyed the benefit of a scheduled service for the previous five years and that it would make money from duty-free sales, catering and car-parking facilities, which had been non-existent up to then. The critics insisted it was too generous a deal to give to Ryanair and would not work for Prestwick, but O'Leary was adamant that it had to work for both. He explained his model to all potential airport partners: he needed them to be profitable to remain open to service his flights. It wasn't a smash-and-grab; it was a long-term strategy to the benefit of everyone. Yes, there might be an initial outlay or loss, but the point of it was for them to move from being low-volume, high-cost entities to being busy, high volume and low cost. He would provide the passengers, but could only do so if he had the low costs to support low fares. Low-cost airlines should not have to pay to bring passengers to airports, he argued, as they are captive retail markets.

O'Leary's first year as CEO was productive and fast-moving. He knew what he wanted and he was going after it, and he was largely let at it by a board that was comprised of Ryan family members and nominees. But there came a change in early 1995, when Tony Ryan, abroad for much of the past twelve months, and still recovering from the trauma of the GPA debacle, decided to come home and join the board as chairman-designate. He wanted to get back into the fray, and nobody could tell him that he wasn't going to be allowed to take the position, not when he had funded the airline since its inception. O'Leary understood that, but it still created an immediate concern for him: Ryan had always been in regular contact, but he might want to 'get in his hair' now that he had more time to do so.

Tension was already building between Ryan and O'Leary about the cost-cutting approach. Ryan had been somewhat embarrassed when friends and associates began to complain to him about what they regarded as shoddy service on Ryanair flights. Whenever he brought this up with O'Leary, he received very short shrift on the matter. While the chairmanship was a part-time or non-executive role for Ryan, it was still important, because it would mean chairing board meetings, and calling O'Leary to account in front of the other directors. It also would mean that Ryan would have a formal say on strategy, and history showed he wasn't short of opinions. O'Leary bristled at the potential for what he saw as interference, and he made a pre-emptive strike to prevent that.

In a memo prepared by O'Leary that angered Ryan greatly, the CEO wrote: 'In your capacity as chairman, you have the potential to substantially improve, or equally substantially damage, the larger controllable items here.' O'Leary emphasized the importance of cost control, stating 'the mission is ruthless.' He hammered home the point that low cost equalled no frills, and that this would be enforced 'at the expense of charm, style and elegance if necessary', deliberately highlighting three words he knew Ryan held dear. He gave his chairman very clear instructions: toe the party line at all times in interviews, speeches or appearances, have 'tunnel vision in pursuit of making money' and do not fall prey to distractions or coups. It's no wonder the domineering Ryan was angry – what O'Leary was effectively saying was 'You're not in charge here, and it's not going to be done your way.' He was laying down a marker, and it was up to Ryan to respond.

For his part, Ryan must have retained trust in his CEO's instincts because he fell in with the message in his public comments. In his first interview as chairman of Ryanair, with the *Irish Times*, he called O'Leary 'probably the best chief executive I've ever worked with', and he specifically praised O'Leary for the idea and implementation of a cost-saving measure Ryan abhorred: stopping free food on flights. 'The family was appalled,' he said. 'We told him the passengers would go spare. He went ahead anyway and nobody complained. The time saved in serving food is now spent selling duty-free. I think Ryanair is now the biggest retailer of Jameson [whiskey] in the world.'

Ryan's new focus became the idea of a commercial airport at Baldonnel, a military airbase on the outskirts of Dublin city. He received support from the business community, but at Ryanair his big idea was dismissed out of hand. In an interview with this author, for the *Irish Independent*, O'Leary didn't pull his punches: 'Ryanair has no plans, no interest and no intention of moving to Baldonnel.' Given that Ryan had said the exact opposite on the national airwaves, I decided to ask for his response before filing the story. I met Ryan at the Irelandia office in Merrion Square. I expected a volcanic reaction from Ryan to what his supposed underling had said, but instead he roared with laughter. He then proceeded to repeat his vision for the airport.

While Ryan was looking west towards Baldonnel, O'Leary was looking squarely at Dublin Airport: he wanted a second terminal built that would offer cheaper prices to Ryanair than applied at present. He made sure everyone knew this was the lynchpin of Ryanair's future plans: 'It is important that the Ryan family's plans for Baldonnel do not cloud this debate. Baldonnel is not, and does not, form any part of Ryanair's growth plans.'

Ryan's efforts came to nothing. Then Minister for Transport Michael Lowry put an end to the proposal for a second terminal with a statement in January 1996. Ryan was furious and threatened to review all Ryanair expansion plans out of Ireland. O'Leary simply ignored his chairman and within months announced three new routes out of Ireland, and the following year another four.

Somewhat surprisingly in retrospect, alongside this expansion O'Leary was also continually looking for a likely purchaser for Ryanair, to see what kind of deal might be on offer. Ryanair remained a small airline and would need large amounts of capital to expand. O'Leary's ambition was to make money, for himself and the other shareholders, not to build what Ryanair would subsequently become. If the money could be raised quickly through a sale of all or part of the airline, he was not against the idea of doing that, especially as there was no guarantee that he would be able to realize the wealth he desired by maintaining the existing ownership structure of the airline.

There were three significant occasions when Ryanair entered into detailed discussions with potential investors or buyers. British Airways, Aer Lingus and Virgin all looked into the possibility between 1990 and 1995. Tony Ryan explored the possibilities seriously each time, but potential investors were sometimes nervous of dealing with him, and older representatives of interested parties sometimes found O'Leary and Declan somewhat brash and similarly unpredictable and demanding in their approach to any deal.

In late 1989 the Wall Street bank Goldman Sachs approached Tony to say it had several clients, international airlines apparently, which might be interested in investing in Ryanair. Tony decided it was too soon – that Ryanair had not developed sufficiently to get the best price possible – but in mid 1990 he changed his mind. Declan and O'Leary met with representatives of the American bank and gave it a mandate to 'locate an international partner who might acquire a minority stake' in Ryanair. Tony gave the project the code-name Project Swan, an allusion to changing Ryanair from an ugly duckling, and oversaw the writing of a negotiating document. He knew Ryanair needed more investment but, whatever about his ego, he was not willing to put more money into the airline without the prospect of getting it, and more, back.

British Airways looked likely to take an equity share, but eventually it withdrew from the talks and gave up on the Dublin–London route itself, which didn't augur well for Aer Lingus or for Ryanair's expansion plans. Aer Lingus entered negotiations with a view to investing in Ryanair, but the slow pace of its negotiating team infuriated Ryan, and Goldman Sachs, and talks were terminated. O'Leary had held a very low opinion of Aer Lingus for years, but this consolidated his view: it was too slow moving and monopolistic in its behaviour. That opinion would mark all of his dealings with Aer Lingus in the future.

In fact, Aer Lingus was struggling badly and in 1993 required a state rescue investment of £175 million to keep it afloat. That money came with strict EU conditions as to its use, many of which were put forward by Ryanair. As O'Leary had hoped, Aer Lingus was still on the ropes. This was the case, too, in terms of how it was operating. As Aer Lingus grappled with its legacy structure and tried to reduce costs, all the while restricted to flying on routes it had served prior to the injection of state cash, Ryanair was in expansionary mode, benefiting from its lower costs and flexibility. Year by year, Ryanair was steadily becoming profitable.

Ryan was still toying with the idea of selling Ryanair, but he didn't just want to realize cash for himself; he also wanted a strategic partner to help its continued expansion. He entered talks with Virgin, the airline founded by the high-profile entrepreneur Richard Branson. Virgin was established on the Atlantic route, but wanted to build its European business. One of Branson's partners in a separate business was David Bonderman, an American who was the founding partner of the very profitable investment vehicle Texas Pacific Group (TPG). Branson was trying to get Bonderman into Virgin as an investor. Bonderman was introduced to Ryanair by the new GPA boss, Patrick Blayney, and it was Bonderman who floated to Branson a proposal to buy 51 per cent of Ryanair in association with Virgin. Bonderman's idea involved changing Ryanair's name to Virgin and to 'expand into Continental Europe while retaining as much of the existing cost structure, method of operations and management as possible'.

It might have been a good idea, but Virgin and Branson were 'distrustful' of Tony. O'Leary insisted that he was in control of the management of Ryanair, not the Ryan family, but that sense of distrust remained nonetheless. O'Leary also found it hard to develop a relationship with Branson, who was simultaneously courting the smaller and far less successful CityJet. In the end, the negotiations went stale, and no deal between Ryanair and Virgin could be consummated. Afterwards, O'Leary spoke publicly about the newly formed European venture Virgin Express losing money, and Branson responded with a terse fax, reading: 'Dear Michael, Bollocks, Kindest Regards, Richard'. Tony saw the fax and responded in kind: 'Dear Richard, the correct spelling is Bollix. Warmest Regards, Tony.' He attached a cutting from *The Times* on a new dictionary of Irish slang to prove the point.

There was never going to be a deal with Virgin, but there was a positive outcome from the talks. Bonderman's interest in Ryanair as a personal investment had been piqued. He had also been taken by what he'd seen of O'Leary. He decided not to proceed with an investment in Virgin and to buy into Ryanair instead. Things moved quickly, and a deal was done in August 1996. It was drawn up with the specific intention of being a prelude to selling shares in Ryanair on international stock markets. Bonderman provided more than just money. His investment demanded greater growth and therefore focused minds on the need for a strategy to achieve it. First, though, a restructuring of the ownership of Ryanair was required.

The company that owned the airline, Ryanair Limited, was owned by CDS Trust for the Ryan family. O'Leary had no part in the ownership, although he had long-established rights to a profit share from Ryan, which was paid annually. On foot of the new investment deal, the Ryans, Bonderman and O'Leary set up a new company, Ryanair Holdings, which bought the airline from the trust for £56.7 million. There was a complicated set of transactions that included O'Leary getting a 22 per cent share of this new company for a personal investment of just £900,000. He gave up his right to the secret deal that gave him an annual share of a quarter of all Ryanair profits over £2 million in return for this discounted purchase of the shares. This deal would not be revealed publicly until the following year. Bonderman paid £26 million for his 20 per cent stake, and the Ryans were left with shares worth £80 million, with the overall company valued at £130 million . . . for now. It meant that O'Leary had achieved his ambition to be super-rich. His investment was now valued at £28.6 million, and he was only in his early thirties.

It was a deal that cemented Ryanair's financial position and its future potential. But, as so often in the history of Ryanair, the happy moment was followed by a crisis. O'Leary wanted Bonderman to become chairman, as a replacement for Tony Ryan, and he wanted Ryan removed from the board altogether. It was, as ever with O'Leary, purely strategic, not personal: 'We needed to get rid of the Ryans, or at least downplay Tony and the rest of the Ryan influence if we were going to seriously float the company on the London Stock Exchange. It was only a few years from the GPA mess, so Tony can't float it. You have to take the Ryans down.'

Family businesses always struggle with succession, and Ryanair was no different. The 'father–son' relationship of Ryan and O'Leary was also a tug-o'-war for the leadership, and neither man was the kind to give way easily. On this occasion, however, Ryan let O'Leary have the battle, presumably thinking the war was still his for the winning. While he was upset by O'Leary's approach, he knew that giving up the chairmanship made sense. His financial need was greater than his ego. Ryan's resignation as chairman and Bonderman's appointment was announced on 19 November 1996. O'Leary's concession was that Ryan remained on the board.

O'Leary was always clear that Ryan's removal was necessary, but with hindsight he could appreciate that those were tough times for his mentor. Many years later he admitted: 'It was tough for him, because he deserves a lot of the credit for Ryanair. It wouldn't have been there if he had followed my advice and shut it down. But he wasn't going to get any credit for it – the great success, the comeback and the rest. He had to bite his lip. As it turned out, he was happy to take the money.'

Now that Ryanair had the right structure and Bonderman's investment was in place, it was time to go to the markets. The Ryan family were no doubt haunted by the events of 1992, when GPA had failed in its IPO bid, a failure that had had far-reaching repercussions. Could Ryanair pull off what GPA had been unable to do?

It was decided to sell the shares in Dublin and New York and to avoid London because of the GPA legacy. It was to prove a wise decision. Bonderman was well known and highly respected in the USA, and his imprimatur gave Ryanair an impetus it would not otherwise have enjoyed. Ryanair was a very small airline, after all, unknown to American investors. It had thirteen routes between Ireland and the UK, one domestic UK route, and two routes from Ireland to Continental Europe. It was promising to open just two routes immediately: Kerry–Stansted and Stansted–Stockholm. It was small beer to the Americans.

In a bid to drum up support, Ryanair embarked on a road-show of potential investors in the USA, among big investment funds that had no idea what Ryanair was and would not necessarily have been interested in something as small, operating so far away. This was an important moment in the development of O'Leary's management style, because at these, admittedly private, meetings he stepped fully out of the shadows, on to a brightly lit stage and by all accounts was an excellent performer. This was his time to shine. The events were accompanied by press briefings and the Irish media began to gain an appreciation of who the Wizard of Oz at Ryanair was. It wasn't quite the start of what he later called 'all the cheap PR stunts' that would characterize his steward-ship of Ryanair – and indeed he promised he would retreat to the shadows for the next ten years, once the flotation was completed – but it was the unveiling of the new face of Ryanair. That promise of stepping back turned out to be one he was either unable or unwilling to keep.

On the investor roadshow, O'Leary gave detailed financial presentations about the performance of the airline and its potential and had an answer for every question. His manner fascinated many of the potential investors. He refused to wear suits, let alone a tie, preferring casual checked shirts and jeans. This was the pre-dot-com era, where such attire was still the exception. He also peppered his presentations with expletives. The advisers at Morgan Stanley were worried about this, but soon relaxed when they realized it was not causing offence but rather attracting attention. They were also impressed by his reasoning for flying his team on economy flights between locations in the USA and staying in dingy, cheap hotels: he expected pilots and crew to stay in low-cost accommodation, so he wasn't going to allow management to live it up.

When details of the share sale were announced, revelations of the company's profitability stunned observers. Ryanair made profits of £23.6 million in the 15 months to March 1996 and £26.09 million in the following 12 months. Nobody had dreamt it was making as much money as this. Nor had anyone considered that O'Leary was taking as much of the profit as was now revealed. In those two years, before the restructuring of the ownership, O'Leary had received a profit share just shy of £20 million. Jaws dropped in many places.

'O'Leary is living proof that nothing motivates the human spirit more than naked greed,' wrote the *Sunday Times*. 'The greed that permeates the Ryanair boardroom is in danger of giving capitalism a bad name.' His pay deal was compared to the excess that was now considered as having been fatal to GPA. 'There is a feeling that Ryanair's best days are behind it.' It made a comparison with GPA and 'the type of negative publicity that punctured Tony Ryan's attempted £1 billion flotation of GPA in 1992. Investors who desire to catch this flight should keep their seat belts tightened.'

The horror was shared within Ryanair, because staff were

certainly not being rewarded in anything like the way their CEO was. They endured a lot in serving O'Leary, who was like Ryan had been at GPA in his way of delivering his demands at Monday morning management meetings. Insiders spoke of 'spin the bottle' meetings at which O'Leary would randomly select a victim. It was rare for the selected target to be able to fend off O'Leary's assault because he was so well prepared and so vicious in the delivery of his point. Arguing back might only make things worse. It was bullying, but as far as O'Leary was concerned it got the right things done.

Now, thanks to the share sale, O'Leary's long-suffering colleagues were aware of the extent to which all of this – the shouting, the swearing, the incessant demands – were feathering his nest. It came as a shock. The deal offered to the senior management team of Conor McCarthy, Howard Millar, Tim Jeans, Brian Taylor, Maurice O'Connor and Michael Cawley was 100,000 share options each, worth £1.4 million between them. When Millar confronted O'Leary about this, O'Leary reacted viciously, telling him to 'take it or fuck off'. Cawley was not seen around the building. Not only did O'Leary refuse to back down, he added Charlie Clifton to the pot, diluting it further for existing members.

The rest of the staff, all 698 of them, were offered a £1.9 million bonus payment and promised that 5 per cent of the airline's shares would be put into an employee share-option scheme, distributed individually. For most of the staff, this translated into either 2,500 share options or £2,500 in cash. Many preferred to take the upfront cash, which was a mistake.

The offering was more than eighteen times oversubscribed at the opening price of 195p per share. O'Leary's American sales pitch had worked wonders. The price immediately went up to 250p per share, and then to 315p by evening. The company was now valued at £380 million and O'Leary's shares were worth £71 million, up by £27 million in a single day. If his intention had been to say to Ryan, 'This is how you do a flotation', it had most certainly been achieved. It was an enormous success.

The Ryan family was ecstatic. Having lost nearly everything, it was now rich again. As O'Leary and Ryanair management celebrated at a rare party at HQ, Ryan stayed in his Irelandia offices in Dublin to savour his financial resurrection. He sent O'Leary a fax with a short, simple message: 'A remarkable triumph. I send my congratulations and thanks.'

10. The blame game

When Michael O'Leary went to Southwest Airlines and brought home a ready-made business model, he chose to leave out certain elements, such as customer service. But, more importantly, he decided not to copy its approach in dealing with trade unions. Southwest had always dealt directly with the unions, for better or for worse. O'Leary took on the Southwest package almost wholesale, but he decided that Ryanair wouldn't have any truck with workers' unions. It was a decision that was to have far-reaching consequences throughout Ryanair's development, eventually exploding in its face in 2017.

O'Leary never wanted to deal with trade unions. It was partly ideological and partly practical, but it became dogma. O'Leary was an Über-capitalist, who believed that capitalism provided prosperity better than any other model, but that sharing the proceeds of profits equally was not fair – because the risks were not taken equally and because it undermined the incentive to make those profits. He was not alone among businessmen of his era in blaming unions for affecting profitability by making unreasonable demands for improving pay and conditions without offering suitable productivity in return. O'Leary believed in personally working whatever hours he could and he believed others should do the same, although, as his new riches emphasized, he was reaping far greater rewards for doing so than would ever accrue to his staff. He also believed that the agreements signed between employers and unions reduced, or even removed, the flexibility he sought, especially the speed at which he wanted to cancel or introduce routes. In short, pesky trade unions would slow him up and get in his way.

For years he enjoyed the benefits of the non-union culture at the airline. The early employees had little interest in being represented by the unions that already looked after Aer Lingus workers and lobbied loudly on behalf of that airline, seemingly putting its workers' interests first. Many Ryanair staff members felt, or were persuaded by management to believe, that the unions wanted to restrict their working hours and earnings in order to protect the agreements in place at Aer Lingus. Indeed, they shared, perhaps with some justification, management's fears that the unions supported the Aer Lingus desire to put Ryanair out of business. Membership of a union wouldn't help the unemployed.

The share sale in 1996 was a turning-point because the revelation of the full extent of the airline's profits, and O'Leary's incredible profit share, undermined his authority and argument significantly. The pilots had never really forgiven him for the savage pay cuts of 1990. Now the discontent spread, albeit not as much as people outside the organization might have expected.

The baggage handlers ended up being the vanguard. They had a few reasons to feel aggrieved. They found out just before the flotation that they were being paid less than handlers at other airlines and airports. Their working conditions were worse than those of similar workers at Dublin Airport, who benefited from the use of conveyor belts for automated unloading and transportation of luggage. For the sake of speedy turnarounds, Ryanair required its workers to shift bags manually, which often left handlers with back and other injuries. If they were unable to work, they received no sick pay. Paul O'Sullivan of the Services, Industrial, Professional and Technical Union (SIPTU) – who was to take the union fight to Ryanair and become something of a national figure in doing so – alleged that 'bad conditions do not apply to pay alone. Regarding staff, Ryanair operates like a revolving door. There is little or no job security and a climate of fear operates.'

The weekend after the successful stock-market flotation the baggage handlers demanded significant pay increases. O'Leary met them directly – without union representatives – and promised concessions. But he didn't deliver to the extent or as quickly as they wanted, and SIPTU, one of the country's largest trade unions, stepped in to capitalize on this, accepting all but one of the sixty Ryanair handlers as new members by year end. It threatened strike action for January 1998, but, in characteristic fashion, O'Leary refused to engage. Instead, handlers were quietly told they shouldn't join the union and were made further promises.

They didn't believe them. On 9 January 1998 baggage handlers engaged in a three-hour strike that left O'Leary and other managers to pitch in to keep bags moving for passengers.

SIPTU continued with a series of similar stoppages over the next month, to largely sympathetic treatment from the Irish newspapers and broadcasters, much to O'Leary's anger. He didn't like this media publicity – almost uniformly negative as far as he was concerned – but insisted that flight operations were not disrupted. All of the rest of Ryanair's 950 staff turned up for duty as normal – including the pilots.

At this point, an effort was made to force Ryanair to attend at the Labour Court for mediation. O'Leary refused, saying Ryanair had not requested it to 'investigate or intervene in the action of a tiny minority of our ground-operations people'.

To do so, O'Leary argued, would 'only prolong the misleading and failed media campaign being waged by SIPTU and detract from the calm, ongoing dialogue being conducted within Ryanair with both the 97 per cent of our 954 people who are working normally, and the minority engaged in limited work stoppages'. O'Sullivan replied that the stance 'presents very serious questions for the government when a publicly quoted company can ignore or try to ignore an institution of state'.

O'Leary's belief that he was the target for a bigger issue was confirmed when the Irish Congress of Trade Unions (ICTU) – the umbrella group of all unions – weighed in to praise the handlers for their 'courage' in standing up to senior management's 'bullying and psychological warfare'. Jimmy Somers, president of the ICTU, pronounced that it was time to confront 'extremists' among employers who were attempting to 'tear down' institutions that brought about industrial peace, assisted in the resolution of conflict in industrial relations and served the community well. He called for the introduction of emergency legislation to enable the Labour Court to issue findings in the Ryanair dispute that would be binding on the company.

Instead of remaining neutral, the National Union of Journalists (NUJ) declared support for the workers and, in a move that enraged O'Leary, suggested a boycott of the airline by NUJ members. Newspaper coverage, which was far more significant in that pre-smart device era, was somewhat one-sided – hugely so, to O'Leary's mind – and he was as much the target as his airline. He felt that his side of the story – that the vast majority of Ryanair workers supported him – was not being reported properly. Politicians in the non-governmental parties jumped in, too, with their criticism of him. His back was up. He was spoiling for a fight. Everyone was about to learn how stubborn O'Leary could be if he felt that right was on his side.

O'Leary did not believe or fear that his company would be the victim of a national boycott as long as his airline offered flights at prices the public wanted. But he sensed that his company was becoming a Trojan horse in a battle between the union movement and all employers in the private sector – who were increasingly dealing directly with employees instead of unions – and he was determined not to be compromised, especially not for someone else's agenda.

There was a dramatic escalation of hostilities at the start of March. Opinions differed as to what exactly happened or who was at fault, but Ryanair withdrew the security passes and mandatory insurance for the thirty-nine baggage handlers who were still in dispute. 'In effect,' O'Sullivan alleged, 'Ryanair locked the staff out.' Ryanair denied that there was 'any lock-out of Ryanair baggage-handlers at the airport', and a spokesman said, 'Security clearances will be restored to each of these employees once they confirm they will resume normal work.'

In response, SIPTU asked its 4,000 members at Dublin Airport – no matter what company they worked with – not to pass the handlers' picket at the three main entrances to the airport. O'Sullivan was confident he had enough support and prematurely mocked O'Leary: 'He said there were only twenty or thirty involved in the dispute. Maybe he can't count, or maybe he can only count in millions.'

By the following morning – a Saturday – about 2,000 people had mounted a picket, and taxi drivers and public-transport workers refused to pass it. The only people left working were at Ryanair. By lunchtime, Aer Rianta shut the airport because emergency fire workers had walked off the job and there was no security at boarding gates. The airport was shut for the weekend.

This was now the biggest story in the country: the national airport brought to a standstill by angry workers. The government was drawn in not just because of that but also because of its partnership arrangements with the trade-union movement in a national pay deal. It was to be the first real public example of how maverick O'Leary was in his approach. Taoiseach Bertie Ahern was furious when one of his officials rang O'Leary's office to organize an urgent meeting at Government Buildings with the Ryanair boss, and O'Leary reacted most unexpectedly.

'The only thing that Bertie wanted on the Sunday when it was closed was for me to come down to Government Buildings at six o'clock,' he said later. 'He wanted me there in time for the TV news, so that the message would be, O'Leary summoned to Government Buildings for crisis talks. So I said "No, fuck off. Go fucking open the airport."' It wasn't a response Irish government leaders were used to, but that was about to change.

Ahern had gained his political reputation a decade earlier as a fixer of industrial disputes, a brilliant middleman in negotiations, but this event tested him severely. He sought to buy time. He convinced the handlers to return to work on the basis of there being an official inquiry into the causes of the dispute. O'Leary eventually agreed to take a phone call from Ahern – which reportedly culminated in another blazing, expletive-smattered row – but he eventually accepted that part of Ahern's recommendation. There was another detail he wouldn't accept: he refused to concede any ground on union recognition as a precondition to the talks process.

He said he would close the airline before he would negotiate with a trade union.

In truth, SIPTU had made something of a mess of things, overstepping the mark and losing public support by closing the airport. 'Ryanair arguably came out of the weekend with its image in better shape than it had any right to be,' former government minister and EU commissioner Máire Geoghegan-Quinn wrote in the *Irish Times*. 'Its decision to remove the thirty-nine workers' security passes should have lost it the PR battle. To effectively lock out your staff, particularly in Jim Larkin's* Dublin, was a startling misjudgement. But it got away with it because of SIPTU's next move.'

The airport may have reopened, thanks to Ahern's intercession, but the dispute wasn't over. Not for the first or last time the media was more critical of Ryanair than it was of the unions. An *Irish Times* editorial tut-tutted: 'For Ryanair, the awkward truth is that it has only itself to blame. There are two options. It can – like many US multinationals – choose to give its workers generous terms and conditions within a non-union environment. Or it can grant union recognition and negotiate with its workers in the traditional way. What it cannot do, as a rich, successful company, is reject both options and give itself the best of both worlds. The continuance of an industrial-relations policy that would be more in keeping with the Victorian era is hardly in the airline's best long-term interest.'

As the investigators began Ahern's promised work,

* A reference to the legendary trade-union organizer and founder of the ITGWU, a forerunner to SIPTU. Larkin is renowned for his part in organizing the dispute that led to the 1913 Dublin Lockout, when employers locked out 20,000 workers who had sought the right to unionize – a landmark event in Irish social and labour history.

Ryanair laid off five of the ground-handling staff who had been on probation when they joined the dispute – despite there being a 'no-victimization' clause in the truce that had been negotiated. O'Sullivan later complained that Ryanair 'did not desist from making public pronouncements on the issue, in effect prejudging the determination of the inquiry team', despite having been told specifically not to do so.

The union wasn't mollified when O'Leary subsequently claimed Ryanair's handling of the dispute had been a PR disaster. He said he 'put his hands up', that it was all his fault . . . and already people were starting to wonder if he should be taken seriously when he claimed to be contrite. Then he announced that the near-1,000 employees of Ryanair were to receive options of nearly four million shares, worth £20 million. Pointedly, however, the shares were to be given directly to the employees, rather than being held through a share-option scheme managed on behalf of the workers by their unions, as was becoming the trend at state-owned commercial companies.

The report into the dispute was completed and published in July. Not surprisingly, Ryanair was criticized for its attitude towards trade unions, and SIPTU was criticized for allowing things to get out of control. The report made no binding recommendations about low pay and union recognition, but was more in favour of the workers than it was of Ryanair. O'Leary was incandescent when SIPTU immediately demanded implementation of the findings about both, threatening a new strike. Ryanair immediately launched a legal challenge at the High Court in Dublin, claiming the conclusions drawn in the report were 'erroneous, arbitrary, unreasonable or irrational'. It led to a series of hearings, going as far as the Supreme Court. Ultimately, the issue went in Ryanair's favour – providing it with the right not to deal with unions if it did not want to do so, a judgment it would benefit from for nearly two decades and that O'Leary would cite regularly as justification for his actions and behaviour in insisting that he would deal only with employee-representative councils at individual bases, with no trade-union representatives accompanying them.

There was another outcome of this spat, and that was how Ryanair – really meaning O'Leary – would deal with public officials in the future. In the Trump era, we have become used to bad behaviour, questionable language and an un-edifying level of disrespect from public officials, but those things weren't the norm twenty years ago. There was a certain decorum that was observed in public matters, and it was expected. O'Leary blasted through that, shattering traditional conventions and protocols as he went.

The trade-union dispute marked the start of a long and bitter conflict between O'Leary and Ahern's government. Ahern was shocked by O'Leary's intransigence, but for O'Leary it was simple: workers at other companies had hijacked the airport and it was Ahern's job to fix that, not to put pressure on him or to take the side of the unions. Most businessmen are cautious in their public comments about elected officials. O'Leary was quite the opposite. The level of disrespect O'Leary showed Ahern – both publicly and privately – was unprecedented. When, just months later, Ahern complained about 'people who weren't around ten years ago' who had been 'jumped up a bit' by economic growth and 'who are now telling us how we achieved what we collectively achieved', it was assumed he meant O'Leary. Ahern did make one direct reference to O'Leary, criticizing his pursuit of 'tooth and claw capitalism'. O'Leary was unperturbed; to be described that way was a badge of honour.

He would engage in regular conflict with Ahern for the

next decade, until Ahern's resignation from office in 2008. The issue was always the same: what O'Leary regarded as state-imposed charges at Dublin Airport and Ryanair's desire to provide competition by building, owning and operating a second terminal. Instead of lobbying ministers politely, he chose to ridicule and harangue the government, appealing instead to the ordinary voters and travellers, to whom he promised lower fares if inefficient state monopolies were broken down. The media lapped it up, as O'Leary regularly made public attacks on the man he called 'prime minister', refusing to use his official title of taoiseach, something that many Irish people felt was disrespectful. He labelled Ahern an appeaser of the trade unions and, worse as far as O'Leary was concerned, a 'ditherer', somebody who couldn't make a decision about anything that was difficult. Ahern clearly didn't like it.

It was markedly, strikingly different from how Tony Ryan and his ilk did things. Ryan developed relationships with leading Irish politicians, made political donations and dangled board memberships as prizes. This was the way it was done: with civility, a whiskey and a smile. O'Leary sneered at what he saw as unnecessary sucking-up to politicians. His experiences with Ahern during the airport dispute only copper-fastened his beliefs that politicians were ineffectual time-wasters, and they weren't going to waste his, at least not now.

The traditional way of doing things had led to questionable practices, though. In the late nineties the papers were thrilling to revelations of lobbying behind closed doors, donations for favours and allegations of secret payments directly into politicians' pockets. Minister Michael Lowry and former Taoiseach Charlie Haughey both fell foul of such allegations.

O'Leary felt much of the criticism was overdone, however. 'I have never yet come across a politician who will make a political decision in your favour or against your favour unless it was in their interest, or in what they consider to be the national interest,' he said. 'They just don't make decisions based on the fact that you sponsored something, or that they stayed in a holiday home of yours.' Later in his career, O'Leary would be happy to make financial contributions to political parties, and he and Ryanair did so: 'If the party is going down the right road, we should try and support it. The only two I wouldn't give a contribution to would be Sinn Féin and Labour. Sinn Féin are a bunch of mindless morons and they have the economic policies of a two-year-old. Labour have my sympathies, but that'd be about the height of it.'

Mary O'Rourke, Ahern's first minister for transport during his 1997–2002 government, and Aer Rianta chairman Noel Hanlon wouldn't even get sympathy from O'Leary. Instead, he went to war with them. Reports of the meetings between O'Leary and Hanlon became the stuff of legend, with colourful accounts of how they swore and shouted at each other over their one lunch meeting. They fell quickly into mutual loathing as each sought to push their position at the expense of the other.

O'Leary decided that he would campaign for a second terminal in full view of the public, a very unusual tactic at the time. In November 1998 he set the agenda by writing to the *Irish Times*, launching a £200,000 initiative for the public to become involved in supporting his campaign for a second, privately owned terminal at Dublin Airport. If they voted in favour of his plans, they would be entered into draws for free flights. He told anyone who would listen that Dublin Airport was the most expensive location at which Ryanair operated, that he was paying £10 million in fees each year when he could build his own terminal, attached to the same runway but with different management and lower charges, for £20 million. He said this competition would drive down prices from all airlines, to the benefit of passengers.

John Burke, the Aer Rianta chief executive, responded with his own letter to the same paper, arguing that 'airport charges are one of the smallest elements of the costs involved, accounting for just 3 to 4 per cent of airline-operating costs. It is not credible to suggest that a charge which is lower than the local bus-fare to an airport would influence a decision on whether or not to take a holiday. This debate has much more to do with Ryanair's profitability than it has to do with tourism . . . Ryanair, on the back of a spurious tourism argument, is lobbying for its current average payment of £1.93 per passenger to Aer Rianta to be reduced to a flat 50p. A 50p airport charge would do little more than cover the electricity and gas bills at Dublin Airport. No other airline is looking for, nor would expect, such a deal.'

O'Leary's adversaries had no idea of the nature of his tenacity. He was completely committed to getting that second terminal, and he would do everything possible to achieve it, and he would be relentless. No whingeing officials or parliamentary committees or adverse publicity would stop him. They meant nothing to him. As he had told Tony Ryan years before, making money required 'tunnel vision', and that was his expert skill.

He waited until autumn 2000 before reigniting the war with Aer Rianta, by way of an interview with the *Wall Street Journal*. He said the best way to settle his differences with the state-owned airport authority was 'with Semtex', the notorious explosive used by the IRA during its bombing campaign. He said it would be used, 'preferably during a board meeting'. Aer

Rianta refused to 'stoop so low as to respond to that remark', but one of the company's directors, Rita Bergin, did: 'Here we have an individual worth well in excess of £100 million behaving in a shockingly irresponsible manner.'

O'Leary was unrepentant, using the following week's Ryanair AGM to condemn conditions at Dublin Airport's only terminal as 'shambolic'. 'They've spent £50 million on a five-storey extension that nobody wants to use,' he claimed, adding that the new baggage hall was 'something designed by Russian architects', while 'Pier C was designed by Aer Rianta to win an architectural competition rather than serve the needs of airlines.'

If the row with Aer Rianta caused plenty of comment, the escalation of hostilities with Minister for Transport Mary O'Rourke caused outrage. He had no respect for her and was not afraid to make it known, even though, or more likely because, she effectively had the power to say yes or no to whatever Aer Rianta planned. O'Leary came to loathe what he saw as O'Rourke's indecisiveness and lack of ability, and said so in derogatory and insulting fashion, going as far as describing her as 'an idiot': 'Most politicians are idiots, but if you look on the scale of idiocy, she'd be right up there at the top.'

In January 2001 O'Rourke's husband of forty years, Enda, died suddenly after suffering a brain haemorrhage. To everyone's surprise, O'Leary joined the mourners at the funeral. To everyone's horror, just days later he ran a newspaper-advertising campaign mocking the newly widowed O'Rourke. She had been on national radio some time previously and had said, in her often informal manner, to the amusement of the listening public, that she had heard some important news one morning from the radio while soaking in the bathtub. O'Leary's advertisement, complete with cartoon depicting her in a bath, ran,

'Mary, Mary, quite contrary, how does your monopoly grow?' O'Rourke was greatly upset. 'He did it four days after Enda died . . . you would say nobody could be that cold or that horrid, but he was. He didn't care.'

Nor was he reprimanded by his board for his insensitivity. Not long afterwards, on 21 March 2001, the Ryanair board decided to mark his fortieth birthday by arranging for a surprise visitor to the board meeting. In marched O'Rourke, unannounced, to berate O'Leary. Except it was the male actor Alan Shortt from the RTÉ satirical show *Bull Island*, who dressed up to play the part of O'Rourke and give the team a laugh.

O'Leary did back off from slagging off O'Rourke, but issued a public statement calling on her to support him in his plan to deliver 20 million new passengers into Ireland and 500 new jobs at the airports. 'I hope she will respond magnanimously in the national interest,' he wrote. He refrained from further antagonistic public comment, realizing that nothing was likely to be done before the general election, due in 2002.

This may have been influenced by the friendship, as well as the business relationship, he enjoyed with P. J. Mara, the high-profile former government press secretary under the Haughey regime; his first private sector gig after leaving office had been with Tony Ryan and GPA. Mara was a highly controversial character, a fixer who provided a link between politics and business, and who had many clients who ended up in some of the country's biggest scandals. However, O'Leary enjoyed Mara's irreverence, wit, charm and outrageous storytelling but, in common with others, valued his judgement and his contacts as well. Mara also had a remarkable talent for maintaining friendships with both sides when powerful and wealthy men went to war with each other. Mara was very close to Ahern – serving as Fianna Fáil's director of elections under Ahern's leadership – and he urged O'Leary to show some patience, at least until after the 2002 general election was out of the way.

Mara's counsel proved wise because O'Leary's patience was rewarded when O'Rourke, somewhat surprisingly, lost her seat in Dáil Éireann in the general election, despite Fianna Fáil returning to power. Instead, Séamus Brennan, key to saving Ryanair nearly fifteen years earlier, was returned to the portfolio. It seemed like a godsend for O'Leary. Brennan immediately set out to meet with O'Leary, with reports that he wanted 'to make peace' with the Ryanair boss.

Brennan proved to be a sympathetic ear, and in July 2002 he introduced proposals for temporary facilities at Dublin Airport for low-cost airlines until permanent facilities could be built. By August he had invited tenders for expressions of interest in developing a new terminal. O'Leary was thrilled, but wasn't particularly interested in winning the deal for Ryanair; he just wanted Aer Rianta stopped. 'If nobody would do it, we'd pay for it, we'd build it, we'd give it to somebody else to operate it. We just want some competition with Aer Rianta out there and we have been consistent in that for years.'

O'Leary's ambitions had increased. He said he would be able to build a facility for €114 million, would be able to handle 10 million passengers a year and would be operational by 2004. Brennan most probably was inclined to allow Ryanair to get on with it, but he was pragmatic enough to realize that the trade unions and Aer Rianta (now to be renamed Dublin Airport Authority (DAA)) were determined to hold on to their power at the airport, and that if anyone else were to disturb it, it would not be O'Leary and Ryanair.

It was not until May 2005, a full ten years after O'Leary started demanding it, that a decision was announced: the DAA, still under the chairmanship of Hanlon, would be allowed to build a second terminal.

O'Leary was angry, to put it mildly. 'The Taoiseach dithered for three years on providing a second terminal at Dublin Airport. As a result, Dublin Airport today is not just a slum; it is a testament to the failure of Bertie Ahern to keep his own election promises . . . Another terminal provided by the people who brought us the Black Hole of Calcutta is not competition, it's still the Black Hole of Calcutta. The government has been forced to open up telecoms, electricity and other sectors to competition, and airports shouldn't be any different.'

He threatened and began a legal challenge that was doomed to failure. 'We'll go to the Competition Authority and the European Commission and challenge this on the basis that it contravenes competition and public procurement rules. It's time for the monopoly to be tested in the courts and in Europe. It's a state monopoly and it's illegal. Competition works but Bertie giving in to his buddies in the trade unions doesn't.' His formal complaint alleged that Ahern had 'entered an arrangement with the trade-union movement in relation to union work practices', and that Ahern 'wrongfully and in breach of duty' had imposed the agreement on his minister for transport. To make things even worse for O'Leary, the DAA announced that the project would cost €1.2 billion and would not be completed until 2009. He was furious with this proposal: 'We, as the largest airline in the country, have not been consulted on either the location, the cost or design of this terminal. It's an absolute bloody disgrace that it's not going to be here until late 2009 and how you can spend €1.2

billion when the private sector has offered to build it for €200 million with no extra cost to the taxpayer is equally a disgrace . . . It's a shambles.'

O'Leary had got what he wanted, but not in the way that he wanted it. At Ryanair, he could be the sole controller; he could shout and demand and things would happen as he said, and quickly. It was deeply frustrating for him to deal with outside forces that wouldn't bow to his will, like the trade unions and the government. As far as he was concerned, he was right and they were wrong. The only good thing was that every step of the way, every letter, every insult, every public mud-slinging, every angry editorial, was all publicity for Ryanair. At least there was that.

11. A European affair

Michael O'Leary gets bored easily. He is a restless individual, fizzing with an energy that comes out in interviews as fidgeting and impatience. He is never still, and the same goes for his mind, which is always working, plotting, seeking out the next opportunity. There's never a cigar, only the constant treadmill of work, work and more work. It's as if he's afraid that if he slows down, he'll stop.

Joining the stock market was just the beginning. It made him rich, yes, which would have sated many, but, in common with other businessmen of his type, he wanted more. And Ryanair needed to do much more if it were to grow as its founders and new investors wanted. The answer was fairly obvious, at least to him if not others. O'Leary saw all of the 300 million citizens of the then twelve member states of the European Union (later twenty-eight) as potential customers. Ryanair would become the low-fares European short-haul airline, that was the ambition.

The Open Skies Directive came into force in 1993, and it meant that all airlines – even small players such as Ryanair – could fly to a greater number of destinations across the entire EU, without having to receive the formal permission of individual states to fly into their airspace or land at their airports. This meant, in effect, that a single EU air-transport market was created. The old rules had been designed to protect incumbent, often state-owned airlines from new competition, but, in a swoop, these were gone. Existing airlines could move into new markets; and new ones could be established to make their pitch to customers. The new competitors could also set their own fares without requiring regulatory approval and fly as many times a day as they wanted. Not only that, but competition rules were introduced to stop bigger airlines from using predatory pricing to keep new airlines out of the market. New conditions were imposed to limit the amount and number of cash injections each government could make to support state-owned airlines. It was a revolution, and one that had been set in train by an Irishman, Peter Sutherland, when he was an EU commissioner. It was to prove to be one of the most far-sighted and beneficial of EU moves, and it allowed the likes of Ryanair to assist in a veritable cultural shift: Europeans could travel all over the Continent for work and leisure on low fares.

O'Leary spotted the opportunity the EU was presenting to airlines, as long as they knew how to take it. The model Ryanair employed in the Irish and British markets could be extended to Continental Europe. He believed that most citizens were 'paying outrageously high air fares'. He wanted price-sensitive passengers who used road, rail and ferry links to switch to flying Ryanair and decided they would do so if the price were cheap enough. 'When the restrictions on airlines are lifted, short-haul, cost-efficient, point-to-point airlines will sprout up throughout Europe,' he predicted. 'They will, in a short space of time, change the face of European air travel.'

It didn't happen immediately, however, even if he would be proved correct eventually. He watched as airlines set up once full deregulation had been introduced failed, mainly because they couldn't control their costs. In 1994 alone, fifty-seven new airlines opened in Europe, but thirty-seven were closed within two years. It confirmed for him his stance that low costs and low fares were the key to survival and success.

To this end, he hit on a strategy that drew much criticism: yet again, following the Southwest example, Ryanair decided to hunt out new airports to serve. These were so-called secondary airports that were not as near to final destinations, but, crucially for Ryanair's purposes, they could offer extremely cheap prices and quick turnaround of planes. There were plenty of options among the secondary routes, so the problem would be to provide enough planes and flights to keep a daily schedule working almost round-the-clock. O'Leary went back to Boeing and put in a new order. This time, Ryanair wanted to upgrade to the 737-800s because they offered the capacity to carry fifty-nine additional passengers to the existing number.

In a bid to avoid waste, O'Leary asked Boeing to fit out the aircraft interiors in the most basic manner possible, with few or no nods to the type of comforts many passengers took for granted. He did away with reclining seats, window blinds, Velcro-anchored headrest covers and even the seat pockets where most airlines put the safety notices and free magazines. The thinking was that the pockets would become a space for refuse, which meant extra work for the stewards that might hamper the quick turnaround O'Leary demanded. The comfort of his passengers – especially the larger ones – was not a concern. It was all about the cheap ticket.

And so to Europe. The first major decision was to fly to Beauvais, described by some as little more than a runway with a shed. It was located 40 miles west of Paris, with no rail connection. Flights from Ireland and Britain to Brussels went to Charleroi, 30 miles south. When flights started from Stansted to Sweden, they went to Skavsta, 60 miles away from the capital, Stockholm.

Many of the incumbent, legacy airlines across Europe scoffed, dismissing Ryanair as not knowing what it was doing and giving its customers a laughably poor service. The media dutifully printed these criticisms, giving Ryanair exactly the type of publicity it wanted for its new services. Much of the media failed to understand the genius of doing deals with obscure airfields. They cost a fraction of what the so-called primary airports charged and signed long-term deals at those reduced rates, sometimes for as long as ten to twenty years. They offered discounts, sometimes to the extent that there were little or no landing or handling charges, reckoning they could make money from retail units at the normally empty airports. They even paid some of the promotional costs for the routes. Competitors couldn't believe that Ryanair would use Hahn in Germany for its flights and call it Frankfurt when it was a two-hour drive away. (Lufthansa mounted a legal challenge to the description, which produced more beneficial publicity.) There was only one important consideration for O'Leary: the availability of cheap facilities that could handle the needs of a low-cost airline.

Ryanair realized that it had enormous power in its dealings with the airports. There were so many of them, desperate for business, that they would do deals on Ryanair's terms. If any tried to change the terms and conditions, Ryanair simply left and set up a new route to a nearby airport. Rimini lost all its flights in 2001 when Ryanair, annoyed by the Italians' attempt to change the T&Cs, simply moved its business to Ancona, an hour's drive away. The message went out loud and clear that Ryanair would walk away from a deal if it felt it was being mistreated. It would also depart if a destination was not providing it with profits. As O'Leary observed, some airlines gave themselves up to three years to make a profit on a route, whereas Ryanair 'will not enter a route if we cannot break even in three hours and grow the market by at least one hundred per cent'. It was a boast, but it wasn't far from the truth.

The distance of the secondary airports from the advertised eventual destination led to all sorts of media coverage. Sometimes the airports were even in different countries to the final destination, requiring extra hours of additional on-the-ground transport. One British newspaper, the *Guardian*, which disparagingly and condescendingly liked to call Ryanair 'Eire O'Flot', in a nod to the old and derided Russian state airline, Aeroflot, once went so far as to devote a special weekly column to the topic. It ran competitions such as 'My Ryanair Hell' and 'Ryanair-Miles', in which it asked readers to guess which of Ryanair's airports was furthest from its stated destination. The winner was deemed to be Reims (Disneyland), hundreds of miles from Euro Disney.

But as word-of-mouth spread, the customers didn't seem to mind; yes, they had a lengthy commute to follow, often on budget buses rather than more comfortable trains, but that wasn't a problem to most. The Ryanair argument was that the secondary airports saved passengers time, keeping them away from congested runways and arrival lounges, which actually added considerably to the advertised times of other airlines at supposedly more convenient locations. The argument had some validity. The often lengthy extra journey to the final destination might not be as bad as it first seemed, because few primary airports were actually that close to the centre of major cities. So, to everyone's surprise, bar O'Leary's, the approach worked.

O'Leary became the butt of jokes because of his skinflint ways. He was living the old adage: take care of the pennies and the pounds will take care of themselves. It amused people, but it also showed his innate understanding of what 'low costs' entailed. In 1998, for example, he decided that ice in drinks was a frill too far. He estimated that not buying ice would save Ryanair €40,000 each year. Passengers were baffled when cabin crew explained they had no ice, but eventually the supplier of ice, who did it as part of a wider service of food, melted and dropped its price. Dunnes Stores supplied him with cheaper, own-brand St Bernard cola, which he served at full price. Finches supplied drinks for free, but he charged for serving them. At Ryanair HQ, he banned the use of cover sheets on faxes to save on the cost of paper, not for environmental reasons. He told cabin crew to buy their own pens or to take them whenever they were left loose. 'I tell the staff not to buy them. Just to pick them up from hotels, legal offices, wherever. That's what I do.' He banned Post-it notes and highlighter pens. Later, he banned staff from charging mobile phones at the offices because it was an alleged theft of the company's electricity. The saving per charge was estimated at 1.4 cent. It led to much sarcastic media coverage that emphasized the depths to which Ryanair would sink to reduce costs, but it was enforced with zeal – and it did save money, as well as gaining free publicity.

O'Leary was forging the kind of low-fares airline he had been pushing for all along. There was resistance, there was a lack of understanding, there were continual criticisms, but slowly he was educating the airline industry about the nature and scope of a low-cost, low-fares company. He was perfectly placed to carry it off because of his obsession with costs, his belligerence and his confidence. It is a very useful tool in business not to need to be liked, and O'Leary certainly benefited from that. He genuinely didn't care about opinions of him as a man or a businessman. He never, ever dropped his focus on the bottom line.

As a result of his efforts, travelling by airplane became easily affordable for all. There was a huge shift from the notion of flying as a luxury, which it had been, to seeing it as an airborne taxi service. Once the price was right, the passengers came in their droves. This led to a new criticism of Ryanair: that it was making the experience unpleasant by allowing the 'riff-raff' on board. British newspapers ran stories accusing Ryanair of facilitating trips to Europe by 'gangs of lager louts'. O'Leary laughed it off, saying Ryanair carried 'very upmarket' passengers whom he described as 'Chianti louts, heading to villas in Tuscany and the south of France. We expect the Chianti louts, the lager louts and anybody who just wants a stunningly low fare to buy tickets.'

Considerable snobbery towards Ryanair developed as a result. Rival airlines blamed O'Leary and Ryanair for giving the industry a bad name. British Airways, responding to the challenge of the Irish upstart, created its own low-fares competitor, Go. When it started with flights from Stansted to Milan, Rome and Copenhagen (primary airports), its boss, Barbara Cassani, promised that 'low price will not mean low service'. She pointedly said she believed it was possible to run a low-fares airline without being nasty and described Ryanair as being like 'a cheap flying pub', the type of place where people threw beer over your head. 'I would just never work for them,' she wrote. 'I wouldn't want to be treated the way he treats people and I wouldn't want to treat customers the way he encourages his staff to treat customers. Our check-in desks at Stansted were right across from Ryanair's and my assessment of Ryanair is that when everything is going well, it's fine, but when things go wrong, they would literally shut the desks down. I disagree with Michael's philosophy, which is you pay low prices, you get crummy service, and I actually think he has done a disservice to the rest of us. I think the accountancy association of the world should vote him as their poster boy. This is what you can do if you start as a bean counter. You can have a mouth like a publican or a drunken sailor.' It's easy to picture O'Leary reading this offended tirade and laughing himself silly.

Cassani's opinion of O'Leary led her to make the mistake of trying to compete with him on the Dublin to Prestwick and Stansted routes. In her memoir, she was candid about the poor judgement that informed that decision. Like many others before and after her, Cassani had underestimated her rival. 'Of course, we didn't realize Michael O'Leary would take the move as a personal affront. He was screaming and swearing a blue streak when he heard the news.' He slashed fares and ran negative advertising about Go and its 'crap schedule'. He was scornful of the ability of long-haul or legacy carriers to operate as low-cost competitors. 'I know more about flying Concorde than BA knows about flying low fares, which is why Go will not work.' He was proven correct. When Go began to fly out of Dublin, he defended his low-fares monopoly with venom, slashing prices and increasing availability until Go gave up, having lost millions of euro.

Cassani conceded that 'We got a thrashing on the new route as Ryanair slashed prices even further. Going head to head cost us millions and we withdrew wounded. We learned another crucial lesson about discounting. You can't take on someone with lower costs because they dig deeper than you to lower their prices and still make money, while you're bleeding.'

O'Leary had decided on a policy of route dominance, and, even if it meant he was in constant rows with Aer Rianta, he was not going to surrender any of his market share out of his main airport. He would defend volume to the hilt because his profit margins didn't come from ticket-price increases but from squeezing suppliers for better deals and selling things on board to gain additional revenue. As far as O'Leary was concerned, he was entitled to soak passengers for as much additional cash as possible to give him his profits.

Most passengers would live with any inconvenience as long as they got a low-price ticket, but some kicked up and Ryanair's staff bore the brunt of dealing with unhappy customers. Many managers sympathized with staff and tried to improve their lot. Conor McCarthy, during his period as chief operating officer, held focus groups with staff and customers to address recurring problems. Caroline Green, a long-standing executive, tried to introduce retraining for flight and ground attendants. She introduced a system to pay bonuses to staff who went out of their way to be charming and helpful to Ryanair customers. 'What does it cost to welcome a passenger on board and be nice to them during their flight?' she asked. 'The things we are doing differently don't cost a thing, but they could make all the difference to a customer and their experience of the airline. We want people to start going the extra mile in their work.' Ryanair began distributing surveys, asking passengers their views of the airline and how it might improve its services. O'Leary indulged the exercises, but didn't act upon the findings because they didn't suit him.

This was hardly a surprise. He had been dismissive of the early customer-relations guides issued to staff, regarding them as a tiresome and expensive burden, even if they had been established at Tony Ryan's insistence. These were manuals published and distributed to ground operations and in-flight services in the early years of Ryanair. Staff were told to be friendly and helpful to passengers. 'If we are perceived to be friendly, efficient and professional, we will get this repeat and new business which is vital to our success,' one manual said. 'Ryanair is the "value for money" airline. This means we do not rely on expensive perks or extravagance to create the desired impression. If we are professional and friendly people, but are not perceived as such by the passenger, then we have lost the battle.'

Remarkably, given what was to transpire under O'Leary's management, this manual set out the conditions under which passengers could expect to receive compensation or meal vouchers if their journey was disrupted. There was to be a snack voucher – for a non-alcoholic drink, sandwich and biscuit – if the flight was delayed for more than three hours. If the delay was longer than six hours, a meal voucher would be provided. The manual also pointed out that help, rather than compensation, might be the best course of action: 'Being genuinely concerned for the passenger's plight and offering assistance with practical things, such as phone calls, baggage, queries and directions, will often by valued more highly and save the company a considerable amount of money.'

That all changed when O'Leary took over. His targets were purely financial; they didn't involve happy, smiling customers. That was purely incidental. As was a shouting, frustrated or upset customer. They simply weren't factored into the equation because the only thing that mattered about them was how much money they were parted from in getting from A to B. In case any staff members were still affected by the old thinking, O'Leary insisted he had the final say as to when such money should be spent. Any staff members recommending payments had to prove to him that the expenditure was absolutely necessary. He made this so difficult that staff members became reluctant to approach him to seek authorization, fearing his wrath. It quickly reached the stage that few ever dared. A corporate dictatorship had been established.

12. The World Wide Web

The presence of a middleman between Ryanair and the passenger infuriated O'Leary. In Ryanair's early years, travel agents could claim 9 per cent of the ticket price from any airline for providing a relatively simple service, and that commission stuck in his craw. It was top of the list of unnecessary costs he wanted to consign to the dustbin. His ambition was to cut them out entirely, and to sell directly to the public. He did what he had done before: found an innovative model to steal. Once again, he looked to easyJet, which was controlling its reservations directly via a call centre. What easyJet could do, Ryanair could do better.

O'Leary set up Ryanair Direct in 1997, to centralize the airline's reservations. It was a basic use of the existing technology. There were banks of telephone operatives in a warehouse taking bookings from the people who rang in. The stated plan was to process 4 million customers a year and handle 10 million calls, but the real ambition was to dilute and then eliminate the influence of the travel agents.

Even though Ryanair wanted to control its own bookings, it took years before it migrated over to the internet as a way of doing this. The technology, although still underdeveloped, was available in the late 1990s, but O'Leary waited and watched. This reflected O'Leary's own aversion to technology at that time. Legend has it that for many years he did not even have a PC on his desk, and that his view of the internet was that it wouldn't 'catch on'. (He also insisted on all PC monitors in Ryanair's open-floor office being turned towards the central walkway, so he could see at any time what people were doing on their computers.) He also remained unconvinced that the majority of people would transfer to using the internet to make their bookings, believing that they would want to converse with a human, or that it would be too complicated for people to use. He could see the potential cost savings, but feared that revenues would not arrive if he authorized the change. In retrospect it seems like an overly conservative approach, but there was sense to it at the time.

O'Leary held firm and did not budge until the technology improved sufficiently to allow people to print their own tickets conveniently instead of having it done for them. Typically, he became something of an evangelist once he was persuaded to use a PC and the internet: the cynics within the airline bemoaned that he acted like he had invented web bookings once he was persuaded of their merits. O'Leary was lucky that others around him, particularly Caroline Green, the head of Ryanair Direct, brought him to where he needed to be.

The eventual creation of the Ryanair website was of huge significance in the airline's development. It also gave birth to another of the company's carefully created legends, designed to get as much positive publicity on the cheap as possible. O'Leary was distrustful of the many computer-literate types to whom he was introduced – believing in the myth that they all wore cargo pants and ponytails – and he was genuinely shocked by the apparently excessive quotes he received for the cost of constructing a user-friendly interactive website. He wanted the job done on the cheap, no matter how potentially important an investment it might be.

Eddie Wilson, Ryanair's recently appointed personnel director, who had previously worked at Gateway 2000, remembered two bright young students who had worked part time there. He reckoned they could do the job. One was a seventeen-year-old secondary school student, John Beckett, who had been diagnosed with a serious medical condition a year earlier (which led to a kidney transplant in 2010), and the other was his friend, 22-year-old dentistry student Thomas Linehan.

When Wilson rang Beckett, the young man was sitting in a classroom at St Andrew's secondary school, Dublin. Wilson invited him to a meeting with O'Leary and the Ryanair management. 'Ryanair was getting quotes of £3.5 million to design their website and Eddie remembered I was doing this kind of work,' Beckett said. 'I went in after school one day in jeans and a T-shirt and was brought to a senior board meeting with Michael O'Leary and all the lads. I winged my way into winning the contract for £20,000.'

Beckett was thrilled, even though he was beaten down on the price, and agreed to do a job in one month that he felt would take three. In the end the duo were paid only £15,500, as O'Leary, ever the cheapskate, discounted their final invoice. 'Ryanair got millions of pounds' worth of publicity and names in the paper and logos all over the place because we got such wide exposure,' Beckett said. But he had no complaints. He was seventeen, after all, and it was a huge sum of money and an incredible opportunity.

They created a website that was relatively simple, even by the standards of the time. It combined a simple marketing function – information on routes and special offers – with a computerized booking system. While the site allowed Ryanair to sell tickets, it did not allow customer interactivity. The booking process was full of advertisements, it took a minimum of seventeen clicks to book a flight, there were booking barriers such as CAPTCHA codes, and terms and conditions were almost hidden. There was no contact email address for complaints or queries; the Ryanair phone number was included in the small print, but for those who managed to find it there was no guarantee anyone would answer a call. Beckett and Linehan ended up asking for their names to be removed from the site, realizing that the publicity attaching to their involvement did not compensate for the hassle involved in receiving hundreds of emails of complaint from angry Ryanair customers who contacted them instead of the airline about any service issues they might have because their addresses were all that could be found on the site.

That first website was formally launched in March 2000, offering discounts for any passenger who booked online. 'We want to concentrate on being Europe's largest low-fares airline,' O'Leary boasted. 'Selling tickets online will help us cut some £10 million in costs, but there is scope for using Ryanair.com to sell a variety of products. We were approached by lastminute.com, the travel site, but we turned them down because we want to sell Ryanair tickets ourselves.'

Within weeks, Ryanair claimed that it had been visited by six million people and O'Leary predicted it would get 50,000 bookings a week. The new technology also gave Ryanair instant and detailed information about bookings on each flight and each route, and allowed for immediate pricing updates. Whatever about O'Leary's enthusiasm for the possibilities, stockbrokers and investment bankers became very excited, some so much so that, in common with the fashionable trend of the day, they suggested that Ryanair should split in two: to have an airline as well as a dot-com company that could be floated separately on the stock market and attract a higher valuation than if Ryanair were to remain intact. O'Leary, presciently, given that the dot-com bubble was about to burst, refused to be caught up in the hype.

Once O'Leary was happy with how the online-booking system was working, he began to shut down other, more expensive sales channels. He decided to leave Galileo, the international booking system in which all the main airlines were participants, even though about 40 per cent of Ryanair tickets were sold that way. He was confident that the discounted fares would persuade customers to book by phone or online and avoid travel agents. Finally, he would be able to eliminate commissions to third parties.

O'Leary saw other opportunities to increase revenues, too. The former corner-shop owner had long realized that a flight was a marketplace with a captive audience. The pay of cabin staff had been linked for years to the number of duty-free products they sold, along with alcohol and soft drinks, so many were relentless in their selling. By 2001 Ryanair passengers were spending an average of £4 each on ancillary services. He spoke freely to the media – getting publicity all the time – about a range of paid inflight services from satellite television to internet services to gambling: 'I'm working on a cinema multiplex model. They make most of their money from the sale of popcorn, drinks and sweets, not cinema tickets.'

That, however, was not where the real money could be made. The booking process itself provided an opportunity to sell more than flight tickets. Anyone who spoke to a phone representative was offered the chance to hire cars, book hotel accommodation and cover their trip with travel insurance. Ironically, given his desire to cut out the middleman, Ryanair took commission from the companies that provided those services. He could now do the same online, turning it into a one-stop travel website. 'We intend to make Ryanair.com the largest air-travel website in Europe,' he said, predictably enough.

The results were mixed. Ryanair made its website available to any partner who was prepared to pay for the marketing opportunity. As long as they guaranteed cash, either by way of upfront payments or commission, took their own risks and asked nothing of Ryanair management's time, they could piggyback. O'Leary didn't seem to care what products and services were being sold – or about possible reputational damage from inappropriate or poor relationships – as long as it brought in money. One of the more bizarre uses of the website came in 2002, when Ryanair agreed a deal with Bank of Scotland to allow it to sell mortgages on the website via a link to a mortgage broker.

O'Leary may have realized his approach was wrong, or perhaps he simply thought it could be squeezed for more money, but in 2003 he brought in Conal Henry, an experienced commercial director, with the express instruction to increase ancillary revenues. Henry, who later worked in the telecoms industry for over a decade and remains highly admiring of O'Leary, did not regard O'Leary as a brilliant retailer: 'I came to Ryanair from Asda, where I worked for the likes of Archie Norman and Allan Leighton, and Michael isn't cut from the same cloth. He doesn't understand the shopping experience in the way that they do.'

When Henry started in his role, 15 per cent of Ryanair Direct passengers on the phone also booked a car or a hotel or travel insurance. On Ryanair.com, by comparison, just 2 per cent of customers made an additional purchase, even though the offers were exactly the same. The reason for the disparity was simple: a person on the phone was able to make the payment for everything purchased at the one time, giving his or her credit card details just once. On the website, the customer was redirected to the next leg of the transaction and had to re-enter all their credit card details again. It was just too cumbersome or confusing for people to bother.

Henry was determined to transform the website to offer better-quality products – and to make it easier to pay for them. He also wanted to be like Expedia, offering one price for flight and hotel accommodation combined. This would have required major changes to Ryanair's booking system, however, and O'Leary refused to sanction it. Disappointed, Henry turned his attention to the deals Ryanair had in place with Hertz and needahotel.com. He discovered another reason for the failure to complete second transactions: customers were unimpressed by the prices being charged by needahotel.com. It was being charged such a large margin by Ryanair that it had been forced to put up its own prices to give itself a margin, but it had gone too high. The same happened with Hertz, which found that the more cars it hired out via Ryanair, the less worthwhile it was in terms of financial return. It got to the point where Hertz stopped putting cars at the Ryanair airports because it was not profitable to do so. Instead, Ryanair passengers rented from car-rental companies that had no relationship with Ryanair but made big profits from simply being at the Ryanair airports – a situation designed to anger O'Leary. Henry renegotiated both deals on lower commissions, but it meant greater overall revenues.

Henry was credited with doing a good job in getting rid of poor partnerships and replacing them with new revenue streams, even though he stayed for little more than two years. Within eighteen months of his arrival, O'Leary was able to report that ancillary revenues were up 35 per cent in 2003, to just under £150 million, and they would have been even better had sterling been stronger against the euro on the foreign-exchange money markets. It was certainly a convincing case for the future of online bookings at Ryanair. If he had been reluctant at first, requiring someone else to go ahead and show that it could work, O'Leary was now converted. He could see that the level of control provided by its online sales hub would be hugely instrumental in achieving the level of success he wanted for Ryanair – and for himself.

13. Lands of opportunity

As Ryanair headed into the new millennium, Michael O'Leary's ambitions grew . . . and he wasn't afraid to make big predictions, even if they seemed boastful, because he knew they would get attention. 'We expect our profits to grow by 20 to 25 per cent,' he said of his targets for Ryanair during the decade. 'That's not just good, that's practically obscene in an industry in which few people make money. This isn't an airline, it's a drug baron's business.'

Striking evidence of O'Leary's single-mindedness came a year later, when two planes flew into the Twin Towers in New York, shattering the new millennium sense of optimism and hope. Airline bosses across the world were shaken to the core by the events of 9/11 and foresaw crippling problems for the future of their industry. O'Leary, by stark contrast, saw blue skies. This presented a lucrative opportunity.

The fear that other commercial aircraft would be used for further terrorist attacks gripped the Western world. American airspace was shut for days and, when it reopened, everything seemed to have changed. Governments moved to reassure passengers that it was safe to fly, but anti-terrorism security checks were intensified, complicating and lengthening the time it took to get on to a flight. It was anticipated that fear would dissuade large numbers from flying at all. Most airlines were already struggling from declining volumes and revenues in an international recessionary economic environment – one that was likely to be hit further by this

blow to public confidence – and they immediately complained that they would be put out of business unless they
received massive financial support from governments.

O'Leary was adamant that it had to be business as usual:
'The only way to defeat terrorism here is not to be whingeing
with your aircraft on the ground looking for subsidies. It's to
get out there with lower fares and persuade people to travel
more often . . . despite the efforts of terrorists, normal life
continues, with millions of people travelling for normal
leisure and business purposes . . . other companies are
grounding flights, laying off staff, but we're going to fly our
way out of this crisis. Our solution is to get back in the air
with more passengers and lower fares.'

He announced seat sales, his tried and trusted response
to any slowdown. He lobbied the European Commission
against allowing state aid to national carriers who found
themselves in even deeper financial trouble because of this
added shock to the system, arguing that any aid 'should be
applied equally to all airlines and all passengers by means of
reducing passenger taxes or landing and passenger charges
in European airports, rather than straight subsidies to inefficient and loss-making airlines'. If his competitors went out
of business as a result, then all the better.

He could have made a different choice. Ryanair had accumulated a €700 million cash reserve, which meant it had the
means to ride out the storm. Instead, O'Leary decided to be
aggressive. Although, maybe 'decided' is incorrect – he is
aggressive, so it was his natural reaction. He read the aircraft
market brilliantly. Airlines were going out of business or
scaling back, so they wouldn't be buying new aircraft. That
meant the aircraft manufacturers, with their high fixed costs,
would discount the price of newly built aircraft to get stock

off the books and keep their staff busy. Boeing was particularly vulnerable, with 50,000 workers and an order book that halved almost immediately in the aftermath of 9/11. As far as O'Leary was concerned, it was an excellent situation for Ryanair: it could buy loads of aircraft cheaply. Fine, said the few managers internally who were willing to argue the point with him, but what if people don't want to fly? Nonsense, O'Leary insisted. People will always want to fly, as long as the fares are affordable. Hadn't they continued to fly during the Foot and Mouth emergency earlier that year?* They'd take their chances.

The first thing O'Leary did was to announce that Ryanair was cancelling its order to buy five new Boeing aircraft it had agreed to take delivery of between March and May 2003, claiming they were too expensive. He also cancelled options on another fourteen aircraft. If anyone was thinking it was a sign of reduced ambition, they were soon put right. Ryanair placed a full-page advertisement in *Flight International*, offering to buy up to 50 second-hand 737s. Even before 9/11, O'Leary had reckoned these could be purchased at bargain prices. After 9/11, the number of offers increased, and by the end of September he had 600 aircraft from which to choose.

'Demand for aircraft is weak,' said Michael Cawley, then chief financial officer. 'Airlines are getting rid of aircraft. Leasing companies have aircraft on their hands and we are one of the few companies expanding in this situation. There

* Foot and Mouth is a disease that affects livestock and is transmitted by the movement of animals and by people who have come into contact with animals that have the infection. In 2001 it resulted in travel restrictions and led to the postponement, for a number of months, of events that involved travel between Ireland and Britain, including rugby internationals, damaging tourism revenues.

are more sellers than buyers, so the price is bound to fall.' Industry insiders speculated that Ryanair could acquire aircraft for as low as $11 million each, whereas the full list price for new planes was $60 million. For that level of discount, Ryanair would live with the higher maintenance costs on older aircraft.

O'Leary's real game, however, was to put the squeeze on Boeing to drop the price of its new aircraft and then buy those. His public courting of the second-hand market was one ploy, his meetings with Airbus in France another. The European manufacturer was Boeing's biggest rival, and it made planes almost every bit as attractive to Ryanair's needs as Boeing did. Although all Ryanair's existing aircraft were Boeing, O'Leary told Airbus he would consider switching his entire fleet to Airbus if he got a good enough deal on price. He completely played Airbus. It thought it had a deal – had even shaken hands on it, although no contracts were signed, it claimed – and he reneged, sending a letter thanking them for their efforts and apologizing because the Boeing offer was better. Legally, there was nothing Airbus could do.

In January 2002 Ryanair made its big announcement: it was buying one hundred 737 aircraft, with a list value of $6 billion, to quadruple the size of its fleet, with options over a further fifty. It was an extraordinary commitment for O'Leary to make, but even more so when the role of Tony Ryan on the board of Ryanair was remembered. Ryan had been laid low at GPA by a gamble on a massive order for new aircraft at a time of economic weakness; investors, wrongly as it turned out, decided that the market for these planes wasn't there and scuppered GPA. The key difference was that O'Leary didn't need to raise equity to part-fund the purchases. He had cash in the bank and could raise additional finance at a very low interest rate. He was taking a risk, but it was a safer gamble than his mentor had made a decade earlier.

The new aircraft for Ryanair had a bigger capacity and could carry 189 passengers. Crucially, they offered thirty more seats than the Airbus A320, and O'Leary reckoned the extra places would reduce the average cost of each seat. This extra availability would allow him to flood the market with cheap fares. 'We are getting the extra seats almost for nothing, so the challenge is to fill them,' he said. It wasn't just PR spin when O'Leary told reporters that 'We have found through experience that the 737 provides the unbeatable cost economies and reliability you need to be a profitable low-fare airline.'

O'Leary denied that Ryanair was expanding too quickly, citing the 'huge potential' for low-cost air travel, which made up just 4 per cent of the total European market. He said that 18 per cent of the market in the USA was catered for by similar low-fares carriers. He pledged that, within the next decade, Ryanair would carry more than 40 million passengers a year and have more than fifty routes. 'Ryanair is going to be a monster in Europe in the next ten years.' The monster would require a lot of people power: Ryanair said it would need 800 new pilots, 2,000 cabin crew and 400 engineers and operations staff.

O'Leary had enjoyed himself enormously during the negotiations: 'I grew up in Mullingar and farmers know that the time to buy is when everyone else is selling and the time to sell is when everyone else is buying. It was quite simple. We had money. Boeing and Airbus couldn't give away planes. So we went and bought up about two years' worth of production.' It is likely he learnt this lesson from watching his father get it wrong. In a 2018 interview with the *Irish Farmers Journal*, O'Leary described how his father always followed the crowd, and as a result he sold when everyone was selling and bought when everyone else was buying. His son watched and learnt, and was determined not to repeat what he saw as a fundamental mistake.

The value of the deal was not disclosed, but the contract was the biggest single order for next-generation 737s Boeing had ever received. Ryanair described it as 'an exceptional deal' at prices 'substantially lower' than those on the options it had recently cancelled. It was estimated that the cost to Ryanair would be between $4.95 billion and $5.4 billion. According to Alan Ruddock's 2007 biography, O'Leary boasted that 'We raped the fuckers.' (That sort of crass and offensive language was common in business at the time. On the back of #metoo, #timesup and the revelations about abuse by movie producer Harvey Weinstein, it would be highly unusual to hear it today.) Asked how he felt about this, Toby Bright, Boeing vice-president in charge of sales, felt compelled to reply, 'We enjoyed the experience.'

O'Leary was invited to the Boeing HQ near Seattle to address some of the workers. He arrived to discover over 2,000 people present, with thousands more watching on the company intranet. Wearing his trademark jeans and open-neck checked shirt, a bottle of Coke in hand, he strutted up and down the stage, praising the American workers for building 'the best goddam aircraft in the world' and running down Airbus.

Displaying yet again his ability to understand his audience and perform for it, O'Leary hyped up his nationality and comparisons between Ryanair and Southwest: 'Firstly, it's run by the drunken Irish, and we like to pride ourselves on our ability to party, and fly while over the limit,' he claimed. 'Secondly, the Irish and Texans have a number of other things in common, like humility, religion, gun laws.' Gun laws in Ireland were tightly restricted, but he wasn't going to let facts interfere with a story. He finished his presentation by promising to fly a Boeing aircraft into every European airport, 'to kick the shit out of Airbus'; and then he started to dance an Irish jig, shouting that the only reason the Irish drank so much was because there was 'no sex in Ireland'. He got a standing ovation. He had made Boeing workers feel good about themselves, and management feel better about being taken advantage of.

The new fleet was quickly put to use, with twenty-four new routes opened in 2002. Ryanair was expanding in every direction, it seemed, and the shape of the company was changing. O'Leary was very aware that keeping to their growth targets was going to take careful management and leadership. To that end, he kickstarted 2003 by reshuffling his management team.

Michael Cawley and finance director Howard Millar were promoted to the newly created positions of joint deputy chief executive. Cawley also became chief operating officer and Millar chief financial officer, Cawley's old role. Two deputies for O'Leary seemed excessive to many commentators, but the move was designed to reassure investors that Ryanair had more to its management than just O'Leary and that responsible adults, with a strong financial background, were there to provide balance in a period of planned rapid growth.

The managers who made the cut prepared for the coming decade of expansion, but others decided to leave Ryanair. Some of the most important managers from the previous decade – such as Charlie Clifton, Tim Jeans and Conor McCarthy – had left in the previous couple of years, all more or less worn out by the demands of working with O'Leary.

He shrugged it off. He would get adequate replacements. Nobody was indispensable . . . other than him. O'Leary calls his management team 'the Z-team', a silly little affectation designed to puncture any growing egos.

As Ryan did with his executives a decade earlier, O'Leary called in the Z-team each Monday morning and roasted them. The regulars at this point were: David O'Brien (formerly Aer Rianta) as director of inflight; Ray Conway (formerly Irish Air Corps), the chief pilot; Jim Callaghan, head of regulatory affairs; Eddie Wilson, head of personnel; Paul Fitzsimons, head of communications; Caroline Green, head of customer services; Mick Hickey (a veteran since 1988), head of safety; and Bernard Berger, head of route development. They discovered that if they brought problems to O'Leary, they needed to bring solutions at the same time. Fighting with him, as some did, was likely to result in only one outcome: O'Leary would win. He didn't develop strong personal relationships or care whether or not people liked him, although he respected most of his colleagues – if they did their jobs. They all had defined roles, but the whole thing worked through him: he had the final say. He was always pushing them for new ideas to cut costs and raise revenues. It was relentless.

The Z-team selected the new routes, but there was an interesting lack of rigour to this process. O'Leary simply selected routes according to the deals being offered by airports, not by demographic or market research. It sounds a bit 'stick a pin on the map', but it illustrates how cost reduction was the single motivation in all planning. It meant many routes failed – for example, of the forty-seven new routes opened in 2003, ten were closed within a year because they didn't deliver the high level of return O'Leary demanded.

At this time, Stansted emerged as Ryanair's key hub. And

it played an important role in Ryanair's first takeover bid when it sought to buy the smaller rival airline Buzz, one of the very few times Ryanair expanded by acquisition, even if buying growth was popular at many companies. O'Leary led the bid and promptly rebranded Buzz as Ryanair, opening twenty-two new routes from Stansted on 1 May 2003 alone. The deal brought O'Leary into conflict with the British unions when, deal signed and approved, he decided to sack two thirds of the Buzz staff. He also got rid of four of its twelve aircraft and axed fifteen of its existing twenty-four routes, halving the fares and doubling the seat capacity on the nine routes he decided were worthwhile.

As was often the way with O'Leary's major decisions, it was reactive, in part prompted by the actions of others. He was taken by surprise in May 2002, when easyJet acquired Go. The ebullient chairman of easyJet, Stelios Haji-Ioannou, boasted that 'The acquisition will contribute significantly to our objective to become Europe's leading low-cost airline by strengthening our position in important target markets, increasing our management strength and providing a larger, stronger platform from which to exploit growth opportunities profitably.' He was throwing down the gauntlet to Ryanair.

Ryanair's initial response was to condemn the deal. 'Rather than widening choice to passengers, this would eliminate it,' Cawley complained, somewhat predictably. O'Leary was somewhat more sanguine, realizing that it would happen and he had to live with it, calling it 'a ballsy move' on easyJet's part to take on an airline with higher fares. 'I will be taking lessons in humility now that we are – for the time being – Europe's second largest low-fares airline.' He promised that Ryanair would still become Europe's largest scheduled airline. The number of doubters increased, though.

Andrew Lobbenberg, an airline analyst with ABN AMRO, had his doubts, especially about filling all 189 seats on each of the new Boeing 737-800 aircraft: 'Flying from London to nowhere can work, but flying from nowhere to nowhere is a challenge, especially with large aircraft.' He published his views under the title 'The emperor has no clothes' and advised his clients to sell their shares because he believed Ryanair's share price was overinflated by expectations the company would be unable to meet.

The last months of 2003 apparently vindicated Lobbenberg's position . . . for the present at least. Competition had intensified and the European economy had slowed. By December, O'Leary knew he would have to issue a 'profit warning' to the stock exchange. When he did so, at the end of January 2004, it led to a one third collapse in the share price – an unprecedented fall, other than for immediately post-9/11, when all stock markets fell sharply because of those unique circumstances. In its statement, Ryanair admitted that its annual profits could fall by as much as 10 per cent because of a need to cut ticket prices to fill seats. The third quarter of its financial year, October–December, had been bad, but things were going to be worse between January and March, the last quarter of its financial year. Expected yields, or average revenue per passenger, were to fall 25–30 per cent in its fourth quarter to the end of March 2004.

O'Leary took an unconventional approach to this unprecedented situation. Instead of playing things down, he ladled it on: 'We are still very pessimistic on fares and yields. Clearly they are going down much faster than we thought before.' He blamed the reversal on an 'enormous and sudden' decline in yields and fares caused by intense price competition, and the huge increase in seat capacity across the board. Ryanair's average fare was €35.60 in the last three months of 2003, compared with €49 in 2002. In January it fell further, to €30. 'It is possible we could be looking at profit margins of under 10 per cent for the next five years,' he said, predicting a 'bloodbath' as a vicious fare war took hold.

One of O'Leary's strengths in a crisis was that he relished the battle and the chaos and the uncertainty. While others might be rattled by the prospect of difficult times, it seemed to bring him alive in a whole new way. 'I love this,' he said. 'It is much more fun when the world is falling apart than when it is going boringly well. We had been saying fares and margins would fall. What we didn't foresee was that they would come down this bloody quickly. It is our job to show that this is a bump in the road and not some hole we have fallen into. I fully accept that the share price will take a beating today and over the next couple of weeks, but we think it is an investment in the medium and long term.' He referenced Southwest and variability in its profits and share price over the years, and said – correctly, as it turned out – that the same would happen to Ryanair.

The stock-market reaction was a disproportionate response to the news. After all, Ryanair would still be earning profit margins of over 20 per cent, if not near the 30 per cent it had been achieving. However, the track record of unbroken growth was about to go. The share price was a multiple of future profits, but in Ryanair's case the multiple was higher than that of rivals because of the expectation that it could deliver double-digit profit growth each year. O'Leary was hit hard personally: it wiped €80 million off the value of his personal shareholding. 'This is the first major crack we've seen in Ryanair's business model,' said Kevin McConnell, head of equities at Bloxham Stockbrokers in Dublin.

Just as before, though, and as would happen again, O'Leary was looking at the bigger picture. He had an ulterior motive. He knew of further bad news coming down the tracks and wanted to get all of it into the public domain as quickly as possible. He used the occasion of the profit warning to lay down markers for the impact of a big and presumably adverse decision he knew was coming in the following weeks: an EC investigation into the deal he had made to service one of Ryanair's major European airports, Charleroi in Belgium.

The deal at Charleroi was sweet. Indeed, it was O'Leary's public boasting of how good it was that alerted the EC and prompted an investigation. Ryanair paid just 50 per cent of published landing fees but, even better, it was indemnified against any losses it might suffer if airport taxes were to rise over the next fifteen years. The airport paid Ryanair €1.9 million to open three new routes, another €1 million towards staff costs and more for office accommodation. In return, Ryanair had to pay only €1 per passenger for use of the airport's ground-handling facilities, as against an advertised charge of €10.

O'Leary's fear was not just the hit to profits at this one location if the deal were overturned, or any fines were levied. It was the potential for any adverse decision to set a precedent to be applied to regional airports throughout Europe, both those he served and those he planned to serve. He attempted personal negotiations with the EC transport commissioner, Loyola de Palacio, but these failed. He then attempted to pre-empt the likely announcement by claiming there would be no fines and mocking the Commission as 'an evil empire'. This caused considerable annoyance, not just at the EC but among his own board of directors. Ray MacSharry, a former EC commissioner, was especially appalled, and he, Chairman Bonderman and a long-standing director, James Osborne, told O'Leary to be quiet, especially when the Belgian commissioner Philippe Busquin complained publicly that O'Leary was 'terribly irritating and irritates commissioners'. O'Leary's bullish behaviour couldn't steamroll through every institution, it seemed.

Ignoring the combined wisdom of MacSharry, Bonderman and Osborne, who were very savvy operators and knew what they were talking about, O'Leary launched a further pre-emptive strike. He accused the Commission of being lured into a plot by flag-carrying airlines and high-cost airports to 'emasculate low-cost airlines and erase them from the picture. There is a certain element in the Commission that would like to make life easier for Air France and other high-cost airlines. They are trying to come up with a set of communist rules, which means that everybody pays the same high costs and charges the same high fare. It would not be the first time the EC has made a balls of an investigation. This is an attack not just on Ryanair but on the entire low-fares sector. The ultimate by-product of the decision will be to increase air fares.'

Six days after the announcement of the profit warning, the Charleroi decision was handed down: the money given to Ryanair by the owners at Charleroi amounted to illegal state aid; €4 million would have to be returned to the Walloon regional government (which owned Charleroi Airport) as compensation; and a new, shorter contract with Ryanair would have to be drawn up to allow competitors access to the airport. The EC said that the contract had allowed Ryanair to operate in 'entirely stable conditions' that were 'sheltered from any commercial risk', putting rivals at a considerable disadvantage. Commissioner de Palacio, in a clear sign of her frustration at the public baiting in which O'Leary had engaged, concluded that O'Leary 'had overplayed his hand. He thinks this is good for him; I am not sure that it is the best for his company, but that is up to him.'

This did not deter O'Leary from a hyperbolic, yet controlled, response. When he arrived at Charleroi on 3 February, he was met by thirty-five television crews from around Europe and countless newspaper reporters. His impromptu press conference achieved blanket coverage, some of it broadcast live, and increased brand recognition. He made it all about the EC and consumers and positioned Ryanair as the ally of the passengers, standing up to the bullying regulators. He held EU BANS LOW FARES banners for the assembled photographers and pretended to cry. 'We consider this to be a disaster for consumers,' he railed. 'It's a disaster for low-fare travel all over Europe and it's a disaster for state-owned regional airports. We don't accept that we have received any state aid at Charleroi. All we received were discounts, just like Tesco would receive discounts from its cheese suppliers.'

He raged against the 'fucking Kim Il-Jungs' in the Commission who were determined to destroy the low-cost industry. Everyone knew he was referring to the North Korean dictatorship in his comment, although he conflated then ruler Kim Jong-Il with his deceased father, Kim Il-Sung. 'You cannot have civil servants trying to design rules that make everything a level playing field,' he complained. 'That's fucking North Korea, and everyone's starving there. This market works well. The European Commission has successfully followed a policy of deregulation and competition for the last twenty years that has transformed air travel in Europe, and has transformed regional airports. It's a complete fuck-up which is going to overturn twenty years of competition in air travel.'

O'Leary aggressively defended Ryanair and attacked the Commission's decision as incorrect, but speculation started to mount as to whether O'Leary could hold on to his job. The *Financial Times* wrote that Ryanair's 'air of invincibility' had been 'finally shattered'.

When it was put to him at a meeting of stockbroking analysts in London that his confrontational position had hurt Ryanair with the Commission, that 'you had started out saying that you would definitely win this, no problem' and that it might be time to consider resignation, he replied: 'Ultimately, the responsibility rests with me. And it would be up to the board and the shareholders. If they want to change me, they can change me at any time. And, as I think on my feet, I think my defence just over the last twelve months would be that the company is still growing at over 50 per cent. We still have the lowest base in Europe; we have the number one operational delivery in Europe in terms of on-time, fewest cancellations; fewest lost bags; no other airline in the world makes a 20 per cent margin; and we have got €1.1 billion in cash. I accept that some people may question my performance, but I think I am happy to stand over it.'

O'Leary's noise about Charleroi and the profit warnings drowned out the thunder of the turbulence being experienced by the entire industry. He was cutting fares and increasing capacity to make life as difficult as possible for his rivals. Having brought expectations close to zero, the only way now was up. He had manipulated the message, had put all of the bad news into a seven day-cycle. The share price fell but would rebound strongly.

He quickly brushed off any criticism for his handling of the mini-crisis: 'There is absolutely no harm is losing this mythical horseshit that we can walk on water. Given that it was our first profit warning the market went nuts but there is no point whingeing that everybody has got it in for us. Perhaps we deserved a slap around the head. It was inevitable that at some point in our history profits would stop accelerating. Any chief executive who doesn't have a sense of their own mortality is heading for disaster. They read articles describing themselves as visionaries and geniuses. They shouldn't believe it any more than when the press are calling them gobshites and wankers.'

O'Leary's ability to trust in himself, without any doubt, had yet again proved to be a valuable asset. While others were caught up in details in the present day, his mind was already ten years into the future, when Ryanair would have brought down everyone else and it – and he – would still be flying high. Genius, gobshite or wanker? It simply didn't matter.

14. Changing of the guard

The story of Ryanair is largely the story of two men, both very similar and yet very different. Tony Ryan was the instigator, while Michael O'Leary is the operator. They were of a type – aggressive, delighting in confrontation, full of self-belief and confidence that borders on arrogance, and astute business minds that don't suffer fools at all. For all that, they were also markedly different. Ryan cultivated a very particular image, an air of gentility and success, and that public face was very important to him. He might have been a difficult boss behind closed doors, but to the world he projected the image of gentleman CEO. O'Leary doesn't hold with any of that. His style of management is just as confrontational, but he has no desire to be held in high esteem. When they looked at each other, they understood each other instinctively, but they also clashed in a fury of fundamental difference. It was a fascinating relationship.

O'Leary was, to all intents and purposes, part of the Ryan family. In some respects, he was treated better than Ryan's natural sons, according to various sources. 'Tony loved him and it was mutual,' said Jim King, a close friend of Ryan and one of his most trusted colleagues at GPA. 'He loved him like a son and wanted what was best for him. Tony saw raw intelligence in Michael and also decisiveness in implementing a decision, once he had first considered all of the facts. Michael often displayed sheer courage in doing something, he was persistent, dogged, refused to give up and Tony admired all of that.'

People needed strength of character to be able to stand up

to Ryan's tirades, to deliver on his demands, to back off when necessary. They fought, but it was without rancour for the most part. They were able to forgive and forget quickly, moving on to the next challenge. Although O'Leary was only in his mid twenties when they first started working together, he was not afraid to stand up to Ryan and tell him what he thought in expletive-laden rants that were returned in kind. Far from being insulted or angry, Ryan was delighted. 'Tony would deliberately provoke him, like he did with many people, but it was all designed to get those on the receiving end to perform better than they thought they could,' King said. 'He did it with all of us. Tony heaped responsibility on people, you had to prove to him that you could do it. Michael did that in spades.'

For his part, O'Leary was greatly influenced by how Ryan operated. He understood and aped his abrasiveness. At Ryanair he copied the Monday-morning management meetings that had become famous at GPA. He held management to account and was loudly and aggressively demanding of them, to get the best out of them, as he saw it. O'Leary became known for vicious verbal assaults that were described in the company lore as 'hate beams'. O'Leary may not have many people he's loyal to in his life, but he was loyal to Ryan. The arguments and bluster were all surface; beneath that was a steel core of trust and loyalty that saw them through the bad times.

O'Leary saw Ryan's ability to sell and negotiate, and vowed to emulate it. He saw how hard Ryan worked, but also the impact that could have on his relationships. 'The guy's a genius,' O'Leary said of Ryan while he was still alive. 'I learnt an awful lot from him. You get few opportunities in life to learn from someone as rich and successful. I get on with him half the time and I fight with him the other half.' He was also deeply impressed by the way Ryan responded to the

GPA debacle. 'Tony was very mercurial and people like that, who are geniuses, they must have long nights of the soul. But Tony was never a depressive, he was a fighter. The easiest thing at that stage of his life would have been to roll over and die, but he never, ever did that.'

Ryan had picked O'Leary out from an early age, and he knew his gut instinct about him was spot-on. He regularly said that sending O'Leary into Ryanair was the best decision he had ever made. He had thought of pitching him into GPA as chief executive, but O'Leary had no interest in the job at the time it was offered to him, when it was in the depths of crisis. Their relationship changed from the moment Ryan's relationship with GPA changed because of the failed stock-market flotation. That failure led O'Leary to decide that Ryanair was the better bet and would get his full-time commitment and also that he had to assert a greater degree of independence from Tony. It was his turn, his time. He began to prioritize Ryanair over GPA, despite his boss's continued dependence on both.

Not being Ryan's son allowed O'Leary to manage Ryanair in the most profitable way possible. As we have seen, Declan Ryan had stepped back, not because he was without considerable ability but because his name was an impediment in implementing cost savings: somebody always thought that, no matter what Ryan said, he had a pool of money from which he could find extra cash to cover things. O'Leary was firmer that he wouldn't do that and, bluntly, was more talented.

Tony Ryan both loved and hated what O'Leary did with his airline. He loved the money and the scale of its successes, because that reflected well on him, but he hated the bad publicity and the blame that became attached to his name. It infuriated and embarrassed the founder that his creation was associated with rudeness and incivility, no matter how grateful he was to O'Leary for reducing the demands on his personal chequebook. It pained him when other people criticized Ryanair as shoddy. Of course, any attempt to raise this with O'Leary was met with an incredibly forthright opinion on what his friends could do with their observations.

This was the central issue in their relationship, and it persisted throughout the decades: that O'Leary's Ryanair was successful, but it wasn't the Ryanair Ryan had wanted to build. This chasm opened even wider when Ryan assumed the chairmanship of the company on 1 January 1996. Ahead of his first board meeting, Ryan wrote a memo to his fellow directors called 'Ryanair is terrific', and it was effectively his blueprint as to how he wanted the airline to conduct itself: 'I set out hereunder random thoughts as to how to raise the profile of Ryanair and convince the public that the airline offers true quality travel and value. After many years of negative rumours – old aircraft, Romanian pilots, poor punctuality, unacceptable service, bad manners from handling agents together with serious questions on its financial viability – Ryanair needs to address its branding and project the airline as it is managed today.'

He wrote that 'cost cutting is of paramount importance', but added that 'a lean, well organized company also had to command respect and gain the confidence of the traveller'. He carried on to prioritize 'safety, value, cleanliness, friendliness and punctuality' and demanded that Ryanair had to get itself 'a smart image', which would demand a 'concentrated effort by everyone'. He finished by stating that he believed 'Ryanair is terrific but we must make the public believe that Ryanair is terrific.'

O'Leary proceeded exactly as before, not allowing himself to be deflected from the mission he had set out for himself of constant cost reduction. 'We were fighting like cats and dogs,' recalled O'Leary, 'and, to be fair to him, I would say I was an odious little jerk, because I wanted to get rich. Tony was older – more mature – and wanted to give me my head a lot of the time, because I was delivering the goods. But he wished I would tone it down a bit, and he was probably right in that respect, too.' Hindsight is as valuable as it is worthless.

Ryan would have liked it had O'Leary copied all, not just some, of what Southwest did. That airline enjoyed a low level of customer complaints, its crew were under orders to be friendly and entertaining, and it offered not only the lowest fares but the highest standard of service. This was bred into the business; hopeful candidates were tested on a scale of one to five across seven traits: cheerfulness, optimism, decision-making, team spirit, communication, self-confidence and self-starter skills. And, of course, that people appreciation was taking place at the most unionized airline in the USA.

Declan Ryan joined in to support his father when O'Leary produced a strategy document in 1998 'that did not cover the areas of customer service', as Declan saw it. He pointed out how the media was constantly writing articles about Ryanair service that portrayed it as 'tough, uncompromising and unsympathetic'. He pleaded with O'Leary not to dismiss his concerns as merely a proposal to increase costs. 'It is in fact stating that we have gone too far and too cheap.' Tony Ryan later noted that his son may as well have been 'talking to a brick wall'. Declan's dissatisfaction with the response prompted a period of disengagement from the company. When, in 2004, he resigned as a director, some insiders interpreted it as a public show of support for his father and a rebuke for O'Leary. Declan denied this at the time and continued to do so. He insisted that he simply had other business interests to chase, and started selling his remaining shares in

Ryanair. He became highly successful in other businesses, some involving airlines, and, while he increased his wealth enormously, he has given much of it away in Ireland to charitable ventures, becoming the country's most generous known philanthropist. The Clongowes Jesuits would be proud.

The upshot of this fundamental disagreement was that Tony seriously considered leaving the Ryanair board. On 1 October 2004 he wrote to Bonderman, tendering his resignation. In a letter, he put his decision down to the fact that 'The chief executive's lack of interest in directors' views leaves me no alternative but to resign.' Again, Bonderman persisted in trying to broker a resolution between the pair, arguing that the consequences of a public resignation on the Ryanair share price – upon which they all depended for their wealth – would be enormous. Ryan agreed to stay, although he, too, continued to cash in his remaining shares. Ryan and his sons made over €900 million through share sales, but the family's disengagement meant that O'Leary was now the largest individual shareholder in the company.

Bonderman, who had a close view on the relationships involved, explained how he regarded what was happening in an interview with Richard Aldous for his biography of Ryan, *The Aviator*: 'Michael was and is concerned about costs, almost to the exclusion of anything else. Tony was much more concerned with image – the company's and his own. Michael didn't care about customer complaints. He dealt with them, but I think Tony thought you should run the business so well there shouldn't be any complaints. Michael was happy with the "cheap and cheerful" design of Ryanair. But if it was just cheap and not so cheerful, he didn't mind.'

King agrees with this assessment: 'Tony felt that there was a vulgarity to some of what Michael did, that his style was not appropriate. Tony was somewhat defensive of himself, of his reputation. He would not have been human if he had not been a little envious of the way Michael took control of his company and there was a touch of that in him. But he was highly pragmatic and agreed that he could not have done with the company what O'Leary did.' It was amusing in a way, that the man from the working-class background, born into poverty, found the Clongowes graduate lacking in manners and good behaviour.

Ryan took ill in 2006 and was diagnosed with pancreatic cancer. He survived a year, but his physical deterioration was in some ways as difficult for his loved ones to watch as it was for him to endure. This was not the powerful man that they feared at times but loved, and it all happened too young as far as they were concerned.

Ryan was seventy-one years old when he died in September 2007.

Two men delivered eulogies for Ryan at his funeral. One was Ken Rohan, the Cork-born property developer who had been possibly Tony's closest friend outside of the aviation industry. O'Leary was the other.

In Ryanair, Tony was not just our founder, he's the visionary, he's the motivator, he's the mentor, the guiding light. When times were tough and we were struggling, he was our staunchest supporter. When times were good and we were going well, Tony was our harshest critic, always urging us to do more, try harder, lower the fares, improve the service, and for God's sake O'Leary try to make it elegant.

All of us in Ryanair are proud to carry Tony Ryan's name and legacy. We will continue to do so with pride and distinction, for he would demand no less. It may not always be elegant, but as long as the spirit of Tony Ryan survives, it will damn well be successful.

Ladies and gentlemen, Tony Ryan hasn't really died, you couldn't kill that fire or that personality, I should know, I tried a couple of times. For twenty years he was my boss, mentor, tutor, supporter and critic, but through it all my friend.

My abiding memory of Tony will not be the business tycoon but rather the shy, softly spoken, charming and courteous man. Despite all his achievements Tony's greatest pride and joy came from his family. His chest was never bigger than when recounting the successes of his sons Cathal, Declan and Shane. Tony was always there to support, encourage and above all celebrate their success, any excuse for a big party!

Ladies and gentlemen, Tony Ryan wasn't perfect, he wasn't always right. Tipperary is not the centre of the Universe. Matt the Thresher did not become the first of a world-wide chain of Irish pubs. However, his failures were occasional and small, compared to the monumental achievements, which will endure long after his passing. Tony's life was a gift to all of us. He created GPA, he created Ryanair, but he has also left his indelible mark on Irish education, the Arts, Sport and our Cultural heritage not least by restoring Kilboy, Lyons and Castleton. These things will endure. The memory of Tony Ryan will endure, and for those of us fortunate enough to have shared in even a small part of that journey, we can be proud that we walked for a time in the presence of greatness.

More than one of the many people who attended the funeral – from business, politics and the arts, as well as family and friends – saw O'Leary choke back tears as he finished and was embraced by Declan. He'd meant what he'd said.

15. Send in the clown

Ryanair was primed to fulfil its ambition of becoming the biggest low-fares airline in Europe, but of course the key requirement was passengers. If O'Leary was going to get people to fly with Ryanair, they had to know what the airline offered. As far as he was concerned, that was low fares. He had to convey that simple message to as many people as possible, and then convert those people into loyal users of the Ryanair service. The primary way any business gets its message across is advertising, but Ryanair wasn't into slick, expensive ad campaigns. They would somehow have to get the benefits of a campaign on the budget of a cardboard cut-out.

There's an old maxim in business: 'I know half the money I spent on advertising is wasted, but I don't know which half.' O'Leary was disdainful of advertising companies and their big ideas. He resented that agencies charged commission for creating campaigns and then for placing them. He also distrusted the messages constructed by copywriters, many of whom he regarded as 'tossers' full of unwarranted self-regard. Their talk of concepts and subtle brand-building didn't interest him in the slightest. He didn't care about winning awards from others in the advertising industry. He wanted ticket purchases now, not at some stage in the future. He wanted immediate attention and notice for what Ryanair offered, and sales to show for it.

O'Leary's trust in his own instincts and ability meant that Ryanair dealt directly with media companies. To his delight,

O'Leary found that prices for a full- or quarter-page ad in many newspapers could be easily driven down. Even more money was easily saved by writing the copy for the advertisements himself. He rarely agonized over the content of the ads, preferring spur-of-the-moment inspiration. Topicality was important, as long it emphasized the 'low-fares' message.

There were many examples. In September 1996 a Sudan Airways flight was hijacked and flown to Stansted. O'Leary quickly produced an ad showing a picture of the hijacked jet accompanied by the caption: 'It's amazing the lengths people will go to, to fly cheaper than Ryanair.' Cue outrage.

It was the same when another hijacker demanded that Pope John Paul II reveal the so-called 'Third Secret of Fatima' as a condition of releasing hostages (before the hijacker was removed from the aircraft). O'Leary produced an ad with a photo of the Pope whispering to a nun, accompanied by the caption: 'Pope reveals fourth secret of Fatima – Psst, only Ryanair.com guarantees the lowest fares on the internet.' There were many protests, just as O'Leary had planned. The Catholic Press and Information Office said the Pope was not a fit subject for a commercial airline advertisement. It added the ad was 'pointless and without any particular focus'. Ryanair responded that the Catholic Church should 'forget the stuffiness' and claimed it had received supportive phone calls from customers. 'This is light-hearted and fun and 99 per cent of people have taken it that way,' spokeswoman Ethel Power said.

It wasn't just something it did in Ireland and Britain. When it opened the Charleroi route as the first European base, O'Leary decided to make a splash in the Belgian market by targeting the state airline, Sabena. He ran an ad that featured a picture of the famous Brussels statue of a small boy urinating:

'Pissed off with Sabena's high fares? Low fares have arrived in Belgium.' Sabena boss Christoph Mueller, later chief executive of Aer Lingus, took legal action, much to O'Leary's delight. This would keep the row in the spotlight for a considerably longer period, and any legal costs and fines would likely be cheaper than an advertising campaign.

Not everyone at Ryanair was impressed. When Tony Ryan was alive, he was appalled by much of the advertising. One ad, in particular, caused him to complain about what he saw as unnecessary vulgarity. 'Blow me, these fares are hard to swallow' read one Valentine's Day newspaper promotion. There was a blazing row at a subsequent board meeting, when Ryan called the adverts 'crass and rude'. Bonderman had to calm things by asking O'Leary to consider what line he would prefer not to cross in the future and come back and tell the board what it was. He never did.

O'Leary's second key tactic in getting the message out was his stunts, which generally garnered acres of free publicity. On one occasion he donned military fatigues and hired a Second World War tank, which he drove to the entrance of Luton Airport, where easyJet was headquartered. He dragooned Ryanair staff as his troops and led them in formation to the security gates, and, with loudhailer in hand, encouraged them to sing, 'I've been told and it's no lie, easyJet's fares are way too high.' He got all the TV and newspaper coverage he desired.

This personal involvement surprised many of those who had known him before he took the controls at Ryanair. But he had been encouraged by Tony Ryan – and what he had seen of Herb Kelleher – to give his own personality to that of the airline, despite his reluctance to give up his privacy. 'I don't mind dressing up in something stupid or pulling gormless faces if it helps,' he said. 'Frankly, I don't give a rat's arse about my personal dignity.' He made himself available to the media regularly, especially broadcasters, insisting on appearing live to prevent editing. He was rarely deterred from dropping in a succession of advertising slogans as he hammered home promotion of the brand and the mantra of low fares. He rarely went off-message, and the same stories and explanations were regularly repeated, sometimes word for word.

He played the media, although there was mutual benefit. One December, at a time when I was editor of the *Sunday Tribune*, I was told by a taxi driver that he had listened to Ryanair employees in his car complaining that the company's Christmas party had been cancelled, to save money. I rang O'Leary. He immediately confirmed that he had indeed done so. When I asked if he was Scrooge, he agreed enthusiastically. We got a photograph of a Santa Claus and photoshopped O'Leary's head on to it and used it as our main front-page image, along with the line 'The Man who Cancelled Christmas'. O'Leary was delighted. He saw it as free publicity for his airline; I saw it as a means of attracting the attention of people browsing newspaper titles. It suited both of us.

In August 2001 I interviewed O'Leary for *The Last Word* radio show on Today FM. O'Leary claimed that a D. Geraghty had flown with the airline on at least six occasions, and he believed this to be Des Geraghty, the president of SIPTU, who regularly condemned Ryanair. The furious union boss responded that he had never travelled with the airline, 'before, during or since' the baggage handlers' strike, and he demanded a retraction or apology. Instead of doing either, O'Leary asked whether the hard-earned dues of union members were 'being frittered away on higher fares for SIPTU bigwigs'. This led to an investigation by the Data Protection

Commissioner, who said he 'was concerned that Ryanair's public reference to named passengers appeared to be incompatible with the requirements of data protection law'. Ryanair promised that in future it would not refer to any named passengers without their prior consent.

In his time as commercial director, Conal Henry worked closely with O'Leary on selling Ryanair any way they could. 'He had metrics for valuing the publicity he got from our stunts. Most of the demographic we were chasing were people on low incomes, students and backpackers and the like, so we did very little advertising as such. Yet every week we used to buy a sizeable ad on the front page of the *Observer* newspaper in Britain. It wasn't the paper's readers we were targeting, however. Michael had decided that the front page of the *Observer* featured on TV screens every weekend during the reviews of what was in the papers. The ad was designed not to say anything of substance but to be as visible as possible in getting the Ryanair brand on screen. It was our cheapest way of getting on television.'

He became more and more outrageous at his press conferences, gaining attention way beyond the financial pages. There were times when O'Leary was assumed to be joking, but many thought he was deadly serious. 'Anyone who thinks Ryanair flights are some sort of bastion of sanctity where you can contemplate your navel is wrong,' he said once. 'We already bombard you with as many in-flight announcements and trolleys as we can. Anyone who looks like sleeping, we wake them up to sell them things.'

His provocative announcements were designed to rile people up. While most people were wise to him drumming up free publicity from gullible elements of the media, he still got his broadcast coverage and inches of free newspaper space . . . and Ryanair ticket sales increased. When controversy hit, he didn't reach for the apology note – he tried to turn it to his advantage. His treatment of customer Jane O'Keeffe, who won free flights for life in a promotion, led to a court case and enormous publicity that embarrassed the majority of Ryanair employees. O'Leary decided, almost on a whim, to withdraw her entitlement, which she used rarely, a decade after she had received it. When she rang him to find out why, she was rewarded with foul-mouthed invective. She decided to sue and ended up facing Ryanair in a high-profile civil action in the courts, where both she and O'Leary gave evidence and he rejected the suggestion that he had bullied her. 'I'm not sure how it is possible to bully someone on the phone,' O'Leary declared.

Justice Peter Kelly found that an enforceable contract existed and that Ryanair had reneged on a promise into which it had entered freely. He ordered that Ryanair pay €67,500 in damages and costs estimated at €200,000. The judge concluded that he 'found the plaintiff a more persuasive witness than Mr O'Leary and I therefore find as a fact that the version of events given by the plaintiff is what occurred. I reject Mr O'Leary's assertion that he was not hostile or aggressive or bullying towards the plaintiff. I find that he was.'

Nor was O'Leary particularly gracious in his comments afterwards. He claimed that he had decided to go through the court case because she had sought €400,000 in compensation, blithely ignoring that none of this would have happened had Ryanair simply provided the flights at a fraction of that cost. 'I would regret that we put the girl herself through four days of court, which was no great fun,' he said. 'It distracted us for three or four days, we had bad publicity for a few days and now I'm characterized as hating women and all the rest of it.

But four hundred grand is four hundred grand.' He said that the message had gone out that Ryanair would never be 'held to ransom' on any issue and that he would go to war, if necessary. He delayed making the payment until O'Keeffe took a High Court action and secured an order that would have put Ryanair into liquidation unless it settled its debt.

Indeed, O'Leary claimed that the publicity, bad as it was, led to an increase in bookings of 30 per cent 'day, by day, by day', although there was no independent verification of that. This was anticipated by Kelly in his written judgment. 'The whole event was designed to, and did in fact, attract enormous publicity,' Kelly said in a comment about O'Leary's 'media games'.

In January 2004 a judge ruled that Ryanair had breached Britain's Disability Discrimination Act in the case of a man called Bob Ross, who had cerebral palsy. He had arrived at Stansted to take a flight to Perpignan and requested the use of a wheelchair to bring him to the departure gate and to the plane. He was charged £18. Ryanair did not like catering for anyone in a wheelchair because it was difficult to get the person on board. This was down to its money-saving exercise of not using air-bridges to take passengers directly from the gate on to the plane; all passengers had to board by climbing a set of stairs.

Ross brought a case to the courts and won. While his compensation was small, it set a precedent. 'It beggars belief,' said Ross, 'that a company with a £165 million profit last year should quibble over meeting the cost of providing disabled people with a wheelchair. Perhaps before counting their pennies, Ryanair should have considered the cost to their reputation and the distress caused to disabled people by acting in such a discriminatory way.'

Ryanair's reaction stunned people. It announced that, while awaiting the outcome of an appeal, it would be imposing a new wheelchair levy on every ticket sold of 50p or 70c. Analysts quickly spotted that in a year in which Ryanair sold 25 million tickets, as was the case back then, it would raise an additional £12 million-plus in revenues − far more than the cost of providing wheelchairs. The Irish Wheelchair Association complained immediately: 'This levy is low and grotesque, even by Ryanair standards. It is sending out a message that it is the fault of people with disabilities. Society in general has moved far beyond seeing disabled people as a burden, but the attitude of Ryanair is really dragging us back. For Ryanair to put such a stark economic cost on what is an issue of equality is obscene.' O'Leary continued to insist that the airports, not the airlines, should provide the wheelchairs.

There was considerable embarrassment within Ryanair about all of this, although few were willing to speak up for fear of being shot down. There was no good to be taken out of the bad publicity. What it did do, however, was to send out a message that Ryanair would be as ruthless as it needed to be in its chase for profit. And it would not be told what to do by bureaucrats. O'Leary's dislike of those who regarded themselves as somehow morally or intellectually superior to him was genuine.

O'Leary took pleasure in deliberately upsetting environmentalists. When, in 2005, a number of airlines formed a 'sustainable aviation group' to address the concerns of environmentalists with regard to global warming, O'Leary chose not to join. Instead, he decided to mock it and any green critics. He said that Ryanair intended to increase its carbon dioxide emissions and that if any customers were worried about the environment, they should 'Sell [their] car and walk.' It was the beginning of regular baiting of environmentalists.

'We want to annoy the fuckers whenever we can,' he declared. 'The best thing you can do with environmentalists is shoot them. These head-bangers want to make air travel the preserve of the rich. They are luddites marching us back to the eighteenth century. If preserving the environment means stopping poor people flying so the rich can fly, then screw it.' In response, Richard Dyer, aviation campaigner at Friends of the Earth, said that 'His contempt for the impact of his actions on the world's climate shows how important it is that the aviation industry is brought under control.'

The irony was that Ryanair had assembled one of the most fuel-efficient and environmentally friendly aircraft fleets in the world, whose planes produced half the emissions, burned about half the fuel and made half the noise of most other fleets. Anyone else would have been shouting this information from the rooftops, answering their critics with a positive news story, but not O'Leary. As far as he was concerned, good corporate and social responsibility were not just self-indulgent but gained no worthwhile headlines. As ever, he was able to maintain a single-track 'tunnel vision' on his needs and outcomes. It's yet another illustration of how little he cares about what other people think.

When the media became interested in an aspect of his personal life, this, too, was offered over as a means of pushing the Ryanair agenda. O'Leary employed a chauffeur, which wasn't unusual for a man in his position. It allowed him to work on the hour-long journey from his home in Mullingar to Ryanair HQ at Dublin Airport. It also meant he wasn't behind the wheel, which was a good thing: in 2003 he received a conviction for an incident in which he overtook fifteen cars on a blind bend while speeding. The interesting thing about O'Leary's chauffeur arrangement was that he had bought a taxi licence for his black Mercedes. The taxi sign on the car's roof allowed his driver to use the restricted bus and taxi lanes to move quickly through traffic.

When the story broke, there was a mix of begrudging admiration and outright resentment. Was it fair that somebody with €6,000 to spare could buy a licence and have it for personal use only? O'Leary took advantage of the controversy to go on the radio and tell broadcaster Joe Duffy: 'The problem appears to be that it's all right if I rent a taxi, but if I own a taxi there's a problem.' He managed to get in his customary plug for Ryanair, in mentioning that the taxi fare from Mullingar to Dublin Airport was normally €82. 'Ryanair is a low-cost airline – we wouldn't entertain mileage allowances like that. It's just one of the penalties I pay for the pleasure of living in Mullingar.'

The Westmeath town and its environs are genuinely important to him. He has no desire to uproot, even when tax experts advise that living in Ireland is costing him a small fortune in taxes. He could easily copy other Irish billionaires by declaring an overseas residence and living there for a portion of the year, returning to Ireland most weekends and for holidays, thereby significantly reducing his annual tax bill. But that would require moving the Ryanair HQ out of Dublin, which he doesn't want, and, more importantly, it would impact on the domestic structure he has carefully assembled.

What O'Leary also learnt from Ryan was the importance of a stable family life, or, rather, the effects the absence of one could have. Ryan enjoyed a good relationship with his children as adults, but he was largely absent from their lives when they were growing up because of the pressures of his lifestyle. It also contributed to the breakdown of his marriage. He lived in some splendour but moved regularly. It was a fitful life at times.

O'Leary, by contrast, decided at a young age to return home to Mullingar, despite owning a portfolio of residential property in Dublin. He purchased the Gigginstown Estate outside the town, and redeveloped and expanded it over the years. He added a huge extension to the Georgian building, with a new swimming pool and courtyard, not long before he got married in September 2003, at the age of forty-two to a woman twelve years his junior.

O'Leary had dated regularly for many years, but always seemed too restless to find a partner. He was engaged to be married in 2000, to a secretary called Denise Dowling, but he got cold feet and broke the engagement. In 2002 he met a young woman at a wedding, that of Shane Ryan, Tony's youngest son, to Lorraine Kinsella. O'Leary got talking to Lorraine's best friend, Anita Farrell, an investment banker with Citibank in Dublin. Within a year they decided to marry.

They did so at St Livinius Church in Killulagh, outside Delvin, County Westmeath – the renovation of which O'Leary paid for. It was a small ceremony, with about 120 guests, mainly family and friends, although government ministers Mary Harney and Charlie McCreevy were present with their spouses, and billionaire J. P. McManus was the most notable guest from the horse-racing fraternity. What marked the wedding out from normal country weddings was the presence of security guards, the proof-of-admission wristbands the guests were required to wear, the journalists, the photographers with ladders, the Gardaí and various PR executives.

O'Leary was wily enough to give some access to the media, though it was tightly controlled. He came to talk to the assembled journalists, and, when asked if the bride would be late, quipped, 'Yeah, she will, she's flying Aer Lingus.' His PR people revealed that Farrell was wearing a traditional

Vera Wang dress and photographs were taken as she arrived thirty-five minutes late in a wine-coloured Rolls-Royce. It would be one of the few glimpses into the life of the new Mrs O'Leary that the public would ever be given, although she has a reputation for being well able to put the foot down with her husband, taking little or no guff from him.

The newly married couple honeymooned in Mauritius, which he described as involving 'scuba diving, hanging around on a beach, holding hands, and the usual honeymoon stuff, which bored me stiff and nearly created a divorce. Thankfully the following week we went to the Singita Game Reserve in South Africa's Kruger National Park, which was incredible. It wasn't so much the animals, but the sky at night. There's no light pollution so we'd be camped out each evening watching shooting stars – a true "once in a lifetime" experience. But now I've done a safari once I've no desire to go back.'

The wedding reception was held at Gigginstown, and there was no question but that it would be their family home. They now have four children, with the eldest boy following in his father's footsteps by boarding at Clongowes, having first gone to a local national school. O'Leary is busy during the week, leaving early and arriving home late, but he minimizes the foreign travel. He is around most weekends, accompanying the children to their weekend sports and social events, just like any modern Irish father, and gets them involved as he checks with his farm manager every Saturday morning. It is not an ostentatious lifestyle. Dare it be said about a high-flyer in the aviation industry, but it is seriously grounded.

16. Politicking

In early 2009 rumours spread on the internet that O'Leary had pancreatic cancer and was dying. It came after months of speculation in some newspapers about the cause of his very visible weight loss. It started when an *Evening Herald* (part of Independent News and Media) reporter put in a query asking if the 'rumours' of illness were true. Most CEOs would have reacted with fury to such a blatant invasion of privacy, but O'Leary decided to engage. He said he had 'never been better' and that his 'leaner' look was a sign of the times: 'I've lost a bit of weight, and if you look at the two pictures in the paper there's one from September where I was about a stone overweight. I was getting fat, dumb and happy during the good times. Now there's a leaner, more caring me for the recessionary times. We are all going to have to lose a bit of weight and work that bit harder.'

If he thought that would be the end of it, he was mistaken, although he was pleasant in answering questions from reporters at that year's Cheltenham Festival. 'I'm in blooming health,' he joked. 'Only the good die young so in that case, I'm going to live to a ripe old age.' By May, the cancer rumour was still spreading. It was time to dismiss the claims as 'a complete and utter load of bollocks'. Only then did the rumours die away, as it became clear that predictions of his imminent demise had not come true.

There was no let-up in his schedule, and many of his colleagues wondered how he could spend so much time and

energy on the day-to-day running of business while simultaneously engaging in an increasing amount of high-profile
lobbying. He was constantly moving, holding meetings, making phone call after phone call. He was aware of the dangers
involved in such a punishing routine as he aged. So, with his
fiftieth birthday approaching, O'Leary decided to shed what
little extra weight he had accumulated and become super-fit
again. He increased his gym and exercise routine, becoming
a daily regular at, of all places, the Aer Lingus Social Club
facility in the airport. He returned to running – which had
been secondary to golf in his Clowgowes days, but at which
he had shown real potential – and eventually took up mara-
thon running in the company of friends in Mullingar. It
helped that O'Leary drank very little alcohol and had long
abandoned cigarettes.

He was fighting fit again, and it powered his constant
battles with governments, regulators and rivals. As Ryanair
expanded, his colleagues tried to guess on how many fronts
he would be prepared to go to war. All of them, it seemed.

In 2009 he became prominently involved in a national referendum in Ireland, including debates on radio and television,
the first of which I hosted. He was a few minutes late to the
start of the first live radio debate, which allowed me to make
a joking reference to his failure to match his airline's boasts
about punctuality. The Ryanair boss seemed to take no notice.
He had come to do a job. O'Leary was going to argue that
the Irish electorate should vote yes in a referendum to endorse
the Lisbon Treaty, despite it having decided, eighteen months
earlier, in a previous referendum to reject the latest extension
of powers for the EU.

O'Leary had declared publicly that Ryanair was spending €500,000 on its campaign, making it by far the largest

non-political player in the debate. Typically, however, a large chunk of that spend went on simultaneously promoting a seat sale to reward what he saw as the correct decision. Indeed, with the Fianna Fáil-led government at the time under siege because of its mismanagement of the economy, O'Leary had become perhaps the most important standard-bearer of the 'Vote Yes' campaign.

O'Leary's vehement support surprised many. Up until now, any comments he had made on political issues always had a direct and obvious link to their impact on Ryanair. Over the previous year, however, he had become louder in making his opinions on broader issues known to the general public. His contempt for the EU institutions was well known. He had said the previous year – after the first referendum had rejected the Treaty – that there should not be a second vote: 'It seems that only in the European Union, Ireland and Zimbabwe are you forced to vote twice. The vote should be respected. It is the only democratic thing to do.'

In late August 2009 – prior to his involvement in the live debate – I interviewed him (by phone) on *The Last Word* and asked him how he had voted the previous year. 'Next question,' he said, as though reluctant to admit something. I continued to press him. 'Are you going to be one of those people who switches sides to the "Yes" side?' I asked. He insisted repeatedly on his right to keep his 2008 vote private, creating an impression that he had changed his mind in the interim. Of course, that may have been just a device to catch the attention of listeners.

I had little trouble persuading him to join our live radio debate, held just over a week before the referendum. He didn't care too much about the identity of the politicians who would be present, but he was particularly exercised about the opportunity to debate with Declan Ganley, who was a businessman of unknown but assumed to be substantial wealth. Ganley wore his Catholicism openly and had founded a political group called Libertas. It was socially conservative and demanded EU reform, and he had come close to winning a seat in the European Parliament earlier that year. He had taken it upon himself, like O'Leary, to be a prominent non-elected voice in the debate, and he was firmly against reversing the previous year's decision.

O'Leary arrived laden with books on the Lisbon Treaty, which he promptly distributed to his fellow panellists. He used his ninety-second opening slot to aim straight at Ganley: 'Please don't listen to the lobby of losers trying to persuade you to vote "No" in two weeks' time. They are all a bunch of failed politicians.' Ganley chuckled and promptly reminded O'Leary of his previous criticisms of the European Commission, as 'Stalinist' and 'an evil empire' run by 'morons' and 'gobshites', and his opposition to rerunning the referendum a year earlier. It was water off O'Leary's back, as he rolled his eyes and countered: 'Accept "No" for an answer Declan and bugger off.'

At a subsequent press conference, O'Leary claimed he had read the lengthy Lisbon Treaty: 'It is a fucking pain in the arse of a document. I nearly died of boredom from reading it, but yes I have read the Treaty.' Knowing that he would be pushed on why he now believed Europe was good for Ireland, he had a list of five reasons ready: the country benefited from the EU policy of competition and deregulation because it led to low airline fares; it was necessary to attract foreign inward investment; Europe had come to Ireland's rescue during the banking crisis; without the EU, the Irish economy would be run by 'incompetent politicians'; the 'No' campaign was being run by 'unemployable headbangers'.

He touched a nerve with many people when he said there was no point in voting 'No' to express anger with the government: 'I am equally pissed off with this government, but I still think that everybody, if for nothing other than Ireland's self-interest, should vote "Yes", because we need to be at the heart of Europe . . . I do realize that the first tactic in the defence book from the half-wits and economic illiterates is "This is big business, this is the golden fucking circle of big business rounding behind the Government." Anybody who believes that me and the government, or me and the social partners, are on the same spectrum needs to come to more Ryanair press conferences. I think our current government is incompetent.'

He criticized ten years of economic mismanagement, attributing blame mainly to his long-standing bête noire, former taoiseach Bertie Ahern. Even if he was bashing the government, he wasn't going to leave the opposition from the left of the political spectrum off the hook either: 'Anybody who isn't persuaded by the economic arguments, and I think the economic arguments are compelling, for Christ's sake, have a look at the half-wits arrayed on the "No" campaign and do the sensible thing and vote "Yes" so we can defeat the likes of Sinn Féin, UKIP, the Socialist Party and the Socialist Workers Party.'

Not surprisingly, those parties reacted to the baiting from O'Leary. Sinn Féin vice-president Mary Lou McDonald – who became party leader in 2018 – said O'Leary supported the Lisbon Treaty because it promotes a 'Ryanair approach to the economy, facilitating a race to the bottom in workers' wages and conditions. Voters need to ask themselves, do we really want a Ryanair Europe? The Ryanair business model has been built on the back of low pay, poor working conditions and hidden costs to the consumer.'

O'Leary, who believed he had done more for working people than any politician by offering them cheap flights, was ready for whatever was thrown at him. He said he was 'no great fan of the European Commission', as borne out by his frequent legal challenges. He knew that some people considered him a 'gobshite', but said he didn't get involved in the first referendum because he was confident it would be passed. Now, it was essential that common sense prevailed and the 'Yes' vote won out: 'I think the two compelling arguments the "No" side had the last time was we would lose a commissioner and we would lose control over our taxation.' A subsequent renegotiation by Ireland had guaranteed keeping a commissioner and secured a veto on direct taxation. 'If we vote "Yes", Ireland continues to control both our income tax and our corporation tax rate and that's what drives so much foreign inward investment in this country and so many thousands of jobs in this country. Europe has certainly been good for Ireland. Without Europe's policy on deregulation, Open Skies, Ryanair wouldn't exist. Let's not forget in Ireland we specialize in government-protected semi-state monopolies that are hopelessly inefficient, very bad for consumers . . .'

The Irish electorate endorsed the Lisbon Treaty in 2009 by a majority of 67.1 per cent to 32.9 per cent, with 59 per cent of the electorate voting. This compared with a 53.1 per cent turnout a year earlier, and a majority 'No' vote of 53.3 per cent as against 46.6 per cent. O'Leary's involvement had been significant.

It didn't sate his taste for political commentary. A year later, in November 2010, the second terminal at Dublin Airport was opened, many years after O'Leary had waged his campaign for it to be built. The opening of the gleaming new terminal coincided with one of the most stressful and embarrassing times for the state of Ireland since its creation. It took place the same weekend that Ireland entered into official talks with the Troika of European Commission, European Central Bank and International Monetary Fund for the provision of emergency loans as the country teetered on the edge of bankruptcy. The incongruity of the official opening of such a monument to the boom was not lost on many, including the foreign media, who flocked to Ireland just as the Troika officials flew in.

O'Leary decided to rub salt in the gaping wounds. He wasn't going to pass up the opportunity to embarrass the government when others were watching. Just before Brian Cowen, taoiseach since the departure of Ahern in 2008, arrived to the official opening, as part of the cavalcade of chauffeur-driven state cars, a hearse pulled up at the entrance to the new terminal. Out stepped O'Leary, dressed in an undertaker's garb of black tails, white shirt and black tie, and sporting a small moustache (in support of the Movember campaign for the Irish Cancer Society). A coffin, draped in the national tricolour, was produced and ushered inside, to the mirth of some and the horror of others.

'It's a statement of modern Ireland. A big, bankrupt property development. It's a new place to welcome IMF executives,' gloated O'Leary to the waiting media. Even many of his fans thought O'Leary might have gone too far this time, but his comments attracted attention and support because O'Leary, unlike the floundering politicians, was a proven success.

In 2012, however, he came out with comments that were on the extreme of anything that had been offered in Irish public discourse for many years. During a radio interview in which he bemoaned how Ireland was 'borrowing €15 billion a year just to survive', he advocated that nurses, teachers and other public servants – his customers – should work harder for their money and have fewer holidays. He also alleged that those who weren't working were getting too much money in social assistance and that this was a disincentive to work. All of that may have been plain vanilla right-wing analysis, but his topping was a demand that Ireland needed 'a serious right-wing dictatorship for five years' to sort out its economic woes. Somewhat surprisingly, his comments didn't cause too much controversy. Instead they were largely ignored, as if there were a collective eye-rolling and a muttering that O'Leary had gone off on one again.

However, he showed a certain immaturity in relation to comments of a sexual nature. Amusing though it might have been to some, it was regarded by others as crude and unnecessary, and reinforced the down-market branding of the airline. 'Ryanair brings lots of different cultures to the beaches of Spain, Greece and Italy, where they couple and copulate in the interests of pan-European peace,' he joked. He mocked those who complained about the annual Ryanair calendar, because it featured female staff in bikinis and other states of undress, as having no sense of fun. And, anyway, the profits went to charity, so shut up.

During one interview, he was asked about additions to flight services. 'Probably passengers paying for access to the internet,' he chortled. 'They'll watch whatever's on their tablets – gambling, racing, pornography.' Asked if he would allow the last, he said, 'Of course, if that's what's on people's tablets.' The interviewer suggested that watching porn on flights, in the company of others, including children, was inappropriate. 'Oh, for the love of God!' replied O'Leary.

He couldn't seem to help himself. The words rolled out of

him, and the media lapped it up. The majority of business-people are, in public at least, deathly dull, forever afraid of saying something that might bring trouble upon them or their company. They live fearfully, waiting for the axe to fall. O'Leary, by contrast, is as close to a stand-up comedian as business in Europe has ever seen. He is unashamedly pro-vocative, sweary and opinionated, and revels in foisting 'fake news' on people just to get a reaction – and, of course, pub-licity for Ryanair. His way of doing business is entirely his own, and he gets away with it because he's bullish, humor-ous, intelligent and successful.

At least, he *did* get away with it. The world was changing around him, and his brand of humour and invective was becoming more and more out of step with the times.

PART 3
Breaking the rules

17. Changing it up

In 2013 the catchword was 'change'. The retrospective view is that O'Leary was indeed shifting. The really clever executives are content to change course, once they have come to the conclusion that the existing direction is counter-productive and an alternative is preferable. The big challenge for O'Leary was to prove that he could reposition himself, even reinvent himself, if his airline was to do likewise. But how much can any middle-aged man really change? Although maybe he was tired of the old act himself.

Given his promise to change it up, the first signal O'Leary sent out that he and Ryanair were evolving was a management reshuffle, just as he had done at the time of the major profit warnings of early 2004. Michael Cawley and Howard Millar had been the main beneficiaries of the management shake-up back then, but now they were the first to be ushered out the exit. Both men had put up with a lot. Famously, at one press conference to announce Ryanair's annual results, O'Leary said: 'I'm here with Howard Millar and Michael Cawley, our two deputy chief executives. But they're presently making love in the gentlemen's toilets, such is their excitement at today's results.'

Cawley did not regard stepping down as any great sacrifice. He had always been strong enough to stand up to O'Leary when necessary and had earned his boss's respect, but he was touching sixty years of age and knew many other interesting opportunities would be available to him on a part-time basis if he left Ryanair now, opportunities that might not be available in a few years' time. His instincts were correct, and he was swiftly appointed chairman of Bord Fáilte, the state's tourism agency – much to O'Leary's amusement, given his battering of that body over the years. Cawley also pitched up on the board of another youthful Irish success story, the gambling firm Paddy Power, as well as taking on other part-time positions. He also accepted O'Leary's invitation to remain on the board of Ryanair as a part-time director, although corporate governance experts frowned on that decision, believing it created inevitable and unwanted conflicts. His negotiating skills would be missed – he had an ability to marry easy charm with stern demands – although Ryanair's size meant it now had such power that its negotiations with airports were stacked in favour of whoever represented it.

Millar was something of a different story, however. He was the same age as O'Leary and had made little secret of his ambition to be the boss at Ryanair himself. He had wondered if O'Leary might step up to become part-time chairman on David Bonderman's retirement, although just how he imagined that would have worked for any new CEO, let alone him, might have been wishful thinking. He wondered if marriage and parenthood – which happened only when O'Leary reached his forties – would persuade him to scale back. He noted with dismay that, instead, O'Leary seemed to be spending even more time at the office. When O'Leary devised and authorized *Always Getting Better* in late 2013 and threw himself into its delivery like a whirlwind, Millar concluded that whatever slim chance he had of taking over was gone. He left the following year, although he, too, agreed to stay on the board as a non-executive.

Over the following year O'Leary revamped the Z-team.

Some of the key appointments were internal promotions, such as David O'Brien, who became chief commercial officer. O'Brien, a graduate of the Irish Military College, had followed his military career with positions in airports and agribusiness in the Middle East, Russia and Asia and had joined Ryanair as director of flight and ground operations in December 2002. He would continue to maintain a low profile with the media. Michael Hickey had been with Ryanair since very near its inception, joining its engineering department in 1988 and becoming its director in 2000. He was now promoted to the role of chief operations officer. Eddie Wilson's title was redesignated as chief people officer. He had joined Ryanair in 1997 and been head of personnel and in-flight since December 2002. Polish lawyer and competition policy expert Juliusz Komorek had been appointed company secretary and chief legal and regulatory officer in 2009. Neil Sorahan, previously with CRH, had become finance director in 2006, but in 2014 his position was upgraded to chief financial officer.

There was also a senior role for Peter Bellew, who had come to O'Leary's attention in 1993, when, as general manager of Kerry Airport, he had persuaded O'Leary to run flights to the tiny Farranfore airstrip in Ireland's most southwestern county. Bellew had joined Ryanair in 2006 as deputy director of flight operations and was given more senior roles over time, including head of sales and marketing, director of flight operations and director of training and recruitment.

Working for O'Leary was always going to be difficult and demanding, but those with the right constitution also found it stimulating, and a great springboard into future positions in their careers. He was tough, but he trusted his key people and rewarded them with internal promotions, although some were jettisoned quickly if they did not live up to expectations.

As well as promoting within, he also looked outside Ryanair to fill key posts. The two most significant arrivals in 2014 were John Hurley and Kenny Jacobs. Hurley became chief technology officer in 2014, a job that would be crucial to implementing the growth ambitions O'Leary now harboured. Jacobs was given responsibility for marketing, communications and sales, with an emphasis on innovation through digital technologies. His was effectively a brand-new role, and he set about making it his own with great vigour. He was to the fore at the launch of *Always Getting Better*, becoming the face of the 'new' Ryanair.

Jacobs publicly took responsibility for the Ryanair brand: 'But as the person responsible for looking after the brand, I have at my disposal a great chief executive who is Kryptonite. As the marketing guy, I am delighted to have a chief executive who is a celebrity and a rock star. Michael is never going to be the CEO of a brand like Rolex. He's the perfect CEO for a straight-talking brand like Ryanair because it's the way we operate.'

In the many subsequent interviews Jacobs gave, he constantly made reference to the approval he said he was getting from his boss. 'Michael has been very receptive. He loves the numbers and growth in market share he's seeing off the back of the changes. He's agile in his approach. I have plenty of arguments with Michael, not a week goes by where we don't argue about something. There's always good tension. That's absolutely the way you'd want to have it when you're in a big business and you're trying to change that business. You have to have tension, you have to have arguments. If we didn't, it would be a bad thing.'

While O'Leary, with his focus on costs and revenues, didn't entirely buy into talk of brands and marketing, he appreciated the approach taken by Jacobs and understood it. Jacobs made a convincing argument that Ryanair was a 'challenger brand', similar to ones such as Aldi, Ikea and H&M in retailing, all of which had built their business on offering low-priced alternatives to incumbents and had evolved their models subsequently. 'They started off absolutely focused on low cost and then on top of low cost they added more choice and then they improved the service,' said Jacobs. 'That's a similar journey that the Ryanair brand will go on.' He said the aim was 'to become as liked as we are useful' – sounding an echo of the maligned Ryan approach, which hadn't been heard around the building in some time.

Jacobs started talking about building consumer trust, but on the basis of giving people what they wanted rather than engaging in corporate social responsibility 'nonsense'. 'Customers don't want us to be lovely guys, they want to trust us to give them what we promise.' The airline was chasing not customers' hearts, but their minds. 'I don't want customers to say, "I love Ryanair,"' Jacobs explained. 'We want people to say, "This is a commoditized, functional experience getting from Dublin to London, from London to Madrid."' He said this would be achieved by 'catching up fast on digital' and by becoming a 'digital leader in the aviation category'.

The digital aspect was crucial to O'Leary's plans, but, in terms of *Always Getting Better*, the immediate changes had to come in three areas: on the website, when people made their bookings; at the airport, when people went to check-in and board their flights; and on the flight itself. Many of the proposed changes were actually relatively small stuff for Ryanair to implement, but they replaced what had been a major irritant to customers and a barrier to bringing in business.

The website was overhauled, with the number of clicks

required to make a booking reduced from seventeen to five. The hated baggage fees were amended, with the fine for excess loads cut by 50 per cent, and reduced fees were brought in for storing luggage in the hold. The €60 penalty for failing to print a boarding pass was cut to €15. Fully allocated seating was introduced on all flights from 1 February 2014. The staff on the planes and at check-in desks were smiling, too, something O'Leary supervised personally on surprise visits to the desks and other customer-service points.

The new website would be launched on 10 April, with the phone app to follow in May. The aircraft interiors were updated, to look less garish; there were new uniforms for the cabin crew, also toned down in their colours, and new menus. It looked like O'Leary was truly taking *Always Getting Better* seriously but, as always, there was a hidden motive. All of this wasn't just for the usual customer. It was very much intended to attract a different kind of Ryanair customer: the business traveller, whom, as easyJet had shown, it was possible for a low-fares airline to entice.

This category of customer was what *Always Getting Better* was mainly about delivering, with the higher prices they would be willing to pay. If Ryanair was going to carve out a new market for itself in serving the business traveller, it had to do even more than it had done already. It would have to introduce something it had mocked previously: a business class. This didn't involve erecting a curtain screen to separate the riff-raff from the more 'important' customers. Ryanair couldn't be seen to do that without alienating existing customers. It had to be a more pragmatic version of the luxury class offered on the existing business-class airlines.

Ryanair's first business fare was called Business Plus and was introduced in August 2014. It was a relatively basic product, offering an allocated seat, speedy access through security and priority boarding, as well as greater flexibility to change flight times if needed. It didn't offer free food, drink, hot towels or extra on-board comforts. The price was pitched between the versions offered by rival airlines and its own cheaper offerings: €69.99 was mentioned as a standard. It was reckoned that company accountants would insist their staff use this option for travel instead of more expensive rival options.

'For twenty-odd years, our focus has been to stack the product high and sell it cheap,' said O'Leary. 'We're still going to do that, but we're going to let the customer relax in the process. Just imagine how many more people we're going to carry and how much more money we're going to make when we give customers more of what they want.'

There was another aspect to business travel that led to one of the biggest changes of *Always Getting Better*. The businessman and woman were time sensitive, because of their work schedules, so they had to get to their final destination in the least amount of time possible. Ryanair's far-flung airports didn't answer this need. Accordingly, O'Leary decided to add routes to primary airports. This decision surprised many analysts and industry rivals, until the rationale was explained. It had long been an article of faith for Ryanair that such airports were too expensive, not just because of their higher charges but because they didn't allow for quick turnaround of flights. Now Ryanair said it would use any primary airport at which it could get a good deal. As a result, half of Ryanair's new capacity was to be stationed at primary airports, going into places like Brussels, Madrid and Barcelona. It was a big shift from its previous position and showed the flexibility in O'Leary's thinking when profit margins were on the line.

Some analysts believe it was the single most important part of *Always Getting Better*, because improved customer service wouldn't have worked unless it included airports that consumers wanted.

There was something else remarkable that Ryanair would have to do to attract this higher-yielding customer, another breaking of one of O'Leary's long-held articles of faith. Given his long-standing antipathy to travel agents and reservation systems, and the commission they charged, the decision to return to dealing with both was a surprising turnaround. But the fact was that business customers preferred third-party travel arrangements, rather than clicking about on the Ryanair website by themselves. In 2013 the Irish Travel Agents Association calculated that its members were still involved in between €250 million and €300 million worth of business annually. It was calculated that about 40 per cent of Aer Lingus business traffic by volume came through Travel Management Companies (TMCs) and smaller agents. The proportion by value was higher. In other key Ryanair markets, such as Britain and Germany, it was reckoned that the volume and scale of business bookings made through travel agents was even higher. Ryanair had to deal with them. It signed up to Travelport, a global distribution system used by corporate travel agents, and to other rival platforms, such as Amadeus. It began direct talks with TMCs. It was the first time in a decade it had done so. O'Leary believed this measure would take Ryanair beyond 100 million customers per annum. 'The travel agents will put together very low-cost packages and Ryanair will become a key part of that pricing.'

Not for the first time, O'Leary was accused of stealing all the best ideas from his rival, easyJet. It didn't matter a damn to him: a good idea could be taken from anywhere. Ryanair wasn't trying to be easyJet, no matter how much some analysts pushed this idea. O'Leary could see that easyJet's success in luring higher-paying business passengers was attributed more to the location of Gatwick than to any price or service it could offer. That was the key difference between them: easyJet benefited from flying mainly to and from primary airports. But O'Leary was eradicating that difference, so that ended the advantage for easyJet.

There was one other major change at this time that pointed to a new era at the company. O'Leary had long been dismissive of companies that spent money on swanky new headquarters, believing it to be a sign of a collective corporate ego – or at least that of the top management – spiralling out of control. But even he found the converted hangar near the cargo area at Dublin Airport increasingly uncomfortable. 'It was a sweatshop that smelled of fuel, and shook every time an aircraft passed,' said former IT director Eric Neville. He, and others, persuaded O'Leary that the next stage of development of Ryanair could not be facilitated at the existing building, not when there was a major technological overhaul required.

Neville ended up as the man tasked with kitting out the new company head office at an industrial and retail park in Swords, a few miles from Dublin Airport, built and owned by one of Tony Ryan's closest friends, the property developer Ken Rohan. The new Ryanair HQ opened in 2014 and it was immediately compared with Google, in particular its games room, which included Xboxes, retro arcade machines and a pool table. It was visually dominated by a giant emergency aircraft slide to take people down to reception. There were oversized chessboards, a putting green, and brightly coloured walls and partitions, festooned with flags from dozens of countries. There were paintings and pictures of an unconscious, drunk dog dressed as Father

Christmas, giraffes, Lego men and football teams. One wall was made to look like a stand from Old Trafford, the Manchester United ground, which was surprising, given that O'Leary claimed Manchester City was his team. There were even motivational quotes on the walls, including one that read: 'Unless it's crazy, ambitious and delusional, it's not worth our time.' It all cost €18 million to put together, but it did have real purpose and included the operations room, where a huge screen showed every one of the Ryanair flights in the air at that moment.

O'Leary was now presiding over a massive operation, with huge demands on his time, decision-making capacity and strategic planning. He was more than up for it – he relished the expansion and was on top of every facet. He was made for this.

18. Rewards and respect

The brand-new Ryanair HQ meant that the digital and technology side of the business could be pursued vigorously. The company now had a location where staff could be hired to develop and operate a tech system fit for purpose. The person who was tasked with pulling all this together and turning the ponderous website into a sleek new beast was John Hurley, who was appointed chief technical officer in 2013.

Hurley was quite critical of what he found on arrival. In an interview with a technology publication, he described how the business model had been not to spend money on IT. 'Ryanair was totally focused on cost and in a low-cost environment you simply don't spend money. This meant anybody with any good ideas, no matter what they were, needed to keep them away,' said Hurley, in a damning comment. 'We had been taking a siesta for fourteen years. We didn't just miss the first wave [of digital], we missed the second wave and are probably in the third wave. We are now a technology company and all we want to do for customer experience moving forward is maintain the price, improve the choice and the digital experience.'

Hurley and other techie new-hires were part of a €20 million investment in what was to be called Ryanair Labs. Although Ryanair would still work with expert third parties, O'Leary decided to bring the process of redeveloping Ryanair's technology in-house. This was a job too big for two students and a laptop. Ryanair Labs was populated by experienced website developers from backgrounds in finance, gaming and enterprise software, about 250 well-paid professionals in all. About 36,000 developer hours, calculated by the tech bosses as the equivalent of eighteen business years, was invested in designing a technology that could fill four Boeing 737s every minute at peak boarding times. Ryanair made coming from behind a virtue, avoiding the mistakes made by other airlines. 'We rebuilt the website from the ground up. We replaced every line of code, nothing got reused,' said Hurley. 'What we had was a booking website.'

He developed a way of processing up to 300,000 bookings a day, with more than 40 million people a month visiting the website. Constant redevelopments of the mobile app saw the average booking time almost halved, from 3 minutes 47 seconds down to 1 minute 54 seconds. The opening time of the app also dropped considerably: previously it had taken up to 14 seconds to open, a timeframe beyond the patience of many potential customers, but now it took just a few seconds.

While O'Leary understood and was delighted by all of this progress, the attitude and intent of this new arm of management were something of a challenge to his way of thinking. His new recruits spoke a different language from him, the lingo of the digital era. Whereas O'Leary spoke of keeping costs down, and after that of keeping costs down, the new breed spoke of 'employing customer-focused technology' and 'cutting-edge user experience [UX] design'. While O'Leary was looking to expand Ryanair's services and reach and ability to generate additional revenues, he never lost sight of Ryanair being an airline in competition with other airlines. 'Obviously, as CTO, I believe very strongly that we are now a platform with an airline attached,' said Hurley in one interview. 'When

I say competition, the competition is Google and Amazon, not Aer Lingus or easyJet; our competition is digital.'

O'Leary had been around long enough to remember the dot-com bubble of 2000 and the talk then, which he had correctly dismissed, of separating Ryanair's internet wing from the airline and floating it on the stock market. There was a whiff of this in Hurley's talk. O'Leary did not allow the IT wing to work autonomously. 'We speak every second day,' Hurley said of his CEO. 'He attends most fortnightly demonstrations of our progress, and is not hands-off by any means.' Anyone who might have expected O'Leary to leave a division alone – especially one costing €20 million a year in salaries and other costs – did not know the man.

Hurley learnt quickly what O'Leary wanted. Within two years of arrival, Hurley was able to tell O'Leary that what he called 'small data' projects had saved the company €20 million at the bottom line. He even began to talk like O'Leary. 'Do not do Big Data, it is wank,' he said in one interview. 'It's confusing, expensive and you can't store it. Start with small data. Do small projects, prove to the business the value of small data. Get them hooked on it. You're dealing crack cocaine here. Get them out there and someone who does budgets will start looking up and seeing the value. The key principles with data are if it's not making you money or improving your efficiency, don't do it. Stop wasting your time, stop navel-gazing. Big businesses want to save money, improve efficiency and make money. Nothing else.' Hurley had obviously learnt quickly what the Ryanair culture was . . . and that some things would not change.

Technology was now central to how Ryanair would deliver everything. It had started from a low base, but the numbers downloading the mobile app thrilled the company. But it wasn't just about making life easier for customers. In helping them, Ryanair was also gathering information about them – and it wanted to put this to profitable use. The website got a further overhaul, primarily to increase personalization, which would let customers store information like payment, identity and passport details, and seat preferences. Again, this was to their benefit, but also left them open to Ryanair targeting them with offers and options based on their flight histories and preferences. 'The opportunities for ancillary revenues through mobile are enormous,' O'Leary said gleefully.

The idea was that in buying a flight all Ryanair customers would automatically become 'members' of its website, giving the airline an unrivalled source of data to mine, either for its own use or to be shared with associated third parties, who offered products through the Ryanair website. After decades of refusing to contemplate the kind of reward schemes provided by other airlines, the company unveiled 'My Ryanair Club', offering customers discounts and free flights for using the airline. It was the first customer loyalty card since O'Leary had dumped its predecessor in the early 1990s.

'It's all about the data, sharing the right information, mining it, protecting it. It is also being mindful of people's preferences and anticipating them,' said Hurley. 'Using our platform to perform better for our customers, we're trying to get the line between knowing enough to not annoy you, and use it in a smart way to almost read your mind. It's about being transparent, no tricks. It's about the information we provide about destinations. Families should be warned beforehand if a destination is more suitable for stag and hen parties and suggest they perhaps go somewhere else more suitable. Even providing data about the airport you are going to, whether you are better off getting a taxi or if the bus service is great. We know where you are travelling to, when you are travelling. If you are going to Spain with your wife and kids, we can offer information like child-friendly hotels; that's what people want. They don't want to be getting spammed about hotels for the next five years if they went there once. They want context.'

Customers – or members as they would be called now – were required to log in, engage, interact. And, even if they didn't choose to, there were further opportunities to sell to them on flights. Cabin crew were given handheld Android devices as point-of-sale devices. These provided them with data for proper stock control on each flight, indicating what passengers were likely to buy, right down to food and drink. If there was a record of a person showing consistent preferences on previous flights, then on-board offers could be tailor-made to match those preferences.

The future of Ryanair, according to Kenny Jacobs, was to be a 'travel retailer that specializes in flights', a different description from the one being offered by Hurley. But suddenly O'Leary had a new slogan for the airline, and he and his colleagues pushed it as often as possible. Ryanair wanted to be 'the Amazon of air travel'. It was a lofty ambition, and realistically probably too ambitious for the airline, but, still, it sounded good, and it would become a regular mantra of the airline over the coming years.

It wasn't new either, this goal of providing a whole range of services beyond the actual flight itself. Ryanair already made sizeable additional income by selling other things beyond airplane tickets and did some of this via the internet. The same retailing promise had been made as far back as 2000 and many times since, albeit without the Amazon reference. But O'Leary felt better able to make the claim now, as his confidence grew in what his IT team was doing. He believed only Ryanair had the scale in Europe to do this. 'We see Ryanair becoming a kind of digital supermarket for everything that you need for travel,' Jacobs said.

Critics asked if a Ryanair business model – which was dominated by price points – could earn the loyalty of a broad and diverse customer base, as Amazon had. The challenge for Ryanair was to broaden its product beyond commodity status with added value, understand better what the modern customer wanted and, as one branding expert suggested, 'reimagine travel as a holistic experience'. That was a concept it was hard to imagine O'Leary buying, but colleagues like Hurley and Jacobs spoke regularly about travel being about 'taking the pain away' and using social media to 'build trust'. Of course, the challenge for O'Leary's Über-cost-conscious Ryanair was to provide services at different price points. That would be hard when it was still perceived as a commodity provider. But it had to be done, because 'experience' was the new catchword and everyone was looking for it.

The big move was to offer a full suite of accommodation, again, based on far more than low price. By June 2016 Ryanair was offering its customers a choice of hotels, including five star, hostels, B&Bs, holiday villas and homestay options. It invited accommodation providers to submit proposals to become partners in 'Ryanair Rooms'. The providers could plug into the Ryanair website and take bookings. Ryanair would operate the price-comparison element for those who logged in. 'More and more customers are looking to Ryanair for products other than flights, and we see this as a natural progression towards Ryanair.com becoming the Amazon of air travel,' said Jacobs.

It didn't take long for Ryanair to declare *Always Getting Better* a success. The bottom line proved it, as did the revenue numbers. In September 2015 Ryanair announced that its profits for the year ending March 2016 would be about 25 per cent higher than stock-market investors expected. Instead of being somewhere between €940 and €970 million, the profits would go crashing through the €1 billion barrier and beyond, to somewhere between €1.175 and €1.225 billion, a 40 per cent improvement on the profits reported for the end of March 2015. The shares hit an all-time high of €14.27 and continued going up afterwards. By November 2015 the share price had more than doubled since January 2014.

O'Leary was the biggest winner, his own net worth going up by an estimated €500 million. Not surprisingly, he was exultant: 'If I'd known being nicer to customers was going to work so well, I'd have done it ages ago,' he said at one press conference. 'Every time you're flying Ryanair, you're adding to my share price, you're adding to my profitability,' the now billionaire said at a lunch hosted by the Institute of Directors. 'I need to keep being wealthy. Because if I'm to support one of Ireland's biggest loss-making cattle-breeding operations, and Ireland's biggest loss-making national stud-horse operation, I need everyone in this room to fly Ryanair.'

Not all of the Ryanair surge could be put down to its own brilliance. European airlines, in general, benefited from Europe's modest economic recovery and lower fuel prices. Even Air France–KLM and Lufthansa, flag carriers hit by strikes, achieved record profits in 2015. 'The summer peak this year was extraordinary. In all the twenty-eight years I've been in the business, I've never seen such a perfect summer. Even the incompetent airlines made money,' O'Leary said. 'In the absence of any unforeseen shock, in the next twelve to eighteen months – with the combination of low fuel prices, low finance costs – most airlines will look like they are geniuses run by management gurus, until oil prices tick back up again and, as Warren Buffett said, you will see who is swimming naked and who's wearing trunks.'

But O'Leary's ambitions were growing, and he had everything in place to make them happen. He announced that Ryanair expected to carry 180 million passengers in 2024 – 20 million more than its previous estimate and double 2014's numbers. He wanted profitability of €2 billion each year. Ryanair announced four new bases, in Berlin, Corfu, Gothenburg and Milan, and announced 119 new routes, including a four times daily Dublin–Amsterdam service. It announced it was targeting double-digit growth in Ireland, the UK, Spain, Italy, Portugal, Poland, Germany and Denmark. Previously, claiming those sorts of goals would have seen O'Leary laughed out of the room; now everyone just looked on as he hit target after target and sent them spinning.

The new-found emphasis on customer service was not forgotten either. In March 2015 Ryanair announced the second phase of *Always Getting Better*: an eight-point customer charter that pledged to make it Europe's 'most reliable' airline and to make travel an enjoyable experience. It promised the 'best choice' of destinations, to maintain safety as a priority and to offer lower fares than any of its competitors. Jacobs, not surprisingly, was thrilled, but looked to downplay things. 'In 2014, we got our shit together. We caught up. Three years ago, our average load factor was just over 80 per cent and this year it will be just over 92 per cent. I don't think it was that hard. I think we were pushing an open door on a lot of things: letting people pick their own seat and bring two bags on-board, having a better website and a better mobile app.

This isn't marketing genius. This is just doing the basics, doing them quickly, and doing them well.'

While it was having its desired effect of making money, the new approach was benefiting the Ryanair brand, too. 'According to the YouGov BrandIndex survey in the UK, we were the most improved brand last year in terms of the customer experience,' said Jacobs. 'Before, other airlines have been able to say, "Come with us, pay a bit more because the experience is better." But now the experience on Ryanair is level.' They had cogged enough to transform Ryanair into a value for money service, which of course was what Tony Ryan had wanted all along.

The test was whether people would notice the difference, and the answer to that was a resounding 'Yes'. Ryanair was different, and everyone could see and acknowledge that. O'Leary had constantly picked rows with his rivals – it was a feature of his leadership style – but even that seemed to be changing. Departing Aer Lingus chairman Colm Barrington, who had known O'Leary decades earlier when he was with GPA, admitted that he had spent 'all but two weeks' of his tenure trying to second-guess what the 'mercurial' O'Leary was doing: 'I wonder whether he was just playing a game. Like in backgammon, where the strategy is to keep hitting the other guy and stop him getting on the board.'

Now there was a new level of respect for the man, as well as for the business. In an interview with the *Sunday Business Post* in 2014, IAG boss Willie Walsh admitted that: 'Competing with Ryanair is a really difficult thing to do and having first-hand experience of that definitely sets you up for understanding what you need to do in this industry to be successful. I have always been upfront in acknowledging what [O'Leary] has achieved. I don't agree with everything he has done, but you can't take away the success the guy has had. More than anyone else he has transformed an industry. Even Herb Kelleher – and I know Herb very well – didn't transform the industry in the way Michael O'Leary has. What O'Leary has achieved is unique.'

Interestingly, Walsh spoke about the idea that all had changed over at Ryanair. 'You do have to give them credit,' he said of the *Always Getting Better* transformation. 'I don't think Michael has changed. He is still the same personality that he always was. But without question Ryanair has changed and that makes them in some areas a stronger competitor. But all they are doing is what we said we were doing, so it's nice to know that they are finally admitting that what they were doing was wrong and what we said about customer service was right.'

O'Leary might have been feeling that he could do no wrong at this stage, but there was one desire he could not satisfy: the long-haul market. He had long wanted to break into the profitable transatlantic routes and give them the Ryanair treatment. By early 2015 he had Jacobs talking publicly and excitedly about the possibilities. Ryanair, apparently, was studying plans to fly between about a dozen European and American cities before the end of the decade, with fares as low as €10, although about half would cost €99 or more. A statement given to the media declared: 'The board of Ryanair, like any plc, has approved the business plans for future growth, including transatlantic ... European consumers want lower-cost travel to the USA and the same for Americans coming to Europe. We see it as a logical development in the European market.'

In fact, Bonderman and the board were appalled. O'Leary

had oversold their interest. As industry veterans, they knew the difficulty of achieving this plan. Bonderman did O'Leary the courtesy of listening to his arguments, but was unmoved in his opposition, seeing it as a rare occasion when O'Leary allowed his ego to overcome his business nous. At the AGM in September, O'Leary had to admit that management had scrapped all its transatlantic plans in favour of sticking to its knitting. Many interpreted it as a rare public slapdown of O'Leary by his usually acquiescent board.

For his part, O'Leary was still trying to sell the idea that both he and Ryanair were maturing: 'We are probably moving from what I would call errant teenagers into being somewhat more adult in the way we both interact with our customers and communicate with the outside world,' he told the *Financial Times* in October 2015. Once the rapid growth phase had ended, he said, 'You then need to hand over to somebody who's a bit more respectful of politicians and bureaucrats, talks about caring about the environment and old people, and fucking jungles and fish in the sea and all that shite.' But it was clear that he believed he could continue dramatic growth, until 2024 at the very least.

There were commentators who argued that dullness was what the airline needed now, and what investors demanded, but others felt that part of the premium in the Ryanair share price was due to O'Leary's attention-grabbing behaviour, as long as it was backed up with results. What O'Leary had done to bring Ryanair to this stage was acknowledged as remarkable, but some wondered if those qualities were best suited to the more mature company. He had proven his dynamism – and, to those who looked further, his competence – but, as he aged, would the company benefit from him maturing, or lose from it? Or would it be damaged by a failure to mature? And, having become fixed in his ways, would he be capable of change? Was it possible that the era of consolidating a customer base around the personal brand of a CEO was coming to an end?

O'Leary seemed sensitive to the theory and suggested that he had been hamming things up deliberately: 'Look, I'm a parody of myself, whatever it is, because my function here, apart from driving growth in the business, is to be the PR extreme of whatever message we're pushing at that moment. So, for many years, it was: "Shut up, sit down, we don't care, we've cheaper fares than anyone else, fuck off." And I'd take that to its logical conclusion. You've got to go out and make as much noise as you can yourself. It becomes pretty simple.'

O'Leary's noisiness even applied when he decided, in late 2016, to hire yet another personal assistant. Ryanair advertised on its website what it called the 'worst job in Ireland' – executive assistant to O'Leary. The job – aimed at an 'ambitious, self-motivated qualified accountant' – had some pretty standard requirements: 'The successful candidate will be expected to manage "a wide range of issues" including treasury and portfolio management, investment analysis, tax analysis and returns, project management and property development, and special project work.' However, what caught the public eye was the promise that the job would also involve 'general drudgery', an 'ability to work without sleep or contact with the outside world' and '(ego) massage qualifications'. A collection of bedtime stories was also deemed essential, for reasons unspecified. Candidates were told that they needed to display an 'aversion to bolloxology', a thick skin and a saint-like patience. 'Dubs fans, Man U supporters and cyclists will not only be automatically excluded from the process, but will be tracked down, tortured and shot,' it said. There was no mention of salary.

The capacity to bullshit never left O'Leary, and his own ability, or desire, to rein it in remained suspect. That same month he got plenty more media attention for announcing a plan to introduce free flights as a way of increasing passenger numbers and airport throughput. 'The challenge for us in the future is to keep driving air fares down,' he told an Airport Operators Association conference in London. 'I have this vision that in the next five to ten years the air fares on Ryanair will be free, in which case the flights will be full, and we will be making our money out of sharing the airport revenues; of all the people who will be running through airports, and getting a share of the shopping and the retail revenues at airports.'

What those with longer memories remembered was that O'Leary trotted out this old chestnut every five years or so, whenever he wanted attention from a gullible media. It was a tried-and-trusted method that worked every time.

19. Teaching a lesson

Michael O'Leary might have changed tactics, but that didn't mean he had changed fundamentally. When it came to his core beliefs, it was a case of a leopard and his spots: there was no moving him from the path of cost-cutting. It is a defining feature of the man that he is obsessed with costs, and, no matter what else might change, that never would. If anyone was thinking the new suite of priorities would steal his attention away, they would soon realize they were very mistaken.

In late 2016 O'Leary became involved in a row that gained considerable prominence outside of the business media, in the sports arena. He very publicly and very obviously ended the contractual relationship between his Gigginstown Farm Stud and Ireland's leading trainer, Willie Mullins. The reason: money, but a surprisingly small amount of money.

O'Leary loves horse-racing and has the wealth to finance what is an expensive hobby, one that became more expensive over the years as his success at the track soared and he had over 100 horses in competition. He bought the Gigginstown Estate as his home in the early 1990s, and then he and Anita turned it into a proper family home. He also began the life of a weekend farmer, breeding expensive pedigree Aberdeen Angus cattle under the watchful eye of a full-time farm manager and staff. While he enjoyed that, he also wanted the competitive thrill of racing horses at the biggest National Hunt jump races in Ireland and Britain.

His brother Eddie took full-time control of this operation,

albeit with daily input from the bill-paying older brother who, despite the time he spends with Ryanair, is so involved that he often makes the final call as to how often horses run and where. This is not something all owners necessarily do, deferring instead to the trainers, who have the necessary expertise. Of course, O'Leary's own expertise is that which he trusts the most, so it's no surprise that he micro-manages the farm and stud alongside micro-managing Ryanair.

Ryanair became a sponsor of many races early in his stewardship of the company, including some of the expensive runs at the major festivals. This could have been seen as a way of using company money to partly finance his personal hobby, though indirectly. 'Michael was always very aware of that,' said the late Ryanair director James Osborne, another horse-racing fanatic. 'Michael made it very clear to the board and then arranged it, that he would personally pay for all of Ryanair's horse-racing sponsorships, even though it would cost him six-figure sums every year.' For O'Leary, it wasn't about gambling or breeding or trading – this part of life was for the fun of it.

O'Leary enjoyed many big days as an owner over the years, his most significant breakthrough coming in 2006 when one of his horses, *War of Attrition*, won him the Gold Cup at Cheltenham for the first time. He had various other successes over the years, but 2016 was undoubtedly his best year. That year, Mullins delivered to O'Leary the unprecedented treble of the Cheltenham Gold Cup, with *Don Cossack*, the Aintree Grand National, with *Rule the World*, and the Irish Grand National, with *Rogue Angel*. It was an owner's dream. O'Leary was the first owner to win the three big races in the same year.

The relationship with Mullins, which had started only in

2011, was regarded as the most powerful owner/trainer partnership in the sport in Ireland and Britain. By the end of the 2015/16 season, the combination of O'Leary and Mullins had enjoyed 158 winners. Of those, 16 were at the highest level, Grade One. They had won 11 races at the Punchestown Festival and four at the Cheltenham Festival. According to the *Racing Post*, one out of every three Mullins-trained/Gigginstown-owned runners in Ireland had won a race in the previous five years, an almost unprecedented level of success. In the 2015/16 Irish National Hunt season, Gigginstown topped the owners' table with over €3 million in prize money in Ireland, with an additional £1.6 million coming from British races; jockeys and trainers would each get a 10 per cent cut from the winnings. It was an exceptional year, by anyone's standards.

The late start with Mullins was down to O'Leary's obsessiveness about not spending money unnecessarily. Prior to 2011, Gigginstown's 100 horses were shared among twelve trainers, with placements made largely on the basis of cost as much as on the likelihood of success. The O'Leary brothers decided to hold a very firm line on what they would pay to keep horses with trainers. They ignored whatever prices various yards cited and set down the rate they were prepared to pay: a flat rate of €1,200 per month, per horse. Mullins was among the trainers who said that was not enough, as he charged €1,400. This stance excluded him from the Gigginstown pool, along with other leading trainers.

Later, however, Gigginstown decided to increase the amount it was willing to pay per month to a maximum of €1,500. That brought all of the top trainers back into range, including Mullins. That was the start of a very fruitful relationship. Mullins kept sixty horses for Gigginstown, and they spent, on average, nine months with him, and three months out to grass at

Gigginstown. Mullins was also a gifted horse spotter, and he brought many horses to O'Leary's attention for Gigginstown to purchase. Among them was a horse called *Apple's Jade*, regarded as one of the most exciting finds in years. It was an excellent partnership that benefited both sides.

In mid 2016 Mullins informed all of his customers that his fees per horse were to be increased for the first time since 2007. They would rise 10 per cent, from €1,400 to €1,540. It was the same rate for all customers, owners who included former Barclays executive Rich Ricci and Graham Wylie, co-founder of software giant Sage. This meant that Mullins was looking to charge O'Leary an extra €140 per month – €40 more than the maximum price Gigginstown had set. O'Leary was willing to pay the €100, to bring the price charged up to €1,500, but not another €40 per horse, which would have cost him another €21,600 per year on top of the bill he was willing to pay if he kept sixty horses there for nine months. Mullins was unwilling to give him a discount that he would not give to his other owners, for fear of damaging his relationships with them. Both sides dug in.

Mullins knew that Gigginstown had ditched trainers previously. Only in May 2016, it had removed all of its horses from trainers Sandra Hughes and Tony Martin. In the previous 2014/15 season, Hughes had won an Irish Grand National for Gigginstown. In the year before she trained *Lieutenant Colonel* to Grade One success. But 2015/16 was a poor season, with only 2 wins out of 42 for the Gigginstown horses in her yard. At Martin's yard, Gigginstown horses had run 36 times the previous season, winning 5 times. 'Michael rang both trainers,' said Eddie O'Leary, 'to tell them that we'd be taking the horses away for the summer and that they'd not be coming back. We're very much a results-based business.'

The news of the split with Mullins, which few had seen coming, was revealed on 28 September 2016. All sixty horses were removed from Mullins's yard and sent to a range of other Irish trainers, including Gordon Elliott, Henry de Bromhead, Noel Meade, Mouse Morris and Joseph O'Brien. The aggregate worth of the bloodstock involved was estimated in the region of €10 million. A particular blow to Mullins was the removal of *Apple's Jade*, along with *Don Poli*, *Valseur Lido* and *Blow by Blow*, to Elliott, his young up-and-coming challenger for the title of leading trainer.

O'Leary made it clear that he would work with Mullins again, but only at the price he had set: 'Gigginstown wishes to sincerely thank Willie and all the team at Closutton for the many Grade One races we have won together over the past seven years. We hope that an agreement can be reached at some time in the future which will allow Willie to resume buying and training more graded winners for us. While we part at this time with regret, we wish Willie and all the team at Closutton continued success.'

Mullins was slightly more pointed in his public comment: 'Everyone that comes into my yard is treated the same. We've evolved our methods of training, which obviously costs a lot, and we're not prepared to sacrifice that. They've been very good to us over the years, they've bought some fantastic horses and there's a fantastic team of horses going to whoever is going to get them. They'll be very hard horses to replace. Even with all the money in the world, lots of people try to buy horses like that, but sometimes they just happen. We've put together a fantastic team with Eddie O'Leary and ourselves, but that's it. It's there now and the team is there for someone else to train.'

The racing press had a story to watch for months and

years to come, looking for interaction between the pair at racecourses, looking to see who would win the big races at Leopardstown at Christmas and at Cheltenham, Aintree and Punchestown in the spring. As if to add insult to injury, *Apple's Jade* beat Mullins's charges in the Mare's Hurdle on the first day of Cheltenham 2017, and Mullins went without a winner on the first two days of the event. But when Mullins had four winners on the third day of the festival, O'Leary was one of the first to go to congratulate him and then speak publicly about his success: 'Willie is a gentleman and a genius and I'm sorry he doesn't have horses for me but hopefully he will again. The tragedy is that we're weaker without Willie although the way he's going this week I don't know if he's weaker without us. But it is only business. I don't mind spending a lot of money on horses, but I run a low-cost airline and I try to keep my costs down.'

That was the line that O'Leary's Ryanair colleagues noted. The issue with Mullins had wider implications, but it was also rooted in O'Leary's DNA and would not change. While racing people watched agog – putting the row down to a clash of strong personalities, an unwillingness on the part of both men to be seen to back down – there were knowing nods over at Ryanair. They had a different theory about the very public break-up between Gigginstown Stud and Mullins, believing that it was engineered almost for their benefit. Several Ryanair managers became convinced that in saying no, and in the full knowledge that the matter would get considerable media attention, O'Leary was using Mullins to send them a none-too-subtle message: no matter what they had achieved on his behalf, if they lost their focus on costs, they would lose their jobs. If he could do this to someone who was delivering for his hobby, what would he do to someone perceived as not rigorous enough in dealing with costs in his business? This wasn't just about horse racing; as they saw it, this was a message to them.

O'Leary's attention to managing costs applied to other parts of his life, not just Ryanair. It isn't simply part of the businessman, it is part of who he is. What has long been clear about O'Leary to those who know him is that he always feels there is somebody else who will do the job at the price he's prepared to pay. That attitude informs every situation where he has to spend money. There is no give. This was illustrated to his staff every Friday afternoon – at least in the days when it was possible, before the business expanded dramatically – when a pile of invoices would be delivered to his office for signing. It was not unusual for him to reject many, or to scribble enforced discounts on to the documents. This extended to personal bills as well. O'Leary does not have an extensive range of clothing, owning few suits and preferring open-neck casual shirts under a jacket with jeans when possible, but what he needs he buys from a local menswear shop in Mullingar. It is not unusual for him to mark down the price when the invoice arrives. Most people wouldn't dream of doing this, wouldn't dream they could actually get away with it, but O'Leary isn't most people.

Colleagues came to realize that he worked on the basis of assuming everyone else was trying to rip him off, and that he would do whatever it took to ensure this didn't happen. It didn't seem to occur to O'Leary that he might be ripping off somebody else by underpaying them for the service or product that was being delivered to him . . . or that he might be building up considerable resentment with his approach to paying people.

He was always fast to tell management they would have to

lead by example when it came to addressing costs – which may have been easy for him, given the value of his shareholding in the company, on top of his salary and expenses. It caused consternation and resentment when, in April 2016, he told everyone earning more than €100,000 that they would not be getting pay rises until April 2017, at the very earliest. He cited the impact of terrorist attacks in Paris and Brussels, price competition from other airlines, targets for traffic growth and an expectation that fares would continue to fall after a flat year in 2015. He told them he had 'little room for movement this year on pay', as the company would have to further cut its costs to fund lower fares. If they were shareholders, the restriction on pay didn't matter as much because their wealth soared with the share price. Others were dependent on their salaries, however, and they were incensed by this move: how could a company earning such a big increase in profits deny its employees even a modest pay rise? O'Leary didn't care what they thought. It was his job not to spend company money unless it was absolutely essential.

Planes can't fly without pilots, which, in theory, puts them in a strong bargaining position. Not when they were bargaining with O'Leary, however, who viewed them as just another cost that was trying to nobble him. Hiring the pilots at the lowest cost possible was a policy that involved some creative accounting and employment structures that greatly irritated the pilots, infuriated some investors and seriously interested the tax authorities in various countries. Ryanair chose not to directly employ as many as half of its pilots, preferring instead to hire them through apparently third-party contractors, or requiring the pilots to form their own companies and provide contracts *for* service, rather than *of* service. It was a technical and legal distinction, but it allowed

Ryanair to save significant sums of money, particularly on providing sick pay and taxes. A number of Irish and British accountancy firms and companies handled the processes.

The advantage to the Irish airline, according to a 2013 court judgment in Belgium, was that it paid the wages to the intermediaries (who in turn paid the pilots), and therefore legally avoided responsibility for 'taxation or pay-related social insurance contributions' on behalf of pilots hired under the arrangement. In 2016 a French court ordered Ryanair to pay €9 million in fines and back-payment of social charges for Marseilles-based crew members hired on Irish contracts. The Italians, too, had issues with what went on.

But it was the Germans who pressed the issue most aggressively. German prosecutors began their investigation in 2010, after receiving an anonymous report of a 'letterbox company' called Brookfield Aviation International that was allegedly controlled by Ryanair and was being used by pilots operating in Germany. The following year German prosecutors contacted the UK authorities claiming that Brookfield's relationship with Ryanair's pilots was 'pseudo self-employment, even under British law'. They asked for help investigating claims that Brookfield was involved in tax evasion by withholding income tax and social-security payments for its German aircrew, and sought a search warrant for Brookfield's headquarters, citing an alleged 'especially serious case of tax evasion'. The warrant was granted.

Brookfield was based in the English town of Epsom, best known for its horse-racing track, in a building over a café and betting shop. Pilots went to Brookfield (or another company called McGinley Aviation) for work and were helped to set up small companies – in Ireland, where taxes were lower and labour laws more favourable to employers – in which they were directors. These companies then entered into a contract with Brookfield, which provided the services of the pilot to Ryanair. It was believed that over 1,600 pilots were covered by these various suppliers, ostensibly self-employed, but in reality concealing their employment with Ryanair.

Ryanair declared that 'the German tax authorities have confirmed that Ryanair is not the subject of any tax investigations. Ryanair requires all of its contractors to comply fully with national regulations and authorities.' However, the German prosecutors claimed that, 'quite contrary to Ryanair's statements', the aircrew were not independent subcontractors for tax purposes but employed by Brookfield and leased to the budget airline.

The investigation dragged on, but in July 2016 the German authorities named three Irish accountancy firms in search warrants as part of the investigation into alleged non-payment of income tax and social-security payments involving some Ryanair pilots. This was followed by customs raids at six Ryanair bases in Germany, and at the homes of some pilots. At least thirty-five prosecutors and customs investigators quizzed pilots and other staff about their employment relationship with Ryanair, and then they seized computers, iPads, rosters and other documents. The personnel firms were accused of withholding pilots' salaries and taxes, while pilots were accused of dodging social-welfare contributions.

The Irish accountants at the centre of it said they had worked to an opinion offered by a barrister who specialized in tax law, and that KPMG, the Ryanair auditors, had also approved it. They also said the Irish Revenue Commissioners, worried that pilots were not registering for taxes or social insurance anywhere, had welcomed the scheme when it was set up in 2009. But it was to become a big issue in Britain for pilots residing there, as the Inland Revenue, noting all the publicity, took an interest in the issue, too.

There was little doubt but that Ryanair, for all its bluster, was spooked. In August 2016 Ryanair set up a new company in Dublin called BlueSky Resources, through which German-based pilots flying Ryanair aircraft were to be employed in future. BlueSky was to employ pilots on five-year contracts, deducting income tax at source. The pilots based in Germany were to pay German social-welfare contributions, despite objections from the German pilot organization Cockpit, which claimed the new arrangements were not compatible with EU law. It was done, apparently, with the agreement of the German tax authorities, but that did not bring an end to the issues arising from the previous rows. That would still have to be dealt with, but, as far as O'Leary was concerned, he still maintained control over the relationship with pilots and he was very much the master.

In his traditional manner, O'Leary was nothing if not consistent in his determination to diminish and disregard the status of the unions representing pilots. In one investor presentation, he described pilot unions across Europe as a 'busted flush' who 'preside over the death of many of the flag-carrier airlines', and claimed they were a 'mob whose day is largely dead'. Warming to his theme, he said the airline union activity around Europe is a 'load of bollox' and he was exercised particularly by obstacles to his plans for expansion in Germany: 'If we got a lot of gyp from some pilots at a particular base in Germany, I'd have no compunction about closing the base and moving the aircraft out of there. If they don't want our jobs and our high pay, fine, we'll move the aircraft somewhere else.'

This wasn't an empty threat – he had already done it in

Denmark. Danish unions claimed Ryanair paid its cabin crew half the salary of staff in Cimber, a local low-cost rival, and the courts decided that Ryanair's Danish staff should be covered by a collective labour agreement instead of by Irish law. The courts also agreed that if Ryanair did not comply, other Danish unions should be allowed to mount sympathy industrial action, including blockading its aircraft, even if they were unconnected to the dispute.

'Apparently industrial-relations terrorism is now legal in Denmark,' O'Leary responded. He also hit out at the ruling for allowing what he called 'competitor airline unions' – those active at Scandinavian flag carrier SAS – to blockade his airplanes. He threatened to close Ryanair's base in Billund, home to Legoland and headquarters of the Danish toy company. 'Then we would have to close Billund, even if we don't want to. Copenhagen is more important to us than Billund, even if we love Billund dearly. I've been to Legoland myself,' O'Leary said. He decided that Ryanair would service Denmark using aircraft and crews based in other countries. The mayor of Copenhagen responded by banning city employees from flying Ryanair for official business, accusing the airline of 'social dumping'. Ryanair in turn began a typical campaign advertising low fares, which doubled up as mocking the officials. It was the old tried-and-trusted method yet again.

A year later O'Leary claimed Ryanair was 'going gangbusters' in Copenhagen, doubling the number of flights and customers served. 'So we've shipped our aircraft out of Denmark and we fly in from London, Dublin and Kaunas ... but they can't blockade us because we don't employ people there,' he claimed.

The unions then got investors – many of them managing pension funds of their workers – involved. Up to seven retirement schemes in Denmark and Sweden have either sold their shares or blacklisted Ryanair as an investment. 'We have a general concern about Ryanair's ability to work and cooperate in local markets, and we find Ryanair's understanding of local business practice lacking. This constitutes a business risk,' said Peter Køhler Lindegaard, head of listed investments at Industriens Pension, a Danish investor with €20 billion in assets under management.

O'Leary branded the Scandinavian pension providers involved as 'idiots' for refusing to invest in his airline. 'We don't pay too much attention to pension funds who have excluded us over labour concerns,' he told the *Financial Times*. 'They are misinformed. We don't have any labour issues. We have excellent relations, no strikes and no threat of a strike. If some idiot proxy says, "Don't invest in Ryanair", frankly we couldn't care less. We are not a sensitive organization. This is their loss – not ours.'

20. Outside the tent and pissing in

Ryanair was busy promoting its 'nice' image, but it did not necessarily follow that O'Leary applied this thinking to his public comments. In 2016 he waded into public discourse again and again to offer damning, contemptuous put-downs of politicians and their parties. It was another example of his contradictory nature. He ran the risk of creating resentment with his combative approach and thus losing customers, but he couldn't help standing up and speaking out anyway.

In fact, O'Leary's prominence throughout 2016 and the number and breadth of his political comments led some to wonder if he might be angling for a second act in his career – as a politician. He was questioned regularly about his intentions and continuously denied that he had any – 'I couldn't get elected as a rat-catcher' was his most common dismissal – but then most people with political ambitions deny them until they announce they will pursue them.

After all, 2016 was the year in which Donald Trump dominated media discourse and fostered a sense that anyone could take the political lead. O'Leary shared with Trump a distaste for political correctness, although he was far more articulate and intelligible in his delivery than the American. O'Leary also seemed more authentic – that he believed his views on customer relations, trade unions and political leadership, rather than saying it simply for effect. O'Leary's fans – mostly those with an ideological zeal for unfettered free markets – were always quick to support him for 'calling it as it is'. They'd be out of the traps on radio and elsewhere to declare that O'Leary could run Ireland as well as he ran his business. The idea of it made many people shudder in fear – not least the trade unionists.

O'Leary is not the type to have many heroes, but he is deeply fascinated by one historical figure who had a very significant political career as a second act. O'Leary has read nearly all the books that have been written about Arthur Wellesley, the Irishman who became the Duke of Wellington, one of the great leaders of the British Empire, a commander of the British Army and subsequently prime minister of the United Kingdom of Great Britain and Ireland. Both men loved a fight: Wellington on the battlefield, O'Leary through the skirmishes of business competition. It is striking just how many businessmen compare business to war and cite generals, commanders and war-time politicians as their role models. Wellington, Napoleon, Patten and Churchill are all favourites of an era of businessmen, now aged between fifty and eighty years. They must, like O'Leary, see something that appeals deeply to their sense of self – a type of man that speaks of leadership, self-confidence and success. Perhaps it was Wellington's spirit that led O'Leary on to become a self-appointed, unofficial spokesman for what he thinks of as 'anti-leftism'.

There was plenty of political fodder to get O'Leary exercised in 2016. The outcome of the Irish general election – which saw Fine Gael/Labour lose its comfortable majority and Fine Gael have to do deals with a cohort of independents and with its rival, Fianna Fáil, to form a minority government – did not please him, although he wasn't alone in his assessment. Before Fine Gael formed its new administration, O'Leary let off steam in an unusual place: an interview with an RTÉ radio agricultural programme.

Even though it was very off-topic, O'Leary was asked to comment on a major strike by LUAS drivers, Dublin's on-street monorail system. It may have been a surprise question, but he knew exactly what he thought. 'In the transport sector you tend to get headbangers who want to hold the whole country to ransom,' he said, urging management to sack anyone who didn't turn up for work. Warming to his theme, he spoke about the national debt and lowering taxation for the middle class. He took aim at Sinn Féin's economic policies: 'The idea of someone like Sinn Féin [with a policy that states] well, we'll tax the super-rich – they tried that in England and many other countries; you try to tax the super-rich to some super extent [and] we'll all disappear, we'll all go offshore. I don't want to go offshore, but if somebody in the Sinn Féin party thinks I'm going to pay 80 or 90 per cent tax, I'll simply move, I'll emigrate. It doesn't work.' (Sinn Féin responded that it had never argued for tax rates that high, 'just' an additional 7 per cent on income over €100,000.)

But it was the raft of single-issue, non-party-aligned 'independent' candidates who had been elected who bore the brunt of O'Leary's ire, including those who'd voted for them. 'I have great sympathy for the politicians; the electorate has not served the country well. I think there is a local popularity contest or the local lunatic [contest],' he said of the general election. 'It's all very well for people to be running around electing the local favourite or the local lunatic, but at the end of the day we have got to be a bit more sensible. We need to, whenever the next election comes around, vote in parties who are capable of running the country for a four- or five-year period. Some people get elected and all they want to do is be in permanent opposition. We vote for people promising the most treats.'

In his view, independents are 'grandstanders' and the worst governments in Irish history were those that had been held to ransom by independents. 'We need sensible parties with sensible economic policies. We need parties with sensible economic policies, not strangers promising us sweeties.' He was expressing the views of many, but it raised the usual speculation and questions as to why he did not offer himself for election if he cared so much.

In early autumn 2016 the European Commission announced its finding that Ireland and Apple had struck a secret, anti-competitive deal on corporation tax many years earlier, and that Apple should now pay Ireland €13 billion in unpaid tax, with interest and penalties potentially amounting to another €6 billion. This led to heated debate in Ireland, with some seeing it as a Trojan horse – a way for the EU to undermine Ireland's 12.5 per cent corporation tax rate. Ireland did not want to levy the tax, maintaining its position that it had done no secret, illegal deal, therefore the requirement to collect the tax was wrong. O'Leary's take on the situation was typical, saying the government should write a letter to the EU telling them to 'fuck off'. Even Leo Varadkar, then minister for social protection, who wanted to tell the EU where to go, was of the view that such provocative language was unwise and that Ireland should say nothing that might give the impression it would consider leaving the EU over the issue. Varadkar warned: 'The idea that we should threaten to leave the European Union as suggested this week by Michael O'Leary, a man whose achievements and even style I admire, seems to me to be akin to someone threatening to pull the pin on a hand grenade in an ammunition factory, seemingly unaware that the first person to be killed will be themselves.'

Not long afterwards, Fine Gael invited O'Leary to speak

at an invitation-only breakfast fundraiser at the Shelbourne Hotel in Dublin, just weeks before the announcement of the 2017 Budget. Five Fine Gael ministers were present, including Leo Varadkar (who become taoiseach the following year), Simon Coveney (who become his deputy), Charlie Flanagan and Richard Bruton. It fell to Minister for Finance Michael Noonan to introduce O'Leary in fine style, calling him 'Ireland's leading altogether decent man', which was quite the endorsement considering what was to follow.

O'Leary embarked on an epic rant, to the delight of many of the 200 or so guests who had paid €55 each to Fine Gael to attend. One of his first targets was An Garda Síochána (Irish police service), who were threatening unprecedented strike action. He said he was a 'great fan' of An Garda, who did a 'fantastic job', but that the proposed industrial action was 'immoral . . . If somebody doesn't show up to work, I'd sack them and if it means we've to sack 4,000 guards, I would sack all 4,000 guards. [Former American president] Reagan did it with the air-traffic controllers in America in 1987. Sometimes the state has to stand up and say, "Sorry, you're the army, you're the guards, you knew you couldn't go on strike when you joined."'

He wasn't finished yet. He insisted private bus companies be allowed to operate routes during industrial action by state-owned operators. He accused the Dublin local authority of destroying the city centre through 'nonsensical pandering to bloody cyclists'. He said the state was 'really crap at running the health service' and called for it to be privatized. He called for reduced taxes on business people, on the grounds it would improve the economy. Notwithstanding the welcome he had received from Minister Noonan, he said the government's response to the Apple tax fiasco was 'weak and limp-wristed' and condemned the EU as being anti-competition.

From there, he went on to compare RTÉ to a 'rat-infested North Korean union shop' and accused it of peddling the views of hard-left union Trotskyites. 'I can't turn on the bloody *Nine O'Clock News* without having to see Ingrid Miley's face giving me the latest spew from the Trotskyites and all the rest of it.' This attack on the public-sector broadcaster – and on its industrial correspondent by name – brought about sustained applause and laughter, although it was later condemned by many when word of the event was published in a number of the Sunday newspapers.

Some wondered why he reserved so much bile for RTÉ and conflated it with the trade-union sector. O'Leary's distaste for RTÉ went back decades, although it never stopped him appearing on RTÉ if he had an agenda to push. The genesis of this went back to the 1990s and his early days in Ryanair, when the airline was struggling to survive. He went to RTÉ to take part in an interview and, while waiting his turn in the green room, he noticed posters on the wall encouraging RTÉ staff to boycott use of Ryanair because of its no-union policy. Although many RTÉ staff actively ignored the exhortation, it angered O'Leary greatly and was never forgotten. He may dish it out in spades, but he can have a thin skin, too – and a long memory.

After his appearance at the Shelbourne Hotel breakfast became public news, it provided a platform for the popular historian Professor Diarmaid Ferriter to vilify both Fine Gael and O'Leary for the performance. He wrote an article for the *Irish Times* that pulled no punches: 'Why do Noonan and his colleagues then provide a platform for O'Leary to eviscerate those same public servants, and not only that, but positively encourage it? Why is Fine Gael so keen to fawn over O'Leary?' He noted how Minister for Foreign Affairs Charles Flanagan expressed his delight, via his Twitter account, at soaking up O'Leary's rants: 'Great start today listening to Michael O'Leary sound off in flying form.'

Ferriter noted that O'Leary enjoyed calling himself an 'obnoxious little bollocks', but argued that the main government party encouraging him was a more troubling issue: 'Is it because, in reality, it sees O'Leary as an ideological soulmate; a perfect fit for a party that talks centre but thinks right? Why should Fine Gael go unchallenged in contributing to and endorsing a destructive pitching of public against private sector which has been a hallmark of reaction to the Irish economic crisis of recent years? Likewise, it appears there are no depths to which the unprincipled O'Leary will not reach to excoriate public servants. Long ago he coined his own expletive – "bolloxology" – which, he explained, "should be liberally used in one-to-one print media interviews when referring to any procedure that other airlines claim is complex". In juvenile, privileged and elite O'Leary-land there are no complexities; it is all a simple matter of money, market dominance and pathetic public servants that Fine Gael seems happy to laugh at, too.'

It was simply Ferriter's opinion, and many disagreed, with the think-tank the Hibernia Forum in particular launching staunch support for O'Leary and Ryanair and its achievements. What wasn't known at the time, and was only revealed later that year after the *Sunday Business Post* secured the details in a Freedom of Information disclosure, was that O'Leary's political interests – and desire to involve Minister Noonan in them – ran deeper.

On 24 March, while the formation of the new government was still under negotiation, O'Leary invited Noonan to attend the exclusive, closed-door annual Bilderberg Meeting in Dresden, Germany, that June. The revelation of this raised questions for a number of reasons. One was that O'Leary was applying himself to political discourse that went far beyond aviation policy. Another was that the Bilderberg Meeting was something of a conspiracy theorist's wet-dream. It was founded in 1954 with the stated aim of fostering dialogue between Europe and North America. That may seem anodyne, but it attracted criticism for its non-disclosure of attendees, agenda and decisions. There are no notes taken, no reports issued and no media allowed. The claim has developed that it is an elite of right-wing capitalists, with their defence and enhancement the goal. Membership is by invitation only.

'For my sins, I am now the Irish member of the Bilderberg Steering Committee which allows us to invite two guests of Irish nationality,' O'Leary wrote to Noonan. He promised that the discussions would be 'wide ranging, insightful, interesting and held under strict Chatham House rules [utmost confidentiality]'. O'Leary told the veteran minister that he would have to come on his own, without staff or security or family, and that he would have to commit to being there for the full three days. 'I think you will find it stimulating,' he said. Noonan did go, and the state covered his full €4,000 costs. As confidentiality was maintained, nobody ever found out what went on.

It didn't go unnoticed, however, that O'Leary was in the process of lobbying for the right to build a new, third terminal at Dublin Airport and – in a throwback to more than a decade earlier – was actively lobbying against the state-owned DAA having any involvement in the project. O'Leary had told the Fine Gael gathering at the Shelbourne Hotel that, if permitted, Ryanair would build the new terminal for €200 million – a bargain price, apparently, given it was less than a fifth of what Terminal 2 had cost. As before, his motivation was selfish. If the DAA built it and spent more than that, at the same time as it was building a new second runway in Dublin (which Ryanair endorsed), then Ryanair might have to pay higher charges and pass those on to customers by way of higher ticket prices. It wouldn't be long before Ryanair was back at the door of the DAA, claiming that Ryanair was responsible for about two thirds of all traffic growth at Dublin Airport and looking for a new 15 per cent discount on charges – but offering to add 2 million passengers per year if it got it.

If such relentless chasing of self-interest reminded many people of Donald Trump, it was not surprising. O'Leary was one of the few businesspeople in 2016 to speak positively of Trump before and after he became president of the USA. During the campaign, it emerged that O'Leary had been in contact with Trump to talk about assets Trump had purchased in Ireland, a golf course and hotel at Doonbeg in West Clare. Not long before embarking on his election campaign, Trump revealed that his plans to upgrade the hotel had been prompted partly by a phone call from O'Leary: 'We are applying for [permission to add] a ballroom. Mr O'Leary from Ryanair, who I have great respect for, called me. Michael told me: "No one else will use any other ballroom." We spoke and he told me that I have bought one of his favourite places in Doonbeg.'

O'Leary saw the upsides in Trump's election, namely that it might suit the aviation industry and Ryanair. 'In a bizarre way it is probably good for the airline industry. He'll certainly encourage more fracking,' O'Leary said. 'I think you'll see downward pressure on oil prices, which will be good, I would imagine, for certainly the airline business.' He was among the many wealthy businessmen who hoped Trump would enforce a move to the political right: 'Not since Thatcher and Reagan left the scene at such tragically early ages have I admired any politician. For all the abuse they got, those two fundamentally changed the US and UK economies. Governments since have pissed that away by wasting money on the NHS and all these other useless quangos. Governments never create jobs – they should just get out of the way.'

However, O'Leary did not offer Trump a ringing endorsement. It was telling what he didn't agree with. 'Some of the other stuff I don't understand. Why you care how many showed up to your inauguration is beyond me. You're already the president. It shouldn't matter.' It was classic O'Leary: score the point and move on, ignore all other opinions, what people think of you doesn't matter in the slightest, it only matters that you won. He also described the America First policy as 'nuts. Isolation never works. If it did, North Korea would be a powerhouse of the world economy.'

Yet the anti-regulation, pro-market policies that got Donald Trump elected to the White House were exactly what O'Leary had championed for years. O'Leary continued his campaign against environmental activists at every opportunity. 'Climate change is fucking rubbish because it used to be global warming and now – because they can't stand up global warming any more, because there hasn't been any rise in temperatures in mean terms for the last ten years – they now talk about climate change,' was his unscientific but loudly aired opinion. 'There's this assumption that if we do something about carbon consumption, or taxing carbon consumption, the climate will stop changing. It's complete and utter rubbish.'

The cap-and-trade system, the subsidizing of renewables,

his perception of a 'completely bloody bogus industry created around this climate change' and what he calls 'the inference that if we only taxed someone and we stop consuming carbon, climate will stop changing' – they all added up to unwarranted government intervention in his view. 'In the end, the market will solve carbon consumption,' he told the *Sunday Business Post*. 'We will adapt. The market will solve most things. The market does need to be regulated in the interests of social protection, but you allow competition in the market to regulate these things.'

All of this commentary and angry lobbying inevitably led to the direct question: would he stand for election himself? 'No!' he exclaimed. 'I'm running a successful airline. I have no desire to get into fucking politics in one of the government ministries. I wouldn't survive a week in a government ministry because I don't have the patience to be telling people what they want to hear. I'd be telling them the truth instead.' It showed a self-awareness that many might have thought he didn't possess.

All of his political pronouncements were based on what was good for Ryanair, which was why, when it came to Europe, he was in favour of the single market and trenchantly opposed to political integration: 'Deregulation, liberalization and removing state impediments to competition and consumer choice. We should continue to oppose further political union and be aggressive advocates of the single market. I don't see any great contradiction there.' This position meant that he was naturally on the side of Remain when it came to the Brexit referendum in 2016.

O'Leary's decision to become publicly and prominently involved in the referendum struck some people in Britain as odd, given that O'Leary was not a British citizen and did not have a vote. In addition, he had bleated over the years about what he claimed was inappropriate EU interference in aviation and competition policy. All his opponents would have to do was rebroadcast the video of O'Leary at an EU innovation conference in 2011 and hijacking it with his complaint that the EU 'spends most of its time either suing me, torturing me, criticizing me or condemning me for lowering the cost of air travel all over Europe'.

Willie Walsh was among those who warned him that it wasn't a good idea for businesspeople to get involved in lobbying, but O'Leary decided that it would be bad for Ryanair if the UK left the EU: 'I don't have a vote, but I run the biggest airline in the UK, we're one of the biggest investors in the UK and employ 4,000 people in fifteen different airports, we are also a big taxpayer in the UK.' For him, that made Brexit very much his business.

He adopted many of the same tactics he had employed in Ireland in 2009, expressing his criticism of the EU at the same time as extolling its virtues: 'We all have issues with Europe ... I don't want to be part of a united states of Europe, I don't want to be adopting French social policies, they don't work in France, and they're certainly not going to work here either. We should celebrate the differences that exist between European countries. We should continue to work together as an economic union because it has worked ... It has transformed and improved the lives of citizens right across the European Union. The EU gets a lot of unfair criticism in the UK, but it has delivered much for the UK economy. It needs people, companies like us, to actively campaign ... Too many businesses are too reticent about getting involved.' He argued that the 'Leave' side was taking the contradictory position that the UK could exit the EU and nothing would change. 'If you leave, everything will not stay the same.' It was a prescient comment.

He appeared at various events, and made an appearance on BBC's *Question Time*, where his direct manner was again notable among the more nuanced politicians – and where he also managed to relentlessly plug his airline. He also returned to his penchant of dressing up to make a point. He donned a specially made suit, half in the EU flag, half in the British flag, and a top hat, for a circus-like performance in front of photographers on the banks of the River Thames, across from the Houses of Parliament. Then, with his CEO hat on, he organized a press conference at a Ryanair event at Stansted – the opening of what he called a European Training Centre, which he promised would create more than 1,000 new jobs overall for pilots, cabin crew and engineers. It was attended by Prime Minister David Cameron and Chancellor George Osborne. 'It is exactly this type of investment that will be lost to other competitor EU members if the UK votes to leave the European Union,' he warned.

To O'Leary's shock, on 23 June he was on the losing side as Brexit was passed by 52 per cent to 48 per cent. He was so disbelieving of the outcome, he claimed to be unconvinced that Brexit would actually happen. He gave a forty-minute phone interview to *Fortune* magazine in late June and admitted that he'd got it badly wrong when he forecast 'Remain' would win with 54 per cent of the vote. O'Leary, again incorrectly, feared that Britain would suffer an immediate and steep recession that would result in increased taxes and cuts to government spending. He predicted that Britain would make 'a big, expensive, nerve-racking U-turn, and end up back where it started, as a full member of the European Community'. He is still holding this line – repeating it in an interview in April 2018, even if the immediate economic downturn he had predicted did not take place.

He correctly predicted that the EU would not give the departing British anything easily in negotiations: 'The EU won't do this out of spite. It's a political calculation. It's much more important to the EU to prevent contagion to other countries that may be getting in the queue to leave the EU, such as France and the Netherlands, than to give Britain a good deal. And the UK isn't even in the euro. They won't make it easy for the UK to leave.'

It was the beginning of a series of interviews in which he foresaw woe for Britain and discussed the potential implications for Ryanair: 'We'll receive 50 new aircraft from Boeing over the next 12 months, and we were going to put 10 of them in the UK. Now none of them will go to the UK.' In another interview he stated: 'there's a bunch of headless chickens here, they don't know what they voted for and have no idea where they're going to finish up, so we have to be cautious with our expansion next year, which is a pity.'

He had long anticipated the potential impacts: a fall in the value of sterling, a decline in aircraft traffic between Britain and the EU, which could be potentially serious if the severance deal failed to put in place some sort of Open Skies deal to allow EU airlines access to British airspace, and vice versa. While others were still popping champagne corks, he could see all sorts of regulatory and licensing problems, given that it was a strict condition of EU licences and flying rights that airlines had major ownership and control by EU investors. The ownership figure for Ryanair at that stage was 60 per cent, but once the UK left that number would fall to 40 per cent. Potentially, he would have to jettison some British investors by buying their shares off them.

He was convinced that Britain would have to remain a member of its single market, and this became the most important factor for him: 'Whether the UK leaves the EU or stays, I couldn't care less. The issue for us is whether we stay in the single market . . . staying in the single market is the sensible way forward.'

That was far easier said than done, however. He knew well that staying within the Open Skies area would require the UK to submit to the authority of the European Court of Justice, anathema to the hardline Brexiters. That made it more likely that the UK would have to secure individual, bilateral aviation agreements with EU countries or else an en bloc deal with the EU. That, he noted, would be difficult as it would require unanimous support from all member states.

While his motivation was selfish, O'Leary's analysis was intelligent and clear-sighted. He understood immediately that Brexit went far deeper than many politicians realized. For example, would the airworthiness certificates issued by the British Civil Aviation Authority be recognized by the European Aviation Safety Agency as equal and permissible? If not, airlines such as Ryanair and easyJet might be left to set up two sister airlines, registering some aircraft in the UK and others in the EU, most probably Ireland.

To O'Leary's amazement, the new British PM Theresa May opted for the 'hard Brexit' position. The alternative to Open Skies was to negotiate a bilateral agreement with Brussels. O'Leary pointed out that in this case, the UK would still have to accept freedom of movement and that such a deal would be subject to the approval of the twenty-six other EU member state parliaments. He had raised this with Chris Grayling, the UK transport secretary, and his cabinet colleagues, but they did not accept his argument. 'But if you ask them what their plan B is, they don't have a plan B,' he added. 'They say that they cannot see how European airports are going to survive without British passengers – well, they can survive because they are going to have to.'

He was frustrated by the lack of sense, as he saw it, in the British thinking on Brexit. 'The British were sold a pup,' he said. 'They were told if they leave Europe, nothing will change. They're about to realize that you can leave Europe and everything is going to bloody change and it's going to change for the worse. When they find that they may not be able to fly to Spain or Italy on their holidays, or that they might have to get a visa to get to Spain or Italy on their holidays, I think there's going to be a sea change in the attitude of the average British citizen towards the misinformation on which they voted in the original Brexit referendum.'

He continues to hope for that reprieve, but in the meantime Brexit trundles on towards its 2019 deadline and as CEO of one of the biggest companies in the UK, O'Leary has to deal with the fallout. In October 2016 he issued the company's first profit warning in three years, flagging that profits to year end March 2017 would be about 5 per cent less than expected. He warned that routes out of Stansted that winter would have to be reduced, both in capacity and frequency. At the same time, though, he was loudly calling for the UK government to have a radical rethink of its proposal for a new runway out of London and approve three runways – one each for Stansted, Gatwick and Heathrow. So he was dealing with the aftermath of the Brexit decision, but also planning for a busy and profitable future for Ryanair at its UK bases. Only time will tell if he gets his way on that one.

21. Spreading its wings

Always Getting Better was an almost unqualified success, at least according to the numbers. At the time of the September 2013 AGM it was possible to buy Ryanair shares for €6.30 each, giving the company a stock-market value of just over €9 billion. The company started 2017 with a share price of €14.66 and a market capitalization of €18.85 billion. It was a very impressive feat, and it was down to the surge in profits: in the year to the end of March 2014, the company had €522 million in profits; €866.7 million the following year; a year later €1.24 billion; and over €1.35 billion for the twelve months to the end of March 2017. It was an incredible achievement. Since 2008 Ryanair returned about €5.4 billion to investors through buybacks of shares (making the smaller number of shares then in circulation more valuable) and special dividends.

O'Leary knew it was the strategy of low costs that was responsible for these returns, and he guaranteed that Ryanair would continue to drive down air fares through cost-cutting. He called it 'load factor active, yield passive', language that would mean little to most but was understood by professional investors. It gave him industry-leading operating profit margins of 23 per cent, even though he didn't run the long-haul routes where most rivals made their biggest profits. He was determined to recover additional revenues as ticket fares decreased, having brought ancillary revenues to 27 per cent of sales, with a plan to increase this to 30 per cent.

'The question for us is whether we can continue to drive down costs,' he said repeatedly.

It is an unpredictable industry, though, and there were many things that were beyond his control. Terrorist violence in several countries hit passenger confidence, as did ongoing air-traffic-control disruption, especially in France. The sharp decline in sterling following the Brexit vote the previous June didn't help either. Ryanair took in a large proportion of its fare revenue in sterling, while the vast majority of its expenses were in euro and other non-sterling currencies.

No matter what happened, though, O'Leary's self-confidence never wavered. Ryanair would win out through it all. The efforts of others were seen as paltry by comparison: 'easyJet's profits declined last year by about 25 or 30 per cent. Ours only grew by 6 per cent – so we're doing better than anyone else. There have been years, maybe one out of every four, or one out of every five, that some other idiot is out there splurging on capacity and there's too much capacity growth in the system in Europe.' The competition would impact on Ryanair's bottom line but, in the long run, he believed his lower costs would allow him to prosper as others faltered.

The key strategy for O'Leary now was expansion. Competition might bite, but he put all his chips on the bet that his low-cost base would enable Ryanair to withstand the resulting decline in fares better than its rivals. He was constantly looking for opportunities to expand, to allow his confident forecasts to be realized. He announced further deals with Boeing, which would bring Ryanair's fleet up to 520 aircraft by 2024, with the aim of flying more than 180 million people each year, and possibly as many as 200 million. So what if he had to deal with Brexit? There was a massive continent in

Europe and beyond, too, as Ryanair expanded into Turkey and Israel.

Ryanair took advantage of whatever deals were on offer. Israel offered foreign carriers flying to Eilat Airport a €45 per passenger subsidy, topped up by another €15 per visitor offered by the local hotels association. O'Leary was aware that there was a strong pro-Palestinian sentiment in Ireland – and that some boycotts of Irish business and cultural involvements in Israel had been sought, but usually by the left-wing types O'Leary despised – so he commenced flights to Israel from Krakow, Kaunas, Budapest and Bratislava. He calculated, correctly, that few in Ireland would notice and that his shareholders would offer no objection.

He gave serious consideration to expanding into Ukraine, a country that wanted to join the EU and had signed a special association deal with it. However, Ukraine was having considerable difficulties with Russia, especially over disputed territories in Crimea after an illegal Russian invasion. The country's pro-EU leadership was desperate for Ryanair to provide low-cost flights to Kiev and Lviv, to allow Ukrainian nationals to take advantage of the visa-free travel they had been granted recently by the EU. However, Ryanair withdrew its plans to open four routes to Kiev and seven to Lviv, even though it would have brought it into a market of 45 million people. Chief commercial officer David O'Brien said that the airport had 'demonstrated that Ukraine is not yet a sufficiently mature or reliable business location to invest valuable Ryanair aircraft capacity' and accused the government of looking to 'protect high-fare airlines', including Ukraine International Airlines, the country's largest carrier. It was a further example of how Ryanair always regarded itself as holding the stronger hand in negotiations.

There was a bigger market closer to home that still had to be cracked. Ryanair's failure to make a breakthrough in Germany had more than surprised O'Leary, especially as he once said the Germans would crawl over broken glass to get something cheaply. It was an enormous and lucrative market and he wanted a chunk of it, claiming that Ryanair could be the airline equivalent of what Aldi or Lidl were in the supermarket sector. Yet, by the end of 2015, Ryanair had only a 4 per cent market share and Jacobs weighed in to support his boss, calling Germany 'our single biggest strategic focus'.

O'Leary and Jacobs spoke of quadrupling that figure by 2020 by taking business away from Air Berlin, Lufthansa and German Wings, on the basis that the competitors were not well organized or providing good value for money to customers. The UK had a 60 per cent penetration of low-cost carriers, with Spain and Italy not far behind, but in Germany it was reckoned that only 20 per cent of the market travelled with Ryanair and its ilk. It provided opportunity, but long-standing Ryanair watchers remembered that such ambitions had been outlined many times over the previous twenty years. 'The assumption that they are going to take a big share in Germany is fairly impudent,' said Robin Byde, an analyst at Cantor Fitzgerald in London.

Protectionism was high on the list of reasons why Ryanair hadn't succeeded. The main German airports – as distinct from the secondary ones developed at more distant locations by Ryanair – were very expensive and controlled by local authorities, in conjunction with local trade unions, which did not like the Ryanair work practices. Local airlines like Lufthansa and Air Berlin dominated the available slots and did not surrender them easily. Ryanair pressed into the primary airports from September 2015, particularly Frankfurt, offering dozens of new routes, as well as Berlin and Cologne. It had Lufthansa worried, because it couldn't match Ryanair's average €33 fare and was not used to this type of direct competition at its airports. Ryanair wasn't happy, though – it was building market share, but not at the pace desired.

In 2017 opportunity seemed to present itself. Air Berlin had made a loss in almost every year since 2008, including a record €782 million in 2016, and had debts of more than €1 billion. It was kept airborne by the generosity of Etihad Airways, its 29 per cent shareholder. Etihad had invested a further €250 million in April 2016, but it was wasted money as the airline's passenger numbers went into freefall, crashing by about a quarter in a year. Air Berlin was going bust.

Much to his frustration and indeed anger, O'Leary couldn't take advantage of this situation. This was his moment to sweep in, take passengers, routes, aircraft and airport-landing slots at the expense of yet another failing airline. Instead, the German government handed Air Berlin a short-term loan of €150 million, which O'Leary called illegal state aid. Lufthansa took hold of some of Air Berlin's leases, giving it effective control over the aircraft. 'The German market is one of the biggest prizes in Europe,' O'Leary said. 'Instead of appointing a liquidator and selling it to all the airlines that would clearly want to invest in the German market, it is carved up so that Lufthansa can buy it.'

O'Leary lodged competition complaints with German and EU anti-trust authorities; he alleged Ryanair and other airlines had been excluded from the sales process and called for all interested bidders to be allowed to compete for Air Berlin's assets, including landing slots at Germany's major airports. 'This is a stitch-up. Lufthansa already have 68 per cent of the domestic market and with Air Berlin they get

95 per cent of the domestic market. They already have 47 per cent of the total market and with Air Berlin they go to over 60 per cent. What's happening is that there's a deal being set up for Lufthansa to come in and take out its principal competitor. It's a merger and the German government are not only actively involved in it, they're supporting it and they're now funding it with this €150 million loan.'

To make it worse for O'Leary, easyJet was apparently to be cut in on the deal, to receive a share of Air Berlin's airport take-off and landing slots as a fig-leaf. 'All this is done to prevent Ryanair growing in Germany, but it won't stop us.' He said that Germany was turning into the 'banana republic of European aviation', and added for good measure that Germans would suffer higher air fares as a result, but his complaints got him nowhere.

While arguing about being shut out of the Air Berlin deal, O'Leary was also making overtures to another troubled airline, Alitalia. It didn't seem a good investment, given Alitalia's €3 billion in debts and the fact that Ryanair had already carried 36 million Italian passengers in the previous year but, as always, O'Leary was looking at a bigger picture. He wanted access to 'feeder deals' with transatlantic carriers, and this seemed a good way to achieve that. He offered a deal on the condition that the airline be restructured first, which meant mass redundancies and lower pay for those who remained, something that was never considered likely given the power of the unions in Italy.

It took Ryanair a lot longer than O'Leary had expected to set up 'feeder deals' with the transatlantic carriers. A feeder deal meant Ryanair would bring customers to the airport, where a transatlantic airline would transport them to their eventual destination, one Ryanair did not serve. Such deals were central to his plan to expand passenger numbers and he spoke of garnering 20 million new customers each year through this method by 2025. The legacy carriers were losing out to low-cost operations on European short-haul routes, relying on their transatlantic services for their profits. To O'Leary, this meant feeder deals would be a cost-effective way for legacy carriers to bring their passengers to hub airports for long-haul flight connections.

'The upside for us is in persuading the legacy carriers to stop trying to compete with us on short-haul because it feeds their long-haul,' he said. 'Work with us on short-haul, you lose less money, I'll have less competition.' His plan was that, in time, Ryanair would replace many short-haul services operated by network carriers, encouraging them to focus exclusively on intercontinental routes. He saw a trend already whereby people were 'self-connecting', organizing their own connections, even if it meant extra hassle at the airport. As part of a feeder service, Ryanair could help them avoid the inconveniences of multiple bookings and check-ins.

'There's nothing but upside for the legacy carriers in this, except you've got to persuade them it's not some scam,' O'Leary said. When O'Leary was at the negotiating table, the issue of trust was always a hurdle. Ryanair was viewed with the greatest suspicion, even by those who now formed alliances with it. *Always Getting Better* was working on paper, but Ryanair had generated a lot of ill feeling over the years, and it couldn't be shaken off so easily.

22. Always getting richer

As the Ryanair business grew rapidly, O'Leary kept his management team tight. This had its merits: he was able to communicate with them readily on an individual basis, and group meetings were not overcrowded. The Z-team was much as it had been reconstituted when Cawley and Millar had left and various promotions executed, although Bellew had departed to run Malaysia Airlines in late 2015. It was tight-knit and agile, but, with the expansion ongoing at such a rapid pace, it meant an increased workload for everyone. The traditional oversight – indeed engagement – that O'Leary wanted became more difficult with so much more to oversee. And, for all the talk of Ryanair maturing and becoming a 'middle-aged company', O'Leary also hadn't curtailed his habit of lighting fires instead of putting them out.

The success of *Always Getting Better* had made O'Leary an even wealthier man. While his shareholding in Ryanair was not quite worth €1 billion, it was assumed that he was a billionaire because he had taken significant chunks of cash – tens of millions of euro at a time – out of the business and re-invested it privately. While he spent some on his horse-racing activities and stud in Ireland – as well as the 210-acre Plantation Stud at Newmarket in England – a lot of the cash was used to purchase properties, both in Ireland and abroad. It was known that he owned an office-block in Park Lane, London, and three houses in the upmarket Ballsbridge area of Dublin 4, but there was much else besides. The speculation was that his non-Ryanair assets were worth several hundred million euro at least, although the true value was known only to a very small number of people.

His long-standing policy of not tying all his wealth to Ryanair continued during 2017. He sold four million shares on Friday, 2 June 2017, at €18 each, giving him around €72 million in cash. Whatever happened at Ryanair, he would depart it at some later stage as a very wealthy man. What he did with this money remained private, but the sale was not taken as a sign of worry about the company's prospects or disengagement from its future on his part. He retained 4.1 per cent of Ryanair, making him the third largest shareholder after HSBC Bank, which held 8.65 per cent, and multinational financial services firm Fidelity Investments, which had 5.87 per cent. It was still his airline, and it might have been assumed that its success made him happy.

It doesn't seem to be in his nature to be happy. He was still angry about many things, not just about the airline industry. The promises of less frequent public utterances and a more mature demeanour, made just a couple of years earlier, were clearly not likely to be honoured. He had too much to say, about too many things, although he was in danger of being seen as a prematurely grumpy old man, an Irish version of Victor Meldrew from *One Foot in the Grave*. 'One of the great crimes perpetrated in the UK economy recently is the old Labour attitude of getting rid of competition,' he said in one interview. 'Getting rid of exams, closing down football pitches – idiotic. Life's about competition. We're not all fucking equal. Sadly, there are people who are faster than me and better-looking than me, so I had to find other ways to compete. Kids need to learn those lessons.'

In the summer of 2017 Ryanair got embroiled in the type

of row that was typical of the days before the introduction of *Always Getting Better*. O'Leary did not attempt to mollify – as he was supposed to do, apparently – but instead riled those who objected to the apparently deliberate separation of people travelling together who did not purchase allocated seating. It became one of the high-profile consumer stories of the 'silly season', and brought O'Leary smack up against the promises he'd made to be 'nicer'.

Logic was on Ryanair's side in the debate, but that didn't sit well with the emotional intelligence that Ryanair was now supposed to display in its interactions with customers. The introduction of allocated seating had proven very popular, as it meant no more jostling to board ahead of other passengers. Now, however, according to anecdotal evidence that was shared readily on traditional and social media, Ryanair was deliberately separating families or people travelling in groups from one another if they failed to purchase allocated seating, with everyone put in middle seats, sometimes a plane-length apart, rather than in window or aisle seats. There were angry claims – especially by those with children – that, while empty, presumably unsold, seats were alongside theirs, their travelling companions were seated many rows away. It was perceived by some as a form of punishment for not having spent the extra money on allocated seating.

Ryanair had an explanation: 'We haven't changed the random seat-allocation policy. The reason for more middle seats being allocated is that more and more passengers are taking our reserved seats (from just €2), and these passengers overwhelmingly prefer aisle and window seats, which is why people who choose random (free of charge) seats are more likely to be allocated middle seats. Some random-seat passengers are confused by the appearance of empty seats beside them when they check-in up to four days prior to departure. The reason they can't have these window or aisle seats is that these are more likely to be selected by reserved-seat passengers, many of whom only check-in twenty-four hours prior to departure. Since our current load factor is 96 per cent, we have to keep these window and aisle seats free to facilitate those customers who are willing to pay (from €2) for them.'

Newspapers like the *Irish Times* made a big issue of it, publishing stories of how young children were allocated seats rows away from their parents. 'It is a complete disgrace,' said one passenger, Cathy Dwyer. 'My five-year-old was put at the back of the plane to board through the back door. My seven-year-old in the front but away from me . . . I ended up paying extra for both the outward and return flights to ensure I sat with my kids. It is so irresponsible of this airline.'

Another example came from a man called Daire O'Brien: 'This happened to my partner, our one-year-old child and I recently. We checked in as early as possible but were given distantly separated, middle seats and it has never happened before. Thankfully, the nice person sitting in one of the adjacent seats agreed to swap, allowing us to sit together. This recent change is sneaky and a return to the unfriendly Ryanair of the past.'

O'Leary decided he wasn't having it. It was the middle of summer, his wife, Anita, and children were away in Portugal on holidays without him, and he decided to return fire, going on RTÉ Radio 1's *Today with Sean O'Rourke* to do so. O'Leary denied that families were being separated deliberately. He pointed out that children under the age of twelve would have a seat allocated for free if an adult travelling with them paid the €2 reserved seat fee. 'We haven't changed our policy. If you're not happy to pay €2 for a seat, stop complaining and whingeing. If you want to select a seat, pay €2. People are whining and whingeing, but you can't sit where you want. Sorry, you can't.'

Most chief executives wouldn't have gone on live radio for the first interview, but those who did would certainly have left it at that. However, just a little more than two hours later, O'Leary phoned RTÉ again and demanded to be on *Liveline*, a phone-in show hosted by Joe Duffy and one of the most listened-to programmes on Irish national radio.

On *Liveline*, O'Leary again rejected the allegation that the computer algorithm that seated passengers deliberately dispersed them around the plane. 'Has the algorithm changed? No, it hasn't. It changes automatically on an hourly [basis] – it changes due to demand and because the number of reserved seats has changed. Are you likely to be split up if you select a random seat? Yes, you are likely to be split up because that's what random means. If you want to sit specifically in a seat, then you select a reserved seat for just €2. Less than the cost of the RTÉ licence fee,' he said, in a reference to the €160 annual charge for owning a TV in Ireland. 'Our aircrafts are flying with 96 per cent load factors, there are no empty seats unless a passenger is a no-show,' he continued. 'For about two years we have had a policy of offering people who want to reserve a seat – can do so and people who choose a random seat can have a random seat. I frankly don't know what you're complaining about when you get a random seat. You're not having to pay extra, you chose a random seat so you're getting a random seat. We have more than 65 million people who chose to pay for the seat.'

Liveline put callers on air to vent. 'You're perfectly free to complain,' he responded. But his patience soon evaporated and, wisely or not, he goaded Duffy when he said, 'Sorry, do you have a sensible question?' Duffy, who wears his Dublin working-class credentials on his sleeve, was furious at what he perceived as condescension. 'How dare you,' he snapped, before demanding an apology. O'Leary instead suggested Duffy was feigning anger. In reply, Duffy called the Ryanair boss 'the Hamlet of mock indignation'. The following day's newspapers were full of the row, giving O'Leary another blast of free publicity.

Colleagues said he was chuffed by the support he received from many quarters. One letter to the *Irish Times* that he enjoyed said: 'The level of outrage that Ryanair has elicited by charging €2 for a designated seat is incomprehensible. Most bus fares cost more than that, and don't guarantee that you get any seat at all.'

While Ryanair might claim to be *Always Getting Better*, it was clear some things would never change – and O'Leary was one of them. His naturally pugnacious attitude can be contained only for so long, and then the gloves come off and he leaps into the ring. It happened again later that year, over the old chestnut of cabin luggage.

Ryanair had issued warnings that it felt some passengers were taking advantage of its generosity: 'Only 16 per cent of our passengers are now checking in bags, taking advantage of our policy of allowing two carry-on bags,' Neil Sorahan, the financial director, complained to the BBC. 'We are now seeing two-year-olds dragging along their own wheelie bag to maximize the baggage allowance. Perhaps we are becoming the victims of our own niceness, but we are looking at the impact.'

The *Financial Times* coined the term 'baggadocio', which it called a noun to describe 'arrogant behaviour on the part of low-cost airline passengers who believe themselves entitled to several pieces of carry-on luggage, all of which are larger than yours and would never fit into that funny little metal size-gauge thing they put at the departure gates'. Sorahan agreed: 'I've seen bags twice, three times the size of what a bag should be going on board.'

While the idea amused many – especially the idea that customers were having belated revenge on Ryanair for the charges and misery that had once been commonplace – it did have adverse consequences for everyone. Luggage-laden passengers were delaying flights as they struggled to find overhead locker space. The overhead locker cabin space on a Ryanair flight allows for the carriage of 90 normal cabin bags. If every passenger brought two, that meant 380 bags competing for the limited space. With flights now on average 96 per cent full, this was happening too often.

Ryanair's generosity had rebounded on it, but attempts to solve the new problem would result only in further complaints. There was nothing for it but to wade in anyway. Ryanair announced that, from November 2017, passengers who had not paid €6/£5 for priority boarding would be restricted to one piece of hand luggage. People with priority boarding could carry two bags. To encourage customers to put their bags in the hold, the check-in bag allowance was increased from 15kg to 20kg and the fee was cut from €/£35 to €/£25. Ryanair said these changes would cost it more than €50 million in lost check-in charges. The measure was earmarked for introduction in November 2017, but it had to be postponed. It was overtaken by events.

The summer of 2017 ended for O'Leary with shock and sadness. His friend James Osborne, the senior independent director at Ryanair, a man with whom he had worked for over twenty years and who was a wise and steady counsel, died suddenly on an island off the coast of Donegal where his father was buried and to which he had sailed on his own, in circumstances that remain unexplained.

Osborne had come to Ryanair by way of his connection with Tony Ryan. He had started his career as a solicitor, and, in running the New York office of A&L Goodbody, had done much of the legal and contractual work in GPA's early years of raising finance in the USA and cutting deals for aircraft purchases. Displaying the independence and self-confidence that was to be his hallmark, Osborne said no to the offer of a full-time job with GPA, deciding that the demands Ryan would place on him, and its impact on his lifestyle, would be too onerous. But he joined Ryanair as a non-executive director in 1995 and was regarded by many as essential to the successful stock-market flotation of the company in 1997. He and O'Leary bonded, sharing not just a love of horses but very similar views on how to do business, corporate governance and probity. They shared a natural self-confidence and, like O'Leary, Osborne was often impatient with those who did not share his views or drive, although he was unfailingly courteous in expressing his opinions. He liked that O'Leary was not interested in ostentatious displays of wealth or influence, contrasting his behaviour favourably with other billionaire business associates.

O'Leary was one of many who spoke at a special memorial service for Osborne held at Trinity College Dublin in late August 2017. According to the *Irish Times*, 'O'Leary delivered a funny, but also searingly emotional, tribute to his friend, who, he joked, had "too much personality" to be a solicitor.'

Osborne had been a more than useful sounding-board

and he was missed particularly in the difficult months for O'Leary and Ryanair (for unconnected reasons) that followed his passing. Had he been around, it is possible that O'Leary would not have blundered in the way that put all of the good work of *Always Getting Better* under serious threat.

PART 4
Crisis

23. Mistakes and miscalculations

Michael O'Leary didn't like to be surprised by his management team. If they brought bad news, they also had to bring solutions. That was the rule. Crises were rare because problems were anticipated and solved. Control was rarely, if ever, lost. O'Leary was seldom rendered speechless, but he was on Wednesday, 13 September 2017, albeit only momentarily. He listened as Michael Hickey, his director of operations, confessed that a staffing issue with pilots that O'Leary had been assured was under control was far from it, and that the consequences would be very serious – that Ryanair might not be able to provide all of the flights it had promised to customers. O'Leary realized immediately that he had a headache to treat, but he failed initially to grasp how painful it would become and how long it would last.

Just how it had got to this point also astonished O'Leary. He had known for months that there was a potential problem. It had been flagged. The issue of what was called 'rostering' was a live one with Ryanair's management group from early June, on the agenda for each weekly team meeting and always discussed. The availability of cabin crew was a related issue, so, while Hickey got the pilots to sort out, Eddie Wilson was put in charge of cabin crew. The expectation was that it would be difficult to manage, but possible, and therefore that it would be achieved. That proved to be the case with cabin crew, so why not with pilots?

Every Monday morning, O'Leary was assured that, while

it would be tight, there would be more than enough pilots available to fly the aircraft. After all, Ryanair had flown a record 12.7 million passengers in August, an increase of 10 per cent on the same month last year, and if punctuality was dropping, this was put down to issues such as passengers' misuse of the baggage allocation. O'Leary assumed the Z-team was performing as usual, doing exactly what their boss demanded they do, and it was all business as normal.

Until it wasn't. While O'Leary was furious with others that it had come to this, he was as angry with himself for not paying sufficient attention to the issue and for being too trusting of his staff. He subsequently decided that Hickey was not entirely at fault, that there had been 'a cover-up' by a small number of staff, although loyalty and a desire to limit the damage meant he would not identify those responsible to anyone outside of the airline. 'We get a weekly report saying the rosters for the next four weeks are issued and all duties are covered,' he said. 'It turned out the rosters were issued and all duties were not covered.' Having got through the busy summer months, 'We were surprised and shocked that we fell over in September.'

That was one way of putting it. The truth was that there simply weren't enough pilots available to cater for Ryanair's ever-growing number of flights. It was a shortfall of just thirty, but that was enough to throw a spanner in the works. The pilots Ryanair had available to it – about 4,200 of them – could fly a maximum of 900 hours in a year. Too many had gone over their limit and not enough of them were willing to cancel their holiday plans – many took a month in October at the end of the hectic summer schedule – to fill the gaps, despite generous financial offers to do so.

On the same day that he went to inform O'Leary, Hickey

made a desperate attempt to sort things out, delivered in language that was meant to hide his panic. He sent his pilots an operational update, reiterating the desire to shorten their holiday leave in the last quarter of the calendar year and asking them to fly during their time off because of a 'unique one-off issue'. He blamed capacity delays by air-traffic control across Europe for increasing the hours that pilots spent in the air. He even blamed the weather.

To make things worse, this all happened a day before Ryanair was to be the subject of a major ruling at the European Court of Justice (ECJ). Cabin crew at Ryanair's Charleroi Airport base in Belgium had challenged Ryanair in a local court to have their contracts of employment governed in that country. That might have seemed obvious to most, but it wasn't the Ryanair way. It argued that staff and contractors had contracts with an Irish company, which meant that any disputes had to be adjudicated upon in the Irish courts. That was easier said than done for all sorts of reasons, including costs and language, and laws in Ireland that were often perceived as more sympathetic towards companies, even if rooted in EU law. It gave Ryanair considerable flexibility in the use of its staff, as well as reducing the cost of paying them, with about half of the pilots on third-party contracts, and 40 per cent of cabin crew pay and 30 per cent of pilot pay based on performance.

Daniel Röska, an aviation analyst at the New York stockbroker Bernstein, and someone who had recommended earlier in the year that investors sell their shares in the airline because its growth prospects were limited, was among those who immediately stated that this was a big problem for the airline. He estimated that roughly 60 per cent of Ryanair cockpit and cabin crew were based in jurisdictions with less favourable labour laws for the employees than in Ireland. Ryanair also did long-term deals at individual bases, so as not to give the same pay and benefits in all countries in which it operated. That wasn't the only benefit to Ryanair of the arrangements: crews could return to their home base each night, allowing the airline to avoid costs involved with overnight rest stops.

So, the day after the pilot crisis upended the management team, the ECJ ruled that Belgian staff and other employees based outside Ireland 'have the option of bringing proceedings before courts of the place where they perform the essential part of their duties'. In other words, it seemed that Ryanair could not continue to impose Irish contracts – and, by extension, Irish labour laws – on its pilots and cabin crew, who had to go to Ireland to make their arguments in the courts there. The ECJ ruled that jurisdiction clauses in employment contracts, which sought to prevent workers from taking proceedings before courts in the country where they were based, were not enforceable. It set out a range of criteria for courts to determine the place where employees habitually carried out their work.

It seemed like good news for workers . . . and bad news for Ryanair. Stockbroker analysts who followed the company suggested it could add €100 million annually to Ryanair's costs. Ryanair shares closed down 3 per cent in a day off the back of analysts' suggestion that the ruling could result in new claims from crew in countries other than Belgium to get improved terms and conditions.

Typically, though, O'Leary rejected any interpretation of the judgment as being bad for Ryanair: 'Our contracts comply fully with EU employment law. We expect no change to staffing agreements, contracts or labour costs. This won't change Ryanair's cost base by one cent.' It was an argument with some validity. While the ruling would give local courts more oversight of working terms and conditions, it did not change the legal basis, in Irish law, of those contracts. This was because the ECJ had rejected the claims made by the plaintiffs that the home base of airline crew should be the *sole* determinant of where labour disputes could be heard. Ryanair argued that Irish labour laws, which have adopted all EU directives on employment rights, offered better protection than some other EU countries. 'For example, maternity leave in Ireland is more favourable than in Belgium and the Irish minimum wage is also among the highest in Europe.'

Trade unions disagreed. 'Ryanair's claim that this judgment supports them stretches reality beyond its breaking point. It's pure wish fulfilment. The verdict is clear. They lost. Big time,' said Ruwan Subasinghe, legal adviser to the International Transport Workers' Federation (ITWF), which represents 700 transport trade unions from 150 countries. Geert van Calster, a professor at the Institute for European Law in Leuven, said the Ryanair ruling was not the 'final blow' for the airline but would probably set a precedent in an area where EU governments were becoming more sensitive to the rights of mobile workers.

The events of Thursday, 14 September, caught the attention of investors, but it was what happened the following day that grabbed the media and customers – an event that made September 2017 the most difficult month in O'Leary's career.

The Friday started badly. Ryanair announced, without notice, the cancellation of 82 flights that day, adding that 80 more wouldn't fly on Saturday. The only explanation offered was 'circumstances outside our control'. Twitter went into meltdown, with furious and disbelieving customers wondering what the hell was going on at the airline. Later that afternoon, the big news hit: Ryanair announced to the world that it would cancel an average of 50 flights a day for the next six weeks, about 42 days of disruption, affecting about 315,000 passengers. The clincher was that it could not immediately confirm which flights would be affected. That left 18 million people with a booking and no idea if they'd be one of the unlucky ones who'd be left at the airport. It left everyone else who was planning a trip deciding if it would be safer to book with another airline. The company that had made customer satisfaction the bedrock of *Always Getting Better* had blundered into a communications disaster but seemed blind to it. No matter what they said, the key number was not 315,000 – it was 18 million.

The statement issued to the stock exchange by Ryanair late that afternoon was full of excuses, but they were not convincing and arguably made things worse. It said the cancellations would improve its 'system-wide punctuality, which has fallen below 80 per cent in the first two weeks of September'. Ryanair claimed that by reducing its scheduled flying programme over the next six weeks by less than 2 per cent (of its over 2,500 daily flights), it would create additional standby aircraft, which would help restore on-time performance to its 90 per cent average. 'We apologize sincerely to the small number of customers affected by these cancellations, and will be doing our utmost to arrange alternative flights and/or full refunds for them,' ran the not terribly sympathetic apology. It wasn't exactly a *mea culpa*. Instead, the blame was put on air-traffic-control-capacity issues and industrial strikes, weather disruptions and the impact of increased holiday allocations to pilots and cabin crew. It was in that last point that the truth mostly lay.

It stemmed from a technical issue about which the public

probably cared little – all they wanted was confirmation that the flights they'd booked would be available – but it's worth examining to explain how the biggest cock-up in Ryanair history occurred. The crisis was rooted in a change in the approach to governing the hours pilots spent in the air. The rules, known as flight-time limitations (FTLs), do not allow pilots to fly more than 900 hours per year, and have been applied across the EU for decades. The Irish Aviation Authority (IAA) regulates this in the Republic of Ireland. The regulations also govern how many hours a pilot can fly in a day, week or month. The focus is safety, rather than time off or holidays.

Ryanair had always run its pilot schedule in parallel with its financial year – the twelve months to the end of March. The IAA insisted this be changed to a straight calendar year, January to December. Aer Lingus had made the necessary changes a year earlier, but Ryanair had been granted additional time because of its size. While it was preparing to phase in the new FTL system, Ryanair continued to allow pilots to take holidays in four-week blocks. The combination of the leave and the switch to the new system left Ryanair without enough pilots to man scheduled flights and provide the normal back-up required.

When the news broke of the cancellations, Daniel Röska immediately provided analysis to the media, saying the obvious explanation was that the pilots ran up against the legal limits of air hours and the company was unable to pull people back in from holiday. 'That means someone in the organization made a decision to run the ship very tight, with very little standby crews. That was not only over a short period, the restrictions and the holidays have been known for a while, the rostering software had the data. It is likely that during the week prior, as delays happened and pilots used up more hours, it sent dominos falling. Then it is likely a more economic decision about how you deal with that in the medium term. You could try to roll it through and incur delays and hiccups or you can take a more extreme measure to cancel flights and disappoint some passengers. For them it is likely the cheaper choice.'

There was near-panic at Ryanair HQ over the weekend as the company monitored the pages of negative commentary in the newspapers, which highlighted the problems and gave short shrift to the company's excuses. Worse, arguably, was the stuff circulating on social media, which was harder to combat. There were stories of stranded passengers everywhere, particularly people who couldn't get back home and return to work, ruined wedding parties and outbound holidays, and of Manchester United fans fearing they wouldn't be able to travel to Lisbon for the Champions League game with Benfica the following Tuesday.

Ryanair had made an enormous miscalculation as to how its decision would be interpreted and perceived by the media, investors and customers. By the start of the following week, O'Leary had to go front and central, and face both the media and investment analysts in separate meetings. 'We make mistakes,' O'Leary said. 'This time we made a major boo-boo.' This was one time when bad publicity could not be used to sell extra seat tickets. O'Leary knew he couldn't hide or send Jacobs or anyone else out to bat for the airline. He called a press conference at the Dublin HQ and, separately, organized a conference call for dozens of stockbroker analysts. The tack he chose to take was apologetic. Not for the first time, O'Leary was prepared to say that mistakes had been made, that Ryanair had got it wrong.

But there were signs that the company still didn't grasp just how bad things were. At the press conference O'Leary sat under an *Always Getting Better* banner, as if this were a sales opportunity. He repeated the party line from the previous Friday – allocation of holidays, weather, air-traffic-control disruptions – but to his critics it was the type of blather he would have mocked had it come from competitors. Harder facts were needed, and some were forthcoming. For the first time, he released a full list of the cancellations and said the airline would adopt a 'no quibble' policy when it came to processing the compensation claims allowed for under EU legislation. He said that, by cancelling the flights of 315,000 people over the next six weeks, Ryanair was ensuring that a further 9 million people would not be hit with delays. He said everything would be sorted within six weeks, as if that meant everyone should ignore the six weeks in between.

True to form, he was as much combative as contrite and said he did not expect to lose much business: 'The reality is when you're flying with somebody else you are paying far more money for the privilege, and you will have to put up with more delays. It is clearly a mess, but, in the context of an operation where we operate more than 2,500 flights every day, it is reasonably small, but that doesn't take away the inconvenience we've caused to people. This issue will not recur in 2018 as Ryanair goes back on to a twelve-month calendar leave. Ryanair is not short of pilots – we were able to fully crew our peak summer schedule.'

He may have been confident and combative, but he also had to show some humility – it had gone beyond the point where he could brazen it out. 'This is our mess-up. When we make a mess in Ryanair, we come out with our hands up.' That wasn't going to be good enough for many of those assembled, who remembered how he had denigrated rivals in the past for their shortcomings. When asked if he felt like a clown, he did not dismiss the question shortly. 'I think, given the performance of our rostering department over the last week, a description of me as a clown is appropriate in the circumstances. Yes, it was short notice and, yes, it was unexpected, and for that I sincerely apologize. We did not focus on the concerns or the worries of customers. I say sorry.'

In an unusual move for him, he even accepted that there was reputational impact, and that if any organization that Ryanair did business with had 'made a mess' on this scale, he would have been calling for heads to roll. This was not going to happen at Ryanair, however. He was firm when asked if he would fall on his sword: 'I don't think my head should roll – I need to stay here and fix this.'

In his presentation to analysts that same day, O'Leary repeated much of what he had said to the media but, to what was a more important audience to him, he hinted that he would take steps to increase the size of crew per aircraft and to retain pilots. Röska pointed out that such initiatives could lead to lower productivity and higher wage costs. Robin Byde, transport analyst at Cantor Fitzgerald, noted: 'They have been running their network very hot for some time and are still maintaining very ambitious growth plans. I see what's happened as almost a result of over-trading. This will make investors question their growth plans and margin expectations more aggressively. It's perhaps a bit of a turning point in the growth story.'

It didn't stop there. Ryanair kept having to issue new information. On 20 September – the day before its AGM – Ryanair issued an update, emphasizing that just 2,100 of its 103,000 flights over the next six weeks were cancelled. It claimed that all 315,000 customers had received email notices advising them of their flight changes and offering alternative flights, refunds and EU261 notices (for payment of compensation). It said that by the end of that process, it would have accommodated over 175,000 customers on alternative Ryanair flights, accounting for over 55 per cent of affected customers, and to have administered more than 63,000 flight refunds. It had taken on extra customer-service staff to expedite the backlog of flight-change requests and refunds. It expected to have processed over 300,000 requests (over 95 per cent of affected customers) by the end of the week, or within six days of customers being notified of the cancellations. It seemed it was offering up deft administration as a palliative, but that wasn't going to cut it with inconvenienced and disappointed customers.

O'Leary had a further chance to address the issue at the AGM, which was held at the company HQ in Dublin rather than at a hotel, to save money. AGMs are generally boring affairs, although Ryanair's were sometimes marginally more interesting, if only because O'Leary, rather than his chairman David Bonderman, tended to draw questions and engage with them, another sign of how he dominated the company. It didn't seem possible that this particular AGM could be boring, though. Ryanair had lost almost €1.8 billion in market value in previous days, and the CEO had been forced to defend an unprecedented error that he seemed not to know anything about until it was too late. If O'Leary liked to draw questions and engage with them, it seemed he'd have plenty of chance to do that today.

An unusually large throng of reporters attended, from media beyond Ireland, too, although they were not permitted to record or broadcast the proceedings. O'Leary spent over an hour walking up and down the room, dressed in an open-necked salmon-coloured shirt, blazer and jeans, speaking without a microphone ('because we're a low-cost airline'), as he fielded questions from individual shareholders and provided the further necessary apologies about disruption to passengers caused by the recent cancellations.

'I spoke four years ago about the widespread perception that flying with Ryanair was not an enjoyable experience,' Brian Graham, a small shareholder, said to him. 'You took it on the chin and you changed it – wonderful. But the gung-ho aspect seems to have crept back into the company and in the way that you did not see this coming. Surely that's got something to do with the way that you deal with your pilots. It's not good enough, and I feel it's being done in my name.'

'We have upset people entirely unnecessarily,' O'Leary acknowledged. 'So, yes, we make mistakes. But we are not gung-ho, I promise you.'

Graham continued to press him on the relationship with pilots: 'It seems to me that there are bad relations with the pilots in Ryanair.' Graham pointed out that he had frequently heard that working for the airline was hard and management was a bit 'too severe'. O'Leary replied that Ryanair had recently recruited 125 pilots, who would begin flying with it as they completed short periods of training in coming weeks. It planned to hire 600 between then and the following June and would have little problem finding them. 'There is a waiting list of 2,500 pilots who are gagging to join Ryanair,' he said with his trademark exaggeration.

O'Leary conceded that Ryanair faced some competition to employ pilots, but he insisted that the cancellations were simply due to a mix-up over holiday rosters, although it was a 'mess' and a result of 'serious management failure'. He maintained that 'it was the right operational decision, but was badly handled. I genuinely regret we upset and worried millions of our customers over last weekend because they weren't sure if their flight was going to be cancelled.'

He said it would cost Ryanair about €25 million to fix the problem, and there would be a slower rate of growth as Ryanair would slightly reduce its traffic: 'Our monthly growth from November 2017 to March 2018 will slow from 9 per cent to 4 per cent. Our full-year traffic of 131 million will now moderate to 129 million, which is 7.5 per cent up on last year.' Significantly, he said he still expected that profits would come in at between €1.4 billion and €1.45 billion.

The meeting was not nearly as fractious as had been expected, even though there were other issues that had to be addressed which had the potential for trouble. The previous year, almost a fifth of investors had protested about pay for O'Leary and his management team, the third year in a row they had done so. Ryanair was the subject of campaigns by three advisory companies, ISS, Glass Lewis and PIRC, whose recommendations were used by many asset managers and pension funds when deciding how to vote on motions at AGMs. They said O'Leary's total pay – €3.26 million for the financial year – was not excessive, but expressed concerns about the level of disclosure as to how his bonus was calculated. His pay included a performance-related bonus of €950,000 and basic salary of just over €1 million. 'My view of shareholders voting against my pay package is: if you don't like it, don't vote against it – sell your shares,' O'Leary said bluntly. It passed.

There was another issue that had to be addressed: the composition of the board, and the apparently excessive amount of time some directors had spent on it. The UK's combined code of corporate governance, to which Irish plcs are meant to subscribe, recommended that non-executive directors should serve no more than nine years on an individual company's board. The reason is to avoid the creation of a cosy club, in which directors or management do what they like without sufficient scrutiny, and to prevent any one person becoming too dominant. Bonderman had joined as chairman in 1996 and Kyran McLaughlin, from Davy Stockbrokers, had joined sixteen years earlier. Cawley and Millar were new to the board but had been executives for decades. If Osborne had not died prematurely just weeks earlier, he would have been into his twenty-second year on the board. The only recent appointment was Stan McCarthy, outgoing boss of Kerry Group, who some saw as a potential replacement for Bonderman as chair. There were legitimate questions as to whether O'Leary was too powerful.

In advance of the AGM, a number of advisory firms questioned Bonderman's independence. ISS and PIRC advised against the re-election of Bonderman, blaming the chairman for corporate-governance failures. Bonderman had become something of an obvious target. He had recently resigned from the board of the car-transport innovator Uber after a major controversy following a sexist comment he made during a meeting. He remained on the boards of four other listed companies, including Kite Pharma and Caesars Entertainment Corporation. 'These external time commitments may undermine his ability to serve effectively in his role as board chair,' ISS argued. ISS also expressed concern that less than one fifth of Ryanair's directors could be considered independent. The American teachers' pension fund CalSTRS voted against the re-election of nearly the entire board, including O'Leary. However, shareholders voted all of them in, by majorities exceeding 90 per cent.

The AGM done, and with far less acrimony than anticipated, O'Leary seemed emboldened by the ease with which he had dealt with his shareholders. He strode out of the meeting at its conclusion and invited journalists upstairs to another room for an impromptu press conference. If his ego was the cause of this move, it was to prove a mistake – a big one.

His adrenalin was flowing after his performance and he was in combative form. The journalists gathered and for the next hour he held forth, boasting and parrying: 'Our traffic this year is up 11 per cent. Our share price year-to-date is up 15, 16 per cent. The only thing that is down is our fares. The underlying business continues to operate very well. You guys [in the media] are all excited, the end of the world is nigh, the Ryanair model is fallen asunder. Yeah. We'll just get on with it, delivering 91 per cent punctuality, and we will get back to running the business. And you guys will run off and get excited about something else.'

That might have been the case if he hadn't taken aim at his pilots in answer to another question. It provoked a response from the Tony Ryan handbook of opinions on pilots: 'If you sit in the cockpit of a plane flying at 400, 500 miles an hour going in through landing in 40, 50 feet of visibility, you have untold respect for pilots. That doesn't mean they don't do a very easy job, and they are very well paid for doing what is an easy job. We are in an era now where the computer does most of the flying. They are no longer doing the flying themselves. But they are very skilled professionals. They do a very skilled job and . . . where our pilots demonstrate that skill is landing in thunderstorms or fog. But are they hard-working? No. Are 900 hours a year or eighteen hours a week, on average, likely to generate fatigue? No.'

O'Leary didn't stop there . . . and tellingly, there was no

one from Ryanair confident enough to stop him. When he was on a roll, putting on a show, nobody dared. He accused some pilots of being 'full of their own self-importance' and called them 'precious'. He questioned the requirement for co-pilots, who were only there to 'make sure the first fella doesn't fall asleep and knock over one of the computer controls'. Aer Lingus pilots, O'Leary argued, were 'peacocks' because they were so fond of the status symbols of the job, such as peaked hats. Ryanair pilots were different, however: 'They are really good guys . . . We don't tolerate an awful lot of the peacock nonsense that goes on.' But even though he added the statement that 'You cannot fail but to respect and admire the professionalism of not just Ryanair's pilots, but all commercial pilots', the media cherry-picked from his comments. He had said enough. And that final attempt at even-handedness would be lost in the hullabaloo that was to follow.

24. Omnishambles

If O'Leary initially felt the AGM and press conference were a good day's work and that he could get back to business, he was soon to realize that he had set the stage for further conflict and more chaos. His opinion of pilots was second nature to him, so maybe he thought others agreed, or that it would be taken as humour. Whatever he thought, he was wrong.

As he saw air travel as simply an airborne taxi service, it meant he regarded pilots as no more than taxi-drivers. That piloting an aircraft is an even more intellectually demanding and stressful occupation than driving a car, that it comes with huge responsibility for the passengers and requires considerable training didn't seem to come into it. While he might mention respect every now and then, O'Leary did not like what he saw as the arrogance, entitlement and self-regard of pilots, making demands about pay and conditions as they strutted around in their uniforms. He made them bring their own food and drinks on to flights, but then banned them from using the on-board microwaves to avoid paying the cleaning costs. He rationed paper. He made them pay for their bi-annual medical examinations, which they had to do on their own time, and made a monthly deduction from pay to cover the cost of uniforms. He charged pilots to be trained to fly his aircraft. He repeatedly wrote to pilots warning of the dangers to their careers if they agitated for union recognition.

O'Leary had held the whip hand for years as resentment among the pilots festered, and occasionally broke out into confrontations that ended in the courts. He believed that he was still in control, that he had bent the pilots to his will. At the post-AGM press conference he was asked about a mounting campaign among pilots to secure negotiating rights for their unions. He claimed that Ryanair pilots did not want unionization: 'That may surprise the unions and some of the journalists here, but we don't expect that to change.'

It was a consistent mantra from which there was no deviation. 'We work very hard to keep the unions out of Ryanair,' he told the *Sunday Times* in 2016, although he insisted that Ryanair did not prevent staff joining unions. 'We negotiate five-year pay deals with our pilots and our cabin crew. They are guaranteed pay increases each year. Unions were a force for good at the beginning of the twentieth century. But look at the amount of legal protection people have now in their jobs. All of that legislation came from Europe. Unions add nothing to it any more.' As he ranted in free flow in the heady moments after nailing the AGM, he said 'hell would freeze over' before the airline would allow unionization.

It may have been a bluff, it may have been an unthinking bit of banter, but his colleagues saw it as a fundamental reaffirmation of his position. He was assuming that supply of pilots would not be an issue, not when other airlines – such as Air Berlin and Alitalia – were tottering on the brink of collapse. Their pilots would want to move to Ryanair. This belief is what gave him such unerring confidence in the face of a crisis. But what O'Leary and the airline didn't take into account was that the pilots also held a strong belief that gave them confidence. They believed the balance of power was shifting, according to the laws of supply and demand that O'Leary so loved, and that O'Leary might just be miscalculating.

The reality was that a shortage of pilots was developing in

at least some parts of Europe and that, as the region's biggest carrier, it was a bigger problem for Ryanair than anyone else. It wasn't just a recruitment issue but a retention one, too – although this was the source of much dispute between Ryanair and the Irish Airline Pilots' Association. IALPA claimed that Ryanair had lost 719 pilots that year, up from 407 a year earlier. It was also reported that the average length of service of Ryanair pilots was now as low as four years. Such claims infuriated O'Leary, as much because of who was making them as anything else. The airline retorted that it had recruited and would train more than 650 pilots, 'not only to replace these leavers/retirees but also to crew up for the 50 new Boeing aircraft we will buy' before May 2018.

However, O'Leary was aware that other airlines offered more attractive working conditions: 'If some long-haul carrier shows up in Dublin offering long-haul flights, and says, "You can fly to New York and fly back two days later, or you can fly to Luton four times a day", I can understand why.' Norwegian Air was seeking forty pilots for its routes out of Dublin alone. One Middle Eastern airline apparently had over 140 Ryanair pilots waiting to take up positions as they became available. So there were other airlines to which the pilots could move and, such was the resentment many harboured towards Ryanair, they would move given half the chance.

This mistrust ran deep. The pilots were furious about O'Leary's description of their working hours, arguing that their duties went much further than eighteen hours a week. O'Leary was talking about 'block hours', the hours when the aircraft was in motion. He was not counting the hours pilots spend completing paperwork, working through weather delays or commuting across Europe to Ryanair hubs. The combination of mistrust and anger proved to be a powerful motivator. O'Leary's comments hit home, and provoked an unprecedented response.

The pilots began to organize more effectively than ever before, contacting each other via WhatsApp groups to protect against detection. O'Leary believed he could continue to divide and conquer, and that his immediate problem could be solved with money, much as he disliked spending it. He pointed out that the terms and conditions of the pilots' contracts required them to give up leave if requested, but he tempered it with a sweetener: 'We'll pay supplements in places where either we have a shortage of pilots or we want to recruit more pilots.' His idea was to 'buy back' holidays – in other words, asking pilots not to take their entitlements in return for bonuses of about €12,000 for captains. According to O'Leary, staff had responded positively to the proposal and there were no problems with the representative councils in his key airports of Dublin, Stansted, Frankfurt and Berlin. Apparently they responded with 'delight' at the news of the bonus and 'have been in regular contact with the airline offering to work days off, to work one week of their allocated month of leave, and offering to go public to correct the false claims made about them, and Ryanair, by competitor airline pilots in certain media outlets'. He dismissed anyone who said differently as members of 'anonymous, circular emails that have the same credibility as Twitter feeds'.

The picture he painted was of across-the-board cooperation, but it wasn't as simple as that. Some pilots could not give up holidays because they had already flown as many miles that year as was allowed. Others decided they would not be forced to offer goodwill, especially when they heard some of the carrot-and-stick rhetoric coming from O'Leary: 'We have some goodies to discuss with pilots, but if pilots misbehave, that would be the end of the discussion of the goodies. If there was a blue flu in your base in Bergamo or something, your employee representative council won't get a meeting for the next sixteen months and you can kiss good-bye to any increased pay.'

Eddie Wilson, Ryanair's chief people officer, weighed in, too, threatening pilots that they risked missing out on big pay rises if they were 'misled by the false promises' of unions. He laid down the Ryanair law: 'We will not enter into writing, or meetings, with competitor airline pilots/unions, or whatever they call themselves this week . . . whose sole aim is to prevent you from accessing a big pay increase next month. The only way to ensure that your base shares in this upside – from November – is to support your ERC's [employee representative councils] reaching agreement over the next three weeks. If this doesn't happen, then these pay increases may be delayed until December, or next year, or not delivered at all.' Whether Ryanair realized it or not, it was language designed to antagonize.

What Ryanair couldn't say was how many of its 4,200 pilots had accepted its proposals. It couldn't name all the bases that had agreed to them either. Instead, Ryanair tried to ram through the proposals without negotiations. What was meant to be the appearance of strength began to look like the taunts of a bully . . . and bullies often act as they do because of fear. A company statement read: 'We will not respond or accede to anonymous demands made via unsigned emails for group or regional meetings, or for union interference at these internal ERC meetings. Many of our pilots and ERCs have confirmed that these unsigned letters were drafted by pilots/unions of competitor airlines who wish to pursue an industrial-relations agenda at the expense of Ryanair and its pilots.'

But it was nowhere near as clear-cut as Ryanair claimed. An email from the Stansted ERC to its pilots told them that 'The company made the decision to implement the new additional allowance before the meeting' and, as a result, the Stansted pilots rejected the additional payment, even though it would have made them 20 per cent better off than their counterparts at the airport. They worried that Ryanair had committed to paying the supplement only for the duration of the existing base agreements, many of which would end in 2020, and that it would stop paying the supplements at that point. They wanted the money paid as part of their core pay, as a permanent addition.

To Ryanair's shock, the pilots held firm. The ERCs representing staff at seventeen Ryanair bases said the majority of their colleagues had rejected what had been put forward because it was 'not an adequate offer and is being met with great resistance'. It was quickly announced that ERC members in Dublin, Shannon and Barcelona had joined other bases in rejecting the offer. A letter sent to Michael Hickey stated that the 'pilot market is changing', and Ryanair would 'need to change the ways which the pilots and management work together to ensure a stable and common future for everyone'. The ERCs wanted contracts 'based on benchmarks with comparable competitors for each individual region', arguing this would help pilot retention. It demanded the new contracts by 1 January 2018 and added that, as 'pilots are not trained as negotiators, we will be bringing professional assistance to our negotiations'. In other words, it wanted the unions in the room.

Further reports of a letter being circulated among some pilots calling for a work-to rule by colleagues did little to assuage worries among Ryanair management of further disruptions. It included the line that 'with immediate effect, the pilot workforce at the bases [airports] listed below rescind the goodwill that has been extended toward the company for many years, including working days off and turning up early. In short, we shall now "work to rule".' Goodwill is a very valuable asset in any company, and loss of it can hurt the bottom line. This is something O'Leary was perhaps guilty of underestimating.

This point was taken up strongly by Evan Cullen of IALPA in late September 2017 in a damning article in the *Irish Times*:

The handling of the current disaster shows the ongoing depth of disregard for passengers' most basic interests – to receive the service they paid for and to be treated with respect and consideration. It is IALPA's opinion that Ryanair's pilots have been shown the same level of disrespect for many years and it is reflected in the low average service length of Ryanair pilots.

An aggressive expansionist strategy cannot be built on an unsound company culture that repeatedly drives experienced and committed pilots away to other airlines. Our IALPA members in Ryanair are frontline staff, yet they consistently report an underlying culture of fear, reinforced by a precarious (contractor) employment model for large numbers of pilots. This culture might generate short-term conformity, but hides negative long-term effects, of which the current difficulties are a symptom. It suggests pilots are a short-term, expendable commodity, rather than a long-term company asset. The Ryanair model seems to alienate and drive pilots away, rather than encourage them to remain with the company.

The Ryanair board has a choice: to gloss over these problems, or to strategically change to an employment model that creates a sustainable working environment for Ryanair staff, and a predictable service for its customers.

The problem was bigger than anticipated by Ryanair management, and likely to grow further. Data from Indeed, the world's largest job site, showed that airlines' demand for pilots was already outstripping supply, resulting in more than a quarter of pilot vacancies taking more than sixty days to fill. An economist at Indeed noted that 'According to Boeing's latest outlook report, the airline industry will need more than 500,000 pilots to meet extraordinary demands over the next twenty years.'

As events unfolded, O'Leary quickly realized that he had made a mistake in his post-AGM press conference. Unlike other CEOs of his era – who have a tendency to double down on their mistakes – O'Leary decided he would have to backtrack. He flew to London on the morning after the AGM for an investor presentation to major shareholders, but he was already receiving messages telling him that his press conference performance had backfired and inflamed the pilots. He did not have an easy time of it during the presentation.

He decided that it was time to call upon Cawley and Millar, the senior managers who had retired in 2013 as *Always Getting Better* kicked off and were now part-time directors. O'Leary was astute enough to know that he needed their help and guidance. When he returned to Dublin that Friday afternoon, he went into conclave with the pair – something that was noted among the Z-team, who felt this was an implied indictment of their performances over the previous week. O'Leary already knew what he had to do, but he talked it through with his two colleagues and was bolstered by their encouragement and reassurance. He emerged from that meeting with a number of decisions. He decided that, instead of offering supplements, he would raise the base pay of many pilots from the beginning of October. He withdrew threats to unilaterally enforce leave. It was an olive branch, but would it be enough?

In spite of O'Leary's movement on these key issues, there remained a very pressing problem: who was going to fly all the planes between now and the end of the year? The error that had caused all this in the first place still remained to be addressed and solved. There were lots of unhappy people around the Ryanair HQ as the crisis rumbled on, but unhappiest of all was Michael Hickey, who, despite O'Leary's initial intention to support him, had to become the fall-guy for what had happened.

Removing Hickey was not unfair, given the circumstances, even if O'Leary would have preferred not to do so. He had been with the airline since 1988 – and in his current role since 2014 – so O'Leary wasn't going to shaft him. In an act of loyalty, he gave Hickey an advisory role as compensation, on undisclosed terms, and let it be known, in his public comments, that he wasn't angry with his COO: 'Over the past thirty years Mick Hickey has made an enormous contribution to Ryanair, especially the quality and safety of our engineering and operations functions. He will be a hard act to replace, which is why we are grateful he has agreed to continue in an advisory role to smooth the transition to a successor and to complete a number of large projects he is currently working on, including a multi-year engine maintenance contract and new hangar projects in Seville and Madrid.'

Hickey moved on, but the problems remained. It was as if the pilots had opened a Pandora's box, and all the disgruntled feelings and resentment had come flying out. One crew member wrote a lengthy article for the *Irish Times*, anonymously, that outlined the reasons for the widespread unhappiness at the company: 'We need to get paid for our duty time, not our flight time, and we need to be paid for home standby and rostered flights. Today I clocked in at 5 a.m. and finished at 3 p.m., with a total of five hours in the air. Those five hours are all I will get paid for even though I was at work for ten hours. I have colleagues who were on standby and called in. They had to take taxis to the airport at their own expense because public transport was not running. Then they waited three or four hours, after which the flight was cancelled, so they went home, and they won't get any payment for that at all.'

She told of 'friends working in Ryanair's smaller bases . . . where the number of flights are significantly cut in winter, who have been told that they will have to transfer to other bases in Europe – and cover all the costs themselves – or they will be forced to take unpaid leave for months . . . If we call in sick more than three times we can be called to Dublin to explain ourselves, and if we can't explain then we might be fired.' She described the pressure to deliver onboard sales and unrealistic targets, and the infighting between staff who were not allowed to cooperate and pool resources. 'When we raised this with management we were told that Ryanair doesn't do teamwork: it wants us to compete with each other,' she alleged.

Ryanair provided a brief response in the *Irish Times*, using it, as usual, to talk up Ryanair and put the boot in with unions:

Ryanair cabin crew earn up to €40,000 per annum and enjoy great terms and conditions, including job security, a recently negotiated five-year pay deal with guaranteed pay increases, a five on, three off, roster (a bank holiday weekend every week), a legal max of 900 flight hours per annum (just eighteen hours per week), great sales commissions which further boost pay, free training, sick pay and an annual uniform payment of up to €425. This is why we currently have a waiting list of over 3,000 young people who all hope to join Ryanair's cabin-crew team, at a time when other airlines and their unions are negotiating job cuts, pension cuts and pay cuts. We don't comment on rumour or speculation, especially when it originates from competitor airline unions.

These were just sideshows, however, compared to the need to keep planes in the air. People might have thought it was all about damage limitation now, but O'Leary was about to shock his customers and investors for a second time, by doing something that even just one week earlier he swore would not be necessary: he was going to ground even more flights.

Nearly a week after the AGM, Ryanair issued its most detailed statement yet, and it outlined more cancellations, this time 18,000 flights, though it tried to dress things up as a plan to 'slow its growth this winter'. It announced that from November 2017 to March 2018 it would fly twenty-five fewer aircraft from its fleet – effectively putting them into storage – than intended originally, and then, from April, ten fewer again. The net was thrown out wider, to affect even more than the original 315,000 passengers. Ryanair put a spin on that, too, in its stock-exchange announcement: 'We have less than 400,000 customers booked on these flights (which affects less than one flight per day across our 200 airports over the five-month winter period), and many of these flights have zero bookings at this time.' It emphasized that it was only a tiny proportion of its annual 800,000 flights, and that less than 1 per cent of customers would be affected.

All of the affected customers received an email giving them between five weeks' and five months' notice of these schedule changes, offering them alternative flights or full refunds, and a €40 (€80 return) travel voucher to be used on any Ryanair service between October and March 2018. The same offer was made to those affected by the previous cancellation, in addition to the accommodation and refunds they had already received, because the initial compensation to them had caused enormous controversy.

Chief marketing officer Kenny Jacobs tried to spin a new story to cover this latest debacle, as he sought to reassure and calm tempers: 'Our winter schedule reductions will ensure that no further flights will be cancelled for rostering reasons and our first-wave punctuality has increased further this week to 97 per cent. Our expanded customer-service team are assisting all affected customers with their requests as we try to resolve any problems we have created for them . . . We sincerely apologize to those customers who have been affected by last week's flight cancellations, or these sensible schedule changes announced today. While over 99 per cent of our 129 million customers will not have been affected by any cancellations or disruptions, we deeply regret any doubt we caused existing customers last week about Ryanair's reliability, or the risk of further cancellations.'

It was another blow to Ryanair's credibility and reputation, but what O'Leary's plan achieved was to allow Ryanair to roster all of the pilot leave needed in October, November and December, allowing it to start 2018 with a clean slate. The measures would create twenty-five more spare aircraft and more than 100 daily extra standby pilots from November to March. Ryanair also gave some rare details of its use of pilots, saying that, with 400 aircraft and over 4,200 pilots, after the adjustments it now had a ratio of over 10 pilots per aircraft available to it, when only 4 per day were needed. That, in itself, was a further damning indictment of the mismanagement of the roster.

The company announced that it was awarding pay increases of €10,000 to its captains and €5,000 to first officers at Dublin, Stansted, Berlin and Frankfurt, without strings attached about leave. It said it would meet ERCs at other bases. But it emphasized again that 'Ryanair only meets directly with its people. It will not meet with competitor pilots or their unions.' The statement stressed that Ryanair would still grow, even when using fewer planes than originally planned: 'By slowing our summer 2018 fleet growth from 445 to 435 aircraft, we expect traffic to March 2019 will slow from 142 million to 138 million, a 7 per cent rate of growth.' It put the costs of the entire episode at €25 million. In time-honoured fashion, it announced there would be a series of low-fare seat sales over the winter as it was 'confident that there will be no further roster-related cancellations'.

That was essential. There could not be another round of cancellations or all residual faith in the airline might be lost, both by customers and by investors. But O'Leary had to do more to keep the faith. He had to show that he was open to change and help, and that he was willing to engage other strong managers – the point about the board that had been repeatedly made by analysts and investors, and repeatedly ignored by O'Leary. The extent of the current crisis meant he couldn't ignore it any more. However, he did not want to spend time on an executive search or to take a chance on somebody he didn't know, so he delved into the Ryanair playbook instead. He sought to recall Peter Bellew, who was now chief executive at Malaysia Airlines, also a crisis-hit airline, but much smaller than Ryanair.

Bellew's prior experience at Ryanair was relevant to what O'Leary needed now. At one stage, he was responsible for managing pilots and service punctuality. Ryanair said Bellew would take up a 'specific responsibility for pilot production, training and career development' to ensure problems with pilot rostering 'will never be repeated'. O'Leary was quoted on the official press release: 'Peter will lead a significant transformation in the way we reward and interact with our pilots, improve their working environment and career development over the coming years.'

It was the type of touchy-feely stuff for which Bellew was known. He had a reputation as friendly and 'affable', of placing emphasis on good communications and empathy. In short, he didn't seem to have much in common with other Ryanair executives, many of whom seemed to turn into O'Leary mini-mes over time. '[Bellew is] the opposite in nature to Ryanair. Contrast the abrasion with the affability Peter has,' said John Strickland, an aviation analyst. 'I think he would take a far more conciliatory, pragmatic approach. There would be more of a feeling that pilots are being listened to.' Yet some pilots were not happy with the choice, believing that a new start was required, not the return of an old face, albeit a more friendly one.

Bellew's resignation statement to Malaysia Airlines said he was returning to Ireland as a form of 'national service' for 'Ireland's greatest company', describing his decision as *negaraku*, which means 'my country' in Malay. He said Ryanair needed his help: 'Love for country is pulling me back to Ireland. I am looking forward to being close again to my family and friends fourteen hours away in Ireland.' He admitted that he had told people in late September 2017 that he would not return to Ryanair, 'but a week later the call came and in life we can really never say never'.

Bellew drove a hard bargain to return, according to rumour all around Ryanair HQ, demanding a base salary of €1 million – far more than anyone else on the Z-team was earning, although this could not be confirmed by anybody. It was plausible, though, given that he was giving up a CEO's role, though one at a crisis-hit airline. Even better, the rumour within Ryanair was that O'Leary had pledged some of his own personal stack of share options to Bellew as a further incentive.

In November, Bellew walked back through the doors of Ryanair HQ that he had exited just two years earlier. He brought with him more and wider experience from his stint at Malaysia, and the confidence that O'Leary rated him highly and was looking to him to help Ryanair combat its problems. For Bellew, this was a big moment, and no doubt he enjoyed the sense of coming in like a messiah to save the Ryanair world. Naturally, of course, commentators looked on with great interest, and it inevitably sparked speculation that O'Leary was anointing his successor. Insiders scoffed, believing much of the media concentration on Bellew was exaggerated. Indeed, when I asked Bellew about O'Leary's future with the company in a radio interview not long after he returned to the company, he laughed and said O'Leary would have to be 'carried out of Ryanair in a box' and suggested he would be there beyond the age of a hundred. He may have felt that he had to say something like that, but within Ryanair there were those who felt that is exactly the way O'Leary has it planned.

25. Losing control

As chief marketing officer, Kenny Jacobs should have been to the forefront of communicating Ryanair's position during the cancellations fiasco, especially as he had been given such a prominent role as spokesman for the airline since the creation of *Always Getting Better*. He didn't exactly disappear during the September crisis, but he may have wished that he had.

Jacobs was largely silent after what could be described as a self-inflicted Facebook mishap in the early stages of the rostering debacle. Newspapers surveyed his Facebook account and discovered that Jacobs had been socializing at a hectic pace in the days leading up to the cancellations, including a trip to Barcelona to see a European Champions League game. He listed a series of ten flights over one week, just as Ryanair announced its first raft of cancellations. Worse still, after O'Leary's first press conference, a picture of a half-drunk pint of Guinness appeared on Jacobs's timeline with the caption 'deserved'.

That might have been containable had he not posted to Twitter a photograph of himself – which was taken at a distance, suggesting it was not a 'selfie' – sitting on a toilet, holding a tabloid newspaper as if it were loo paper. The photograph was accompanied by the caption: 'Winding down after a "shit happens" week.' Asked for a comment, Ryanair responded that the post, quickly deleted, was put up 'in jest in response to the barrage of coverage from the newspapers during a week when his full focus was on re-accommodating customers'. It didn't help that in an interview earlier that year, Jacobs had proclaimed himself the 'bad boy' of the industry. He protested loudly in the office that he had been hacked, demanding to know who in Ryanair had access to his account. He received no sympathy from O'Leary, who overheard him. 'What's a 47-year-old man doing on Facebook anyway?' O'Leary barked and everyone in the open office heard, or later claimed to have heard. Given that O'Leary was largely dictating the entire communications strategy, it's no wonder Jacobs had time to make his gaffes.

The announcement of the original set of cancellations had been a mess, and now, incredibly, Ryanair's handling of customers' compensation claims was equally so. Multiple publications across many countries reported stories of passengers claiming they had not received adequate compensation from Ryanair, as set down in EU law, in addition to refunds. Replacement flights were often more expensive and required additional transport if they landed at airports not served by Ryanair. There were complaints that the live-chat function on the website was not available, that it was near-impossible to find a telephone number to call – and if you did, you were left on hold for lengthy periods on expensive premium lines – and that the company's social-media platforms were almost silent. Customers said that they did not receive information about cancellations promptly, making it more difficult to make alternative arrangements. They complained that prices of flights on other carriers soared as those airlines took advantage of the transferred demand.

There were also allegations that Ryanair agents told customers to reclaim money through their own travel insurance, even though EU law stated that the airline should cover all expenses. Yet Ryanair sent emails that said: 'Once the refund option has been accepted, no further liability under EU261 arises.' An internal memo instructed call-centre staff to offer flights with other carriers, provided the price 'does not exceed three times the value of the original Ryanair fare'. Passengers were told they would have the option of using 'agreed partner airlines' – easyJet, Jet2, Vueling, CityJet, Aer Lingus, Norwegian or Eurowings – which didn't necessarily suit customers, but was cheaper for Ryanair.

The company was unable to contain the social-media reaction, which gathered under the hashtag #boycottryanair on Twitter and demanded O'Leary's resignation. Many wrote that they would never fly with the airline again, urging others to do likewise and 'make them go bust'. O'Leary took little notice because it was 'only' social media. But the whole fiasco was the antithesis of the caring, *Always Getting Better* image the airline had promoted so assiduously, and he knew that was a problem. Ryanair was failing its first major test of genuine customer care since the 2013 revolution, and failing miserably.

Regulators on both sides of the Irish Sea and in Europe made Ryanair's customer care a priority issue. The consumer group *Which?*, routinely mocked by Ryanair, waded in: 'Ryanair appears to be plucking figures out of thin air as there is no legal basis for the arbitrary figure they've set. The law says passengers must be rerouted and there's no specified limit on cost. Ryanair is still flouting the law and failing to properly inform people of their rights, so it is good to see the regulator stepping in.'

It was the British regulator, the Civil Aviation Authority (CAA), that really took up arms and went to war with Ryanair. They had form together. The CAA had taken Ryanair to court in 2011 for publishing misleading fares on its website, and again in 2015, when it failed to compensate passengers for delays. In 2017 the CAA was concerned that Ryanair's website and emails to passengers didn't make sufficient mention of their entitlement to flights with other airlines and money back for expenses such as meals, hotels and transfer costs. It said Ryanair falsely claimed it did not have to reroute passengers on other airlines, particularly when there were no other services available. It not only threatened legal action but set a very tight deadline of just days for Ryanair to change its website information to make it clear how it would reimburse passengers.

The CAA chief executive Andrew Haines, in a letter to Ryanair, accused the company of 'persistently misleading passengers with inaccurate information regarding their rights'. He said that O'Leary's statement that he was not going to pay for Ryanair passengers to fly on other airlines was unlawful. Asked on Sky News if he was at his 'wit's end' with Ryanair, Haines responded: 'We are furious. We do take action and when we take that action, the airline complies. There are clear laws in place which are intended to assist passengers in the event of a cancellation, helping minimize both the frustration and inconvenience caused by circumstances completely out of their control. We have made this crystal clear to Ryanair, who are well aware of their legal obligations, which includes how and when they should reroute passengers, along with the level of information it provides its passengers.'

Ryanair responded that it would meet with the CAA and 'comply fully with whatever requirements they ask us to'. Haines retorted that he would take the statement with a 'pinch of salt'. He received staunch support from Britain's aviation minister, Lord Callanan, who personally reprimanded O'Leary: 'I have made clear my disappointment about the service many of their customers are receiving. Despite assuring me there would be no further disruption, it is alarming that Ryanair has announced that more flights will be cancelled. Airlines must fulfil their obligations to customers and ensure they are fully compensated when they face disruption, which is why I very much support the CAA's decision to take enforcement action against Ryanair.'

O'Leary was scathing about what he saw as interference from busybodies, but he also realized that Haines and Callanan could not be ignored. He decided that the way to handle them was with a third party – the Irish regulators. It was a good call, because Cathy Mannion, the Irish commissioner for aviation regulation, seemed more willing to engage with Ryanair on a friendly basis, arguing that regulations about treatment of passengers were 'open to interpretation'. She drew Ryanair's attention to their 'care and assistance' obligations but said that 'Our position is that we can encourage them, but we cannot require them to do so.'

It was a markedly different approach from her British counterparts, but she got the result the British authorities wanted. Ryanair issued a clarification email to all affected customers, outlining their rights to refunds and flight changes, including being rerouted on another Ryanair flight or completing their journey with other providers and receiving expenses. Ryanair confirmed it had taken on additional staff to ensure that all refunds were provided within seven working days and promised to deal with expenses and compensation claims within twenty-eight working days. It agreed to fully implement EU261 and pledged to reimburse any reasonable out-of-pocket expenses incurred by customers as a result of the cancellations, subject to receiving an EU261 claim form supported by original receipts.

In doing all this, Ryanair met the deadline set by the CAA with only an hour to spare, simultaneously sending a letter to the CAA agreeing to meet the requirement for customer clarification on its 'EU261' obligations. Haines was very pleased: 'It appears that Ryanair has capitulated. We will review their position in detail and monitor this situation to ensure that passengers get what they are entitled to in practice.'

Within Ryanair, the reference to capitulation was noted and deeply resented. O'Leary fired off a letter to the CAA, accusing it of not adopting an equally hard-line position against British Airways when a computer meltdown left thousands of passengers stranded. He effectively accused the CAA of double standards.

It felt like the bad old days – customers complaining, watchdogs howling, and O'Leary flinging about accusations and drumming up bad publicity. The question now was whether all the efforts by Ryanair to reform its image had gone to waste and, if so, was that because there was one thing that had failed to change: its chief executive.

One commentator put it succinctly: 'It was becoming a much more popular airline, it was becoming more loved because of the consumer changes it's made, but in the last two weeks Michael O'Leary's management team have unravelled the progress that has been made in the last two years and that is a major issue that they are far from solving. There has undoubtedly been a loss of confidence and it is already starting to hurt them. Once you frustrate passengers they will not be returning, they will choose another carrier.'

Which? waded in yet again, this time through a letter from its chief executive, Peter Vicary-Smith, to *The Times*: 'Sir, At the end of another week in which Ryanair has lurched from crisis to catastrophe, it's hard to ignore the utter disregard in which the company appears to hold its greatest asset: its customers. Almost three quarters of a million passengers have had their flights cancelled, their right to rebook with another carrier arbitrarily constrained and their compensation entitlement hidden. The airline has played so fast and loose with consumer rights and regulations that the Civil Aviation Authority had to step in and point out that it was breaking the law . . . Michael O'Leary must not take customers for granted again: if he does, he should be prepared to face the consequences.'

Vicary-Smith wasn't alone in wondering what those would be.

At the end of October, on publication of Ryanair's half-year results, O'Leary spoke to stockbroking analysts in an effort to emphasize that he and his management were on top of the situation. He conceded that the rate of passenger growth would slow and that Ryanair would face €100 million in higher annual pilot costs, but insisted profits would not be hit and that the 'substantial unit-cost advantage we have over all other EU airline competitors' would not be surrendered. O'Leary talked up the strength both of the Ryanair balance sheet – where the net debt of €600 million was very small compared with the value of the business – and of the use to which strong cash flows were put. In the previous six months, Ryanair had generated enough cash to engage in capital expenditure costing €675 million, make debt repayments of €200 million, and buy and cancel €639 million worth of its own shares. In other words, Ryanair remained a cash machine for its owners.

But he was contrite . . . to a point. He admitted Ryanair 'could have responded sooner to a tightening market' for pilots and that 900 had now been hired, which was 300 more than he'd said a month earlier was needed. There was investment in new operations management and added resources for pilot recruitment, base management and rostering teams. Yet his contrition was on O'Leary terms: 'I'm sorry that our people have had to listen to misinformation about Ryanair promoted by competitor pilot unions, however we have been here before, and we will be again. We understand that the reason they wish to denigrate Ryanair is because their airlines cannot compete with us. As usual when these union airlines fail, such as Monarch, Air Berlin and Alitalia in recent months, their pilots all come to Ryanair seeking jobs that pay up to €175,000.'

When the possibility of industrial action by pilots was raised, O'Leary dismissed it, maintaining that the relationship with pilots remained 'very good'. Employing the language of the bully again, he said that any industrial action would bring 'consequences', and those 'consequences will not be to the advantage of those pilots'. He dismissed workers' 'laughable demands for legacy-type inefficiencies', a reference to what went on at rival airlines, which he regarded as the fault of bowing to union demands. In his usual combative pose, he stated: 'We are fully prepared to face down any such disruption, if it means defending our cost base or our high-productivity model.'

He might have been better off striking a more conciliatory note, but he hadn't arrived at that place yet, even though many of the pilot crews across the eighty-six European airport bases had yet to agree to the new pay packages. As O'Leary spoke confident words to the analysts and portrayed a boss in firm control, a mood of militancy was taking hold among the troops.

26. Capitulation

The pilots knew what they wanted. They were demanding an independent European ERC as the recognized representative body to present their views collectively to management. Ryanair insisted that its position remained unchanged: it would only negotiate with ERCs from individual bases, and would not engage with trade unions as part of those ERCs. The company was determined that it would protect its existing structures of individual negotiation of terms and conditions at each separate base, and the mix of staff and contractors at each.

The pilots weren't just angry, though, they were calculating, too. Many realized that, right now, Ryanair could not afford a strike because of the damage it would do to its reputation, even if O'Leary tried to blame the pilots. Many were so disaffected and so badly wanted to work elsewhere that they didn't really care if they did Ryanair damage. Within Ryanair, there was a growing realization, and horror, that a genuine problem was escalating and that a number of pilots would not be fobbed off with extra money, as expected. The temptation to bully them into submission, driven by O'Leary's long-standing methods, couldn't be resisted, especially when O'Leary was deeply involved in what was unfolding, treating this as his priority. Pilots were told that if they went on strike, they would lose benefits, including guarantees over rosters and pay, and be denied promotion. In Italy, for example, cabin crew were told that action by any one member would result in the entire base losing rights to transfers or promotions.

While negotiations went on at Stansted to Ryanair's satisfaction – in that there was hope of a settlement and little or no threat of strike – the Dublin-based pilots proved far more troublesome. Chief people officer Eddie Wilson warned them that if any of them supported strike action, benefits would be withdrawn along with certain pay and promotion opportunities. However, many of the pilots thought it unlikely that Ryanair would go that far in its response. When a vote was called, about 115 of Ryanair's estimated 390 pilots at Dublin, Cork and Shannon airports agreed to strike on Wednesday, 20 December. Although this was a minority – just 28 per cent, as Ryanair repeatedly emphasized – it was enough to cause mayhem because that number included 90 per cent of the captains, who were employed directly, rather than on contracts, and safety regulations required captains on all commercial passenger flights.

Wilson tried to whip up public opinion in Ryanair's favour: 'We apologize sincerely to our customers for any worry or concern that this threatened action, during the Christmas week, by a small number of very well-paid pilots may cause them.' The company said it would 'face down' the strike and claimed that 'while some disruption may occur, Ryanair believes this will largely be confined to a small group of pilots who are working their notice and will shortly leave Ryanair, so they don't care how much upset they cause colleagues or customers.'

The company promised it would publish contingency plans two days before the planned strike, to minimize disruption. That didn't satisfy customers. O'Leary had promised that the second set of cancellations was Ryanair's last and he couldn't break that promise. If he did, the reputational damage would be extensive. His negotiators returned and said they believed that the action planned for the Wednesday might be the start of a series of strikes, by unions in Ireland and Europe, unless Ryanair entered into dialogue with its pilots.

This was a genuine crisis. It forced O'Leary into lengthy consultation with his management team and brought them towards a conclusion that nobody foresaw, notwithstanding subsequent, unconvincing claims by O'Leary that he always knew dealing with unions was inevitable and that it was merely a question of when it would happen. Within Ryanair, a discussion never aired previously was in flow, and Peter Bellew was central to it. He brought to bear his perspective, gained from a couple of years away from Ryanair, and his new title, which gave him more than just permission to speak up. That O'Leary was listening to Bellew and entertaining a radically new approach came as a shock to the Z-team members, veteran and recent. But, then, they had seen O'Leary execute U-turns before, so they should have known how flexible he could be when the chips were down.

On 15 December 2017, Ryanair made what was possibly the most important and extraordinary announcement in its history: it would negotiate with trade unions representing the pilots in Ireland, the UK, Germany, Italy, Spain and Portugal. O'Leary was the voice of reform: 'Ryanair will now change its long-standing policy of not recognizing unions in order to avoid any threat of disruption to its customers and its flights from pilot unions during Christmas week.'

The company decided to present its position as one of the responsible CEO protecting and championing the consumer. Ryanair issued a written statement in which O'Leary said: 'Christmas flights are very important to our customers and we wish to remove any worry or concern that they may be disrupted by pilot industrial action next week. If the best way to achieve this is to talk to our pilots through a recognized union process, then we are prepared to do so, and we have written today to these unions inviting them to talks to recognize them and calling on them to cancel the threatened industrial action planned for Christmas week. Putting the needs of our customers first, and avoiding disruption to their Christmas flights, is the reason why we will now deal with our pilots through recognized national union structures and we hope and expect that these structures can and will be agreed with our pilots early in the New Year.'

It produced a stunned, scarcely believing response from the pilots, their unions and the media in general. This went against one of O'Leary's core, unshakable beliefs: unions damage business. It contradicted his previous vow that he would rather close the airline than deal with unions, or that he would cut off his arm first. This was the most remarkable of surrenders.

But there was little celebration, initially at least. Immediately, most wondered what the catch was, because, even with his back to the wall, O'Leary did not give away things lightly. This time was no different . . . be careful what you wish for, and all that. There was a significant caveat within the statement, the details of which got somewhat lost in the publicity about the overall announcement. In return for union recognition, Ryanair demanded that the pilots establish 'committees of Ryanair pilots to deal with Ryanair issues, as Ryanair will not engage with pilots who fly for competitor airlines in Ireland or elsewhere'. Ryanair was still trying to control who it negotiated with and continue its base-by-base approach, instead of dealing with one union body representing all the bases. When they read the small print, the pilots wondered what would really change, other than who was allowed to negotiate with the airline's management. The key question was whether the bases would continue to be treated separately.

Investors were not optimistic either, with an immediate fall in the share price, knocking €1.8 billion off the company's market value, which had been recovering slowly since the September crisis. All of O'Leary's old quotes about unions – some uttered as recently as September – were dragged out, and not just by the media but by stockbroking analysts, too. Mark Simpson, an aviation analyst at Goodbody Stockbrokers in Dublin, said that O'Leary had performed a '180-degree shift', having previously described pilot unions as a 'busted flush' engaged in a 'load of bollocks'. Merrion Capital's chief investment officer, David Holohan, told the *Irish Times*: 'I just cannot see Michael O'Leary running a unionized airline. When profits are high, unions tend to negotiate very good contracts; when those profits erode, unions tend to give very little back.'

Andrew Lobbenberg, an analyst at HSBC, questioned the effect on the bottom line: 'If they move to a unionized workforce, I would expect that to lead to normal industry working practices with local employment contracts and permanent employment contracts. A key part of Ryanair's success has been how flexible the business has been. And part of that has been their contractual ability to move people around which has come from their employment structure.' He noted Ryanair's limited room for manoeuvre: 'They were in a place where their natural established behaviour, which is to respond assertively or aggressively to labour or where people are challenging them, was only going to make the situation worse . . . and put them into deeper trouble.'

Lobbenberg also warned that 'industrial relations [might distract] management and investors', and he was very quickly proven correct. The ITWF immediately wrote to Ryanair, seeking recognition for unions representing 8,000 cabin crew members across Europe. Its campaigns director, Liz Blackshaw, said she wanted to deal with direct employment, contracts, pay, rosters and other conditions.

The general consensus was that Ryanair's back was to the wall in a way it had never been before. Daniel Röska noted that it had to 'safeguard the number of employees' in order to maintain flying schedules and reach its 2024 target of carrying 200 million passengers a year. 'That's why they are so adamant in pushing through the wage rises. It's seldom that an employer is so desperate to give people more money. If they don't, people will leave. Unionization is also designed to get people to stay and not leave as quickly.' Up until now, Ryanair had snapped and snarled and intimidated all-comers into submission. But the cancellations crisis had changed its ability to do this. O'Leary was correct in saying that they could be a low-fares airline only with a low-cost base, but he may have sacrificed too much on the altar of low costs. It had created an imbalance in the company, and now he would have to do his penance.

The decisions that had led to this point, along with the decision to give way on the unions question, created an even greater focus on the future of the company. Mark Simpson noted that: 'The reason the stock is down by more than a euro is because it brings complexity and uncertainty and the market hates uncertainty. This is diametrically opposed to commentary from Michael O'Leary, so it has raised question marks in the minds of investors over his longevity.'

The key question for investors was whether this new move

was shifting Ryanair towards the models of other airlines, and therefore robbing it of its USP: 'Fundamentally they are still in a strong position, with a very competitive cost base, high margins and a very strong balance sheet,' said Gerald Khoo, aviation analyst at Liberum. 'It's not going to be crippled by this. The underlying business model is still absolutely viable and successful . . . but the reversal of yet another long-standing and strongly asserted policy would seem to reduce the differentiation compared with legacy airlines.' It seemed an unavoidable consequence of losing ground: 'Ryanair used to say that it would recognize unions when hell froze over. Faced with building straight threats, it has capitulated. A unionized Ryanair will still be profitable, cash-generative and value-creating in our view, but it will be a markedly different company.' Ryanair would be closer to being just another airline, which would mean that it would find it harder to persuade investors to choose its shares over those of other airlines.

Eddie Wilson told the *Financial Times* that the move was merely a manifestation of becoming more mature, which had been the aim of *Always Getting Better* all along: 'We would have fought to have kept the model that we have because it gives you flexibility, but the world has moved on. The business has changed. You have to adapt to it. If you can't win something, then you just have to change.' But he emphasized that the low-cost, high-productivity model would be defended aggressively: 'If suddenly pilots said they only wanted to fly 400 hours a year like elsewhere, then, yes, there would be conflict.'

Once it had made the decision to recognize unions, Ryanair moved quickly. It wrote to the IMPACT trade union (since renamed Fórsa), offering not just proposals on pay and conditions but procedures and dispute resolution for its

Irish-based pilots. It said that it wanted to conclude an early agreement. IMPACT agreed to an early January meeting, to agree a deal that would set out collective bargaining procedures. But this would not be achieved quickly. Trust would not be easy to establish, and both parties were coming from different starting points. Ryanair wanted to retain its flexibility on costs and continue out-sourcing; IMPACT sought greater job security.

Union recognition did not prevent a strike in Germany on 22 December – the first pilot refusal to fly since the airline's creation. Vereinigung Cockpit (VC), the union with which Ryanair was prepared to deal, said Ryanair rejected two of their five union representatives. Ryanair said the two were there to represent Lufthansa unions. 'From VC's point of view this refusal clearly shows that the principles of trade-union autonomy are disregarded by Ryanair and that the company does not truly desire to enter into constructive negotiations.'

Other problems – irritations as far as Ryanair was concerned because it was politicians interfering – emerged in the House of Commons and European Parliament. Two UK parliamentary committees announced investigations into employee working conditions at Ryanair, specifically claims of staff being underpaid, paying for their own uniforms and incurring claw-back fees upon leaving the airline. Rachel Reeves, chair of the Business Select Committee, accused Ryanair of 'trying to wiggle out' of paying the UK's national minimum wage: 'These allegations ... suggest a company falling well short of its duty to the staff who help their planes get off the ground and who spend the flight attending to and serving its paying customers.' Ryanair immediately denied her claims, countering that its cabin crew earned 'more than double the UK national minimum wage'.

At the European Parliament, working conditions at Ryanair were likened to 'slavery' and nobody spoke up on their behalf, not even the Irish MEPs. 'This company mocks us,' said Romanian MEP Maria Grapini.

In subsequent public comments on the decision to recognize unions, O'Leary insisted it was 'not a ruse' and that it was 'in many respects my idea'. He claimed it allowed for expansion into heavily unionized France and Scandinavia. Ryanair had no bases in France, but could put fifty aircraft into the country. O'Leary still strived to be the rule-setter: 'But if someone is being unreasonable and we are being completely messed around by a union, we will still move aircraft away from that base or country. We will still have much lower aircraft costs, much lower financing costs, much lower airport deals. That will all remain unchanged.'

Securing agreement would become a very time-consuming process, just as analysts had predicted. In Ireland, a majority of pilots at the Cork and Shannon bases agreed quickly to the conditions of their pay increases, as did most contractor and new entrants based in Dublin. But about 35 per cent of Dublin pilots refused to vote and were denied their pay increase.

The situation in the UK was sorted relatively quickly, despite Bellew being deeply embarrassed by the unauthorized taping of a remarkable presentation he made to pilots at Stansted in late December 2017, and the subsequent publication of an extract of the recording on independent.ie. During his speech, he admitted that the culture and tone of working at Ryanair 'has gone very miserable . . . even in our head office . . . It seems that there was a culture that people who knew there was a problem . . . that they were not listened to, or they were actively discouraged from even raising the issue. Or not only were they not getting done, they were getting told, "Piss off, I don't want to know about this."' There was only one voice people could hear in their minds to accompany that last comment.

Bellew told the pilots that part of Ryanair's problem was 'we grew too fast' and that a culture shift was needed to introduce 'a certain softness and kindness that we had at a point but we seem to have lost'. It was impossible to believe that O'Leary would have conceded such points.

Bellew empathized, saying he understood people were 'really pissed off' and acknowledged that staff retention was a major problem – something O'Leary had denied consistently. According to Bellew: 'Traditionally in the past where people were leaving, we would have contacted them, or we would have known in advance, and say, "Why are you leaving?" We'd sort them out, and often they'd retract their resignation.' Instead, he admitted, senior management now deliberately encouraged a policy of non-engagement with pilots who had decided to leave. If they were going, they were told not to let the door hit them on the arse on their way out. 'There's a very basic lack of trust I can sense now from the pilots. We have to work very hard to restore that. I don't expect people to accept that overnight ... but I do think we can fix it.'

A pre-crisis O'Leary would almost certainly have had Bellew's head for showing such weakness. As it was, Bellew was only just installed, and he was needed. His soft touch was at odds with Ryanair's way of doing things, but it did seem to strike a chord with the pilots. The confusion was whether or not Bellew was doing O'Leary's bidding or defying him – was it simply a tactic to support the greater strategy?

Whatever the truth of his comments, it helped Bellew

achieve his aim. A deal with the British Airline Pilots' Association (BALPA) was signed at the end of January 2018, covering about a quarter of Ryanair's pilots and aircraft. It gave BALPA recognition as the sole representative body for Ryanair-employed pilots in the UK. The deal came less than two weeks after Ryanair's fifteen UK bases accepted a pay increase of 20 per cent. Wilson said the agreement showed 'how serious Ryanair is about working constructively with unions that are willing to work constructively with us' and demanded other unions 'stop wasting time and act quickly'.

The optics of the BALPA agreement were important. Its general secretary, Brian Strutton, admitted that, while 'initially sceptical' about Ryanair's sincerity, 'our conversations and meetings with them have shown that they are genuine in wanting a constructive trade-union relationship'. Perhaps *Always Getting Better* was the real Ryanair after all?

Epilogue: Onwards and upwards

In personal terms, Michael O'Leary ended 2017 on a high note. His race horses, wearing the colours of his Gigginstown Stud, gave him eight winners from twenty-eight races over the four days of the Leopardstown Christmas Festival, one of the highlights of the Irish jump-racing calendar and a significant precursor to the Cheltenham Festival in March. It was a remarkable success rate. Photographs of a smiling O'Leary in the winners' enclosure, hugging his young daughter, appeared in many newspapers. Winner all right, as the saying in the sport goes.

The same couldn't be said for his business life in 2017. It must have counted as the worst year of his career to date, even if profits and volumes continued to grow at Ryanair. At a distance, the criticism seemed somewhat strange. Most airlines would be thrilled if their passenger numbers grew 10 per cent in 2017, to 129 million, as Ryanair's did. A double-digit growth in volumes was impressive, no matter what. Even after the controversial cancellation crises, the airline carried 9.3 million passengers in December 2017 – a 3 per cent rise over the same month in 2016. It also filled 95 per cent of the available seats on its aircraft, compared with 94 per cent in December 2016. It was the type of failure other airlines and chief executives envied.

O'Leary had always set the bar high, so his 'failure' raised all sorts of doubts as to the company's ability to manage its changed circumstances, its size and its ambitions. His future as CEO had been called into question regularly, and he was accused of being the author of his own – and his company's – misfortunes. His contract as chief executive would expire in 2019, but before now no one had doubted that it would be extended. He was fit in body and lean in weight – having taken up gym workouts in middle age – and undoubtedly still sharp of mind. He showed no sign of flagging under his relentless work schedule, even if some observers were shocked by the amount of coffee that fuelled it, apparently dozens of cups each day. He had never shown any sign of not loving it all, but now, just a few years shy of sixty, he was under more pressure than at any stage since those years when he had urged Tony Ryan to shut the airline, to stem its losses.

Others might have been tempted to throw their hat at it. What more did he need to prove or achieve? He was rich beyond most people's dreams and had engineered a success story that would grant him a place in business legend. None of that seemed to matter to O'Leary. His restlessness and drive demanded that he have a job to go to where he would be in command and control. The idea of O'Leary flitting around other companies in other industries, as a chairman or a non-executive director, where he would not be in day-to-day control, simply did not fit with the man and his way of doing business. Retirement? Not a chance. That would drive him insane. No matter how much he likes his two annual holidays, they are a break and nothing more, not a way of living.

O'Leary has always affected a thick skin, allied to a devil-may-care attitude, and indeed thrived on any opposition levelled at him, but the level of criticism he attracted in 2017 cannot have been easy to endure. As an avid reader of history and biography, he had plenty of knowledge of the stories of the powerful who lost it all. He was not someone who ever took things for granted. He knew well the definition of *Schadenfreude* – the satisfaction or pleasure felt at someone else's misfortune – and could see that many were revelling in his discomfort as the crisis unfolded at Ryanair. He could dismiss the acumen or accuracy of many of those commentators, but, even if he regarded much of it as ill-informed, spiteful and premature, he also knew that momentum could gather, and that things could spiral beyond his control.

O'Leary's list of enemies – and that is not an inappropriate word – is long. Those critics who lined up in late 2017 included scorned members of the media, politicians, airport, aviation and consumer-protection regulators, rival airlines and European Commission officials. Many were still smarting from insults flung their way by O'Leary, even if delivered years ago, and they enjoyed the boot being on the other foot. He took many kicks during 2017 and was bruised badly.

Even his usually loyal investors joined the fray, with some selling shares in response to events, that act itself declaring a lack of confidence in O'Leary and his ability to run the company profitably. As a veteran of the stock market, O'Leary had never been too concerned by sudden falls in the share price. He was confident he could overcome adverse sentiment, even when it was the result of profit warnings by Ryanair. The cold, hard facts of long-term massive profits, enormous passenger numbers and consistent growth always trumped the opinions of those who didn't like the methods by which he achieved those things. Now, however, he had to moderate the company's growth so as to manage it more firmly.

It is not an exaggeration to say that Ryanair finished 2017 in the grip of a crisis, and that much of the work of the previous four years to better the company's image, and sell more tickets, was damaged. O'Leary had never cared much about branding or the views of advertising agencies, but even he must have flinched when Core Media, Ireland's biggest media agency, published research that suggested Ryanair's brand image had plummeted in value: 'As Ryanair's brand sentiment plunged to its lowest point ever, their visibility also jumped to 80 per cent, the highest ever. This tells us that Ryanair stood out in people's minds more strongly than ever before, but for all the wrong reasons.' It added that the crisis had effectively grounded the *Always Getting Better* repositioning of the brand. O'Leary had long treated rows as part of a game he controlled. He believed there was no such thing as bad publicity, or at least nothing that couldn't be solved by a quick seat sale. Now, it seemed, things were different.

His role in the crisis naturally came under scrutiny. 'The ball was dropped,' said Andrew Charlton, managing director of Aviation Advocacy. 'Ryanair is as scary an example of laser-like focus on costs as any in the world. But if there is a lesson, it is probably that you also have to focus on operations and you have got to look after the really tiny bits as well as the big bits. And you can't afford to have any of your staff make this mistake.' Charlton argued that an airline with a less prominent leader might not have received the level of coverage Ryanair attracted during 2017: 'But if you live by the sword, you die by the sword and [O'Leary] lives by the sword. He is paying the price for all those years of celebrity. He mouths off and then finally the smartarse gets it and who doesn't love that? Who wasn't at school when there was a smartarse who finally got a question wrong? Mister O'Leary has been the smartest kid in the room since kindergarten. And every other kid is smirking.'

Others were more sympathetic. 'He has held his hands up, which was the right thing. In the past, airline chief executives

who have shown they can fix it and move on have actually performed better,' said John Strickland, director of JLS Consulting.
'Personal stuff aside, O'Leary has a phenomenal reputation.'

In truth, much as it was bandied about, the idea that O'Leary
could be doomed, given the grip he held at Ryanair, was always
likely to be a gross exaggeration. O'Leary's legion of supporters had a persuasive, factually based argument that O'Leary
was Ireland's most successful ever businessman, and that
Ryanair was one of the country's most extraordinary and
worthwhile companies. In their view, his critics were whining
about emotive issues, like treatment of people and excessive
behaviour, but those things didn't really matter. Of course,
now his critics had facts to support their contentions, but it was
still unlikely to be enough to unseat him. His management
remained in awe or fear of him, his board kept supporting him.

Going into 2018, the belief was that we might see far less
of O'Leary in public, other than at the racecourse, that he
would spend more time managing and would deal with
stockbroking analysts when he wanted to get his message
across. This sort of low profile had been promised previously, of course, especially when Jacobs took a more public
role after joining the company. O'Leary may have been
reluctant initially to become a public figure, but in time he
came to enjoy playing the pantomime baddie and generating
sizeable publicity for Ryanair, and some friends believed he
would be reluctant, or even unable, to return to the shadows.
He would need somewhere to let off steam if the new Ryanair
was having to be nice to staff as well as customers.

Another challenge for the control freak in him was finding an appropriate level of responsibility to delegate to others.
He had reason to fear that, given that trusting others had
caused many of his problems in 2017, but equally the scale of

the business meant he had to let others get on with things and not undermine them. Delegation involved sending Bellew and Wilson to deal with the unions, although few doubted that he would monitor their every move closely and that any agreements reached by them would be rubberstamped only after intense interrogation.

Bellew's high-profile return to Ryanair – and the prominence of his role in the negotiations – led to much speculation that he would be O'Leary's successor, but, again, this was exaggeration. O'Leary brought him back because he had to be seen to be doing something, and hiring an old hand, one he had already broken in, was an easy option. Few within Ryanair thought there was a plan for succession. O'Leary, as the heartbeat of Ryanair and its intellectual powerhouse, would not be leaving, unless a further disaster unfolded. He was, is, and will remain Ryanair.

Those wondering if O'Leary would lose his appetite at a company that had to deal with unions on a formal basis were told that, ever the pragmatist, he would simply adapt to the new circumstances. If Ryanair had to become a more conventional company, both in looks and behaviour, then he'd do it. He wouldn't disappear either. While he reduced his media appearances – and refused requests for an interview for this book – he did a major interview with the *Sunday Times* in February 2018. Asked if union recognition would undermine the Ryanair model, he screwed up his face and said: 'Nooo. The idea that we were this low-paying, Siberian salt mine for thirty years . . . Our average captain earns between €150,000 and €200,000 [£177,000] a year. This is a good deal. A tiny proportion of our cost advantage over our competitors is labour. Unionization is not going to alter that.'

He also made it clear he would not be a soft touch with

unions, deriding a proposal to pay pilots €1,000 when a flight finished after midnight. 'The idea that we're going to start making payments because your flight went beyond midnight? Go to hell. That is never ever going to happen here. You can go on strike for a day, a month, a year – and it would not cost us a thought. We will take the strikes. Unlike easyJet, we won't roll over. We are a low-cost, highly efficient airline and we intend to remain a low-cost, highly efficient airline that pays its people very well.'

The union talks were ongoing, and weren't progressing smoothly. Ryanair spoke of moving quickly, but analysts expected the process might not be completed until 2020 – and that could prove correct. By July 2018 (time of writing) BALPA and ANPAC had signed a recognition agreement, but the Irish pilots again threatened to strike. Ryanair maintained that the European ERC and its communications have 'no legal standing or validity'. Ryanair argues that 80 per cent of Ryanair pilots have already accepted a 20 per cent pay increase that the EERC has opposed. From the EERC's point of view, however, these deals cover only just over half of its eighty-seven bases.

O'Leary was determined not to be curtailed. He remained worried about Brexit, telling the *Sunday Times*: 'Very few people are yet focused on Brexit, which amazes me. Everybody still thinks it's all going to get solved on the night – and it isn't.' He warned that flights between Britain and the EU would likely halt, albeit temporarily, when Britain exits in March 2019. He suggested that grounding flights might be the only way to make people realize the gravity of the situation. In a pre-emptive protective measure, he made an application to the CAA for a British air-operating certificate, to ensure Ryanair would be able to continue flying in the UK after Brexit.

'This may be required for Ryanair's three UK domestic routes in the event of a hard Brexit in March 2019.' Ryanair's three intra-UK routes account for just 2 per cent of its business, but O'Leary doesn't like any business being lost.

Expansion continued as the nuts-and-bolts of union agreements were hammered out. The hard line that had been taken in Ukraine the previous year was justified when Ryanair finally reached a better deal to expand to Ukraine in autumn 2018, offering fifteen new routes between European cities and Kiev and Lviv, making it the thirty-sixth country in which Ryanair operated. The new routes would connect Ukrainians with five Polish cities, as well as with London Stansted, Barcelona, Bratislava, Stockholm, Vilnius, Düsseldorf and Memmingen. It was the perfect example of how Ryanair was now far more European than Irish (or British).

The big expansion announcement, however, was made in March 2018, when Ryanair purchased, subject to EU competition approval, a 75 per cent majority stake in Laudamotion, the airline founded by Formula One champion Niki Lauda. This came two months after Lauda had managed to block an attempt by BA's owner, IAG, to buy his airline as part of the insolvency of previous owner Air Berlin. Lauda then recouped part of the price he paid by bringing in Ryanair as his new partner. Ryanair's idea was to take a 24.9 per cent stake until the all-clear was received from the authorities, and then buy more shares. It was Ryanair's first acquisition since Buzz back in 2003. Ryanair said it would pay 'less than €50 million' for the 75 per cent stake and provide an additional €50 million for year one start-up and operating costs. It subsequently emerged it has an option to buy the remaining shares at a later date.

The idea was that Laudamotion would offer scheduled and chartered services from Germany, Austria and Switzerland to mainly Mediterranean leisure destinations, putting it up to Lufthansa and its Swiss and Austrian subsidiaries. Lauda would chair the airline and Ryanair would provide financial and management support. It is planned that the airline will reach profitability by its third year of operations, if it can fly at least thirty Airbus aircraft. 'The Laudamotion Air Operator's Certificate will support a fleet of Airbus aircraft, which is something we have hoped to develop within the Ryanair group for some years,' O'Leary said, a comment that must have sent a shudder down the spines of executives at Boeing.

It was yet another sign that O'Leary was not slowing down, that he had new ideas to implement and ambitious targets to hit.

There were always new firsts to be achieved. At Cheltenham in March 2018, he enjoyed a bumper festival. He had seven winners in the week, making him the most successful owner at the races. He even won the race he sponsored, the Ryanair Chase, for the first time, with *Balko Des Flos*. A month later he won the Aintree Grand National again, this time with a horse called *Tiger Roll*. He delayed the return flight from Liverpool to Dublin to allow jockey Davy Russell to board it and, in an unusual move, provided personal compensation to other passengers. A video was shared on social media, showing how O'Leary could be generous, but with limits. 'Today we won the Grand National,' he declared on the plane's PA system, 'so, unusually on board this flight, there's going to be a free bar, which I am personally going to pay for, but you're all restricted to one free drink only.' His level of racing success was so remarkable, it raised complaints on some sports pages that he was becoming too dominant in the sport. How he must have laughed at that.

The financial results for 2017/18 that Ryanair announced

on 21 May 2018, were classic of the type O'Leary liked to issue. The profits for the twelve months to the end of March were at the top end of expectations, up 10 per cent to €1.45 billion, despite all the disruption caused by the 2017 flight cancellations. Revenue had increased by 7 per cent to €7.15 billion, and the airline had carried over 130 million passengers. So, at first glance, all was right in O'Leary's world again.

But there was a familiar twist. O'Leary had found clouds to counteract the silver linings. The next financial year would be 'tough', because of rising jet fuel prices, increased staff costs and the risk of a cliff-edge Brexit. Profit growth would stall and fall: O'Leary predicted that Ryanair's unit costs – the thing he always concentrated on – would rise by 9 per cent. He declared himself to be on the 'pessimistic side of cautious' as he reiterated his ambition to have 600 aircraft and, using a word few had ever heard him utter before, '200 million guests'.

The cycle of manipulating opinion and expectations had started again, with short-term expectations dimmed and longer-term improvement emphasized, all with O'Leary, despite the very uncertainties he had highlighted, very much in the corporate cockpit and taking control.

In early July 2018 Ryanair received unwanted publicity of the type O'Leary hated when a flight from Dublin to Zadar in Croatia lost cabin pressure, descended quickly and, after the oxygen masks had been deployed, made an emergency landing at Frankfurt Hahn. Thirty-three passengers were treated in hospital, and there were reports that some were bleeding from their ears, a consequence of the rapid depressurization of the cabin. Some said they suffered great distress during the incident, as that they feared they were about to crash. Ryanair described the drop from 37,000 feet to 10,000 feet over seven minutes as a 'controlled descent' and that the plane landed as normal.

Unsurprisingly, there was plenty of media coverage, not least of passenger complaints that people were not adequately looked after following their ordeal, and that much of the care was left to the airport authorities and the German Red Cross, with few if any Ryanair staff on the scene. Ryanair said it had agreed to pay for hotels for the affected passengers but claimed there was a 'shortage of available accommodation'. Another plane was dispatched to transport the passengers, but many were declared by doctors as medically unfit to fly for at least a week and they were required to take a Ryanair-supplied bus to their destination, one that took eighteen hours. It could have been far worse.

If Michael O'Leary had spent July 2017 making mischief, then July 2018 was a harsh reminder of the new realities he and Ryanair faced in conducting industrial relations and maintaining a reliable service for customers.

The long-running enmity with the Irish pilots contributed to three one-day strikes out of Dublin Airport. Flights between Ireland and the UK were cancelled as the company emphasized the importance of maintaining its service to Continental Europe for holidaymakers. The disruption was minimized – just 30 out of 290 flights failed to go on 12 July, the first day of the strike by fewer than 100 pilots, and fewer flights still failed to go on subsequent days – but the publicity didn't help forward sales.

Ryanair used social media to release statements, knowing it could get its message directly to followers on Twitter and that it would be picked up by print and broadcast media. Ryanair was quite aggressive. It sought to undermine public sympathy for the pilots, pointing out that they had secured a 20 per cent pay increase already, earned up to €200,000 per annum (although this top amount was for a small number of them), enjoyed rapid promotions and 'unmatched job security', and worked five-days-on, followed by four-days-off (which it described as a double-bank-holiday weekend at the end of every week).

It said that Fórsa, the union that now embraced the IALPA, had received written proposals on seniority, annual leave and base transfers, the alleged reasons for this strike. Ryanair claimed Fórsa had 'rejected 21 separate invitations to meet Ryanair to negotiate', all because the union bosses didn't want to go to the Ryanair HQ. It published a letter it claimed IALPA president Evan Cullen – who was also an Aer Lingus pilot – had written to the Dublin Airport Authority on 25 June – ten days in advance of the Ryanair pilots' strike ballot being counted – to warn that they were 'contemplating a series of one- and two-day strikes in July and August'. Ryanair claimed it was 'unacceptable that competitor airline pilots are actively organizing strikes by Ryanair's pilots when these airlines will be the direct beneficiaries of any such disruption'.

It took days to agree a meeting venue. The first encounter in a suite at Dublin Airport came just a day before the first strike was due, too late to reach a settlement. It lasted for over seven hours but direct negotiations took place for little more than two. To the frustration of the Ryanair management, the union officials called many recesses. Ryanair believed that the union delegates didn't fully understand all of the positions they (the delegates) were advocating and when challenged required further briefings from the union officials, who weren't present. In particular, they felt that Cullen – pulling the strings behind the scenes – was being called for direction. For their part, the union officials felt that whatever might be agreed with Wilson and Bellew would still be subject to referral to O'Leary for approval.

The second meeting wasn't much better, even if the adjournments were more limited and shorter. Irish Congress of Trade Unions general secretary Patricia King attended and spoke. 'She made a lengthy speech attacking us and what she didn't like about us and we just sat there,' said one attendee. 'It was as if the unions were getting over twenty years of frustration off their chests, lecturing us on what we'd done wrong and how horrible we'd been, even though it meant little or nothing to the process at hand. It was classic 1980s stuff, a history lesson as they saw it and we didn't have time for it but had no choice but to listen.'

Ryanair was put under pressure to allow for third-party mediation but resisted, saying it would slow things down. It pointed out that in the same week in which it was bogged down with Irish unions it had managed to do recognition deals with cabin crews in Italy and Germany. 'The German unions have the most power but they are most business-like in doing things too,' a Ryanair insider told this author. 'The Irish unions are not engaging and seem to want a slow, drawn-out process, even though they're asking for things that we've demonstrated are not actually better for the pilots than we're offering.'

In the midst of all this, Ryanair had to release financial statements to the stock market on Monday, 23 July, for the first quarter of its financial year to 30 June. It was a combative O'Leary who went on a conference call with stockbroking analysts that morning, as he sought to explain how lower air fares and higher costs left profits at €319 million for the three months ending 30 June, 20 per cent down on the same period in 2017. This was despite revenues 9 per cent higher, at €2.08 billion, and traffic that was up 7 per cent, to 37.6 million passengers. The shares fell by over 6.5 per cent in value on the day as investors digested the news.

While the hour of questions was polite, it was pointed. Many of the analysts focused on the acquisition of Lauda-motion, which O'Leary admitted would lose €150 million in its first year of Ryanair's 75 per cent ownership and would not break even for three years. Airline fuel was costing far more, at nearly $80 per barrel, and, with fuel costs over €450 million higher than previously, this had wiped out the bene-fit from the increase in ancillary revenues. Typically, O'Leary thought the higher fuel costs would do more damage to competitors than Ryanair because of his lower other costs.

O'Leary also grumbled about the impact of 2,500 flight cancellations in the summer months, affecting 450,000 pas-sengers, caused by air-traffic-control staff shortages and air-traffic-control strikes across Continental Europe. It meant a loss of higher-yielding weekend traffic and a steep rise in the compensation to discommoded customers under EU-261 right-to-care rules. Punctuality – upon which Ryanair placed such store – had fallen to 75 per cent on-time, com-pared with 89 per cent a year earlier. He conceded that Ryanair was losing the ability to sell unsold or the last-remaining unsold seats at high yields 'because we're re-accommodating passengers onto those flights from other disrupted flights'.

But if that was outside his control, what really irked him was the impact of the strike in Ireland, no matter how much he emphasized that it was relatively minor in the overall scheme of things and that Ryanair had minimized the disruption.

'Our approach to this has been to confront these strikes,' O'Leary told the analysts. He complained that the strike in Ireland had received 'a disproportionate amount of publi-city' from the Irish media. Still, he threatened that Ryanair would review its winter schedule and that this might 'lead to fleet reductions at disrupted bases and job losses in markets where competitor employees are interfering in our negotiations with our people and their unions'. In other words, he was making a thinly veiled threat to Dublin-based pilots that he could move some of the planes, which would affect their terms and conditions, and, in some cases, jobs.

'It is inevitable that where we have unions, there were going to be occasional strikes,' he told his conference-call audience. 'There will be a period of bedding down when we have to learn our way around dealing with these unions. And also, these unions have to learn that Ryanair is not some legacy airline that's going to roll over every time we're threatened with a strike. We will take strikes in those markets where we think that we are facing unreasonable demands.'

At one stage he conceded that 'I hate the fact that we've signed recognition agreements with pilots and cabin crew in most of our bigger markets,' but he tempered that by saying, 'It's indicative of how serious we are. I think it's important if we're going to preserve our low-cost model and our cost advantage over other airlines. As far as we don't want to invite strikes, we want to resolve these issues by negotiation with our people. We're inviting our people to meet with us. But if we are being dealt with unreasonably, in some cases, by competitor employees interfering in the process, I would be far happier to take a hit to our earnings this year.

'We still have an image of – some lazy media want to characterize us as being anti-union. We're not anti-union. We recognized in December that we were going to negotiate with unions. We're open to doing that, and we're open to reasonable – very reasonable – accommodations with our people, particularly our very well-paid pilots and cabin crew who enjoy very good conditions – terms and conditions of employment, and very favourable rosters. But if we're going to be pushed around by a couple of competitor people trying to distort the process, then it is inevitable that we will take on those strikes. We will or may face more strikes during the remainder of July and August, but we're prepared for them, and we're ready for them.'

Two days after O'Leary's frank comments to the analysts, unions representing cabin crew in Spain, Portugal and Belgium launched the first strike in a threatened series of stoppages. A 48-hour withdrawal of labour resulted in the cancellation of 600 flights and affected the travel plans of almost 50,000 passengers. In an apparent shot across the bows of the striking workers, the morning of the cabin-crew strikes Ryanair issued protective notice to more than 100 pilots and 200 cabin crew in Dublin, saying that it would cut its Dublin-based fleet by 20 per cent. In a statement, COO Peter Bellew referred to the pilots' action in Dublin as a reason for the decision. 'Ryanair operates a fleet of over 450 aircraft from 87 bases across Europe. We can only do so if we continue to offer low fares, reliable flight services to our customers, and if our reputation for reliability or forward bookings is affected, then base and potential job cuts such as these at Dublin are a deeply regretted consequence.' Within a week pilot unions all over Europe notified Ryanair of a plan to take coordinated strike action.

As July drew to a close, speculation about O'Leary's future restarted, this time not in the media, but at Ryanair's HQ. Rumours spread of a dinner with Willie Walsh in London earlier in the month. There was nothing unusual in that. O'Leary's respect for his fellow Irishman had grown over the years and the two met regularly to discuss airline issues.

But rumour spread that O'Leary had spoken of his own retirement in 2019, when his contract is due to expire, and had raised the idea of Walsh ditching IAG to return home to Ireland and Ryanair. Only the two men know what transpired during their July meeting – what sort of suggestions O'Leary made and how Walsh responded – but within Ryanair there was a realization that if O'Leary was going to hand over the reins, it would not be to someone within the organization but to somebody who had proven himself elsewhere and who, even if by being in competition with it over decades, understood the Ryanair culture.

Age has not diminished Michael O'Leary's hunger or his ambitions. But Ryanair getting bigger does not make it any easier to handle. There is ever greater complexity to manage, and the struggle to maintain Ryanair as the lowest-cost operator in the airline business gets more difficult with every year. Of course, that's exactly what O'Leary relishes. Whatever he does, he wants to be bigger and better than everyone else. So, though there is new speculation about his future, the expectation remains that he will sign a new contract in 2019 and continue to run what may be Irish business's biggest success since the creation of Guinness.

The Michael O'Leary story is far from over.

Acknowledgements

I have to offer my thanks and appreciation to many people, so excuse me for any I have left out.

Firstly to my family, for putting up with yet another interruption to my time with them (although they might secretly appreciate that).

To my work colleagues at Today FM on *The Last Word* (Mary Carroll, Diarmuid Doyle, Juleigh Ni Ghaibhain, Daniel Cahill and Robyn Keleghan on my production team) and at TV3 on *The Tonight Show* (Siobhan Russell, Siobhan Nic Uidhir, Nadine Maloney, Sally McLoughlin and Amy O'Brien on the production team and of course my co-presenter Ivan Yates), if they have felt that my concentration has wavered because of my commitments to the book. I hope it didn't and that the time-management was done correctly, but for when I fell down in that regard I apologize.

To my brilliant editor Rachel Pierce, who was a wise and skilful head on this project, and a patient one, too, and to Donna Poppy for the final copy-editing. To Patricia Deevy and Michael McLoughlin at Penguin Ireland for encouraging me to take up the idea and for keeping me on track with their sound advice and encouragement.

To those people who spoke to me for the book, many on condition of anonymity, and some on-the-record, and who provided the guidance that enabled me to tell the story as accurately as possible, I owe you my thanks, too. I should also acknowledge fine books written previously about Michael

O'Leary and Tony Ryan by the late Alan Ruddock, Siobhán Creaton and Richard Aldous.

I can't thank Michael O'Leary for any contribution because he chose, politely, twice to decline the opportunity to be interviewed specifically for it, despite our many interviews for broadcast and print media in the past. He doesn't like business books, especially when they are written for the gratification of egotistical businessmen. In some respects this made it easier for me to be as straight down the line in the telling of the story and offering an assessment as I could be, without allowing him any element of editorial influence or control.

Index